50-34

THE MALE SINGING VOICE AGES EIGHT TO EIGHTEEN

by

Frederick J. Swanson, Ph. D.

author of
Music Teaching in the Junior High
And the Middle School

LAURANCE PRESS
CEDAR RAPIDS, IOWA

MT
915
.59

PREFACE

Forty years ago I became a teacher of vocal music in a rather large junior high school. Forty years ago I first encountered "the boy problem". At first it was "How can I get these boys to sing?" Then it was "Why can't I find music that fits the voices of my boy singers?" When I organized the youth and victory choruses during World War II and toured the army camps and hospitals and bond rallies the question became "Why can't I find enough tenors and basses?" When we organized the summer music theater it was "Where can we get MEN to take the important leads?" Always in over thirty years of church choir directing I asked "Why can't we find men singers enough to balance the lady singers?"

Thirty years ago I began my case studies, keeping records of the vocal development of boys as their voices changed. Year after year I made tapings, drew voice graphs, and kept records of vocal and physical growth, racial background and economic status. I began with boys in my own school, then added cases during each of the eight summers when I was "boy specialist" at the University of Illinois summer music camps. Whenever I conducted a workshop or directed a demonstration group I made "on the spot" voice checks. Even to this day, as I work with private students, I add to my collection of voice tapes and graphs.

By 1956 I was ready to return to the University of Wisconsin to analyze my data, to use the resources of a large library, to discover what others had written on the subject and to come to some conclusions. The result was "Voice Mutation in the Adolescent Male", a dissertation* dealing with the phenomenon of voice change and how to direct the singing activities of boys during that period.

As a part of this reasearch I was given an entire eighth grade class of 85 boys to organize into experimental groups as I desired, to measure and record vocal development and related physical growth, to experiment with various song materials and vocalises and to draw conclusions.

Results, educationally speaking, were so encouraging that for the past twenty years the three junior high schools in my city have segregated the boys from the girls in eighth grade vocal music classes. I have seen the excellent results when dedicated, cooperative teachers have followed the recommended procedures; I have seen the failures when an ill-prepared or less than genuinely sincere teacher, or a less than co-operative administrator has not followed through.

In 1948 I organized THE MOLINE BOYS' CHOIR for other than investigative reasons, but I soon discovered the tremendous potential of the boy treble voice in choral and solo singing during the four or five years preceding voice change (ages 8 to 12/13). As the choir grew from a modest 39 into a 200-voice four-unit enterprise, I saw the attitude of a whole community change. The touring unit sang music of great worth and beauty to bring admiration and prestige to a small

---

* Available on microfilm

iii

mid-western city. More important to me, an educator, was the discovery that not only could these young lads attain a great proficiency and a remarkable singing technique, but they usually went through the voice change easily, sometimes even spectacularly. I realized with great clarity that voice mutation need not be a time of frustration and vocal atrophy, nor a time to withdraw from singing activities. Rather it can be a time of great challenge, a time when the voice can achieve great range and beauty—when PROPERLY GUIDED.

I remember some golden years when we had almost 120 singers in the ninth grade (freshman) choirs in EACH of our junior high schools, and six choral groups in the senior high (grade 10-12), numbering from 60 to 80 each. We saw the boys from our boys' choir move into the seventh grade "honors chorus", go through the changing voice class, move into ninth grade as tenors, baritones or basses, and continue through high school. We at this time achieved the desirable balance of 70 boys to 70 girls in our ninth grade choirs.

I have also seen this ideal progression break down when one member of the "team" could not or would not function well. This is when I have realized that EVERYBODY concerned with the choral music program from elementary to high school must realize that boys' voices are by nature different from girls' voices and that boys need different teaching than girls do.

In the following pages I try to set down, for the benefit of anyone concerned with the training of boy singers:

parochial and
public school music teachers
administrators of a music program, grades 1 through 12
those who prepare future teachers of music
students preparing to become music teachers
church or community choir directors
professional boy or youth choir directors
private/studio teachers of voice
boys who want to become good singers
parents who want their boys to become good singers
school administrators and curriculum coordinators

those items that I have learned or unlearned in four decades of constant study. I will try to describe those items that have worked and have failed to work for me or my colleagues. I shall introduce some subjects about which I am not yet very knowledgeable, hoping that somebody somewhere will be motivated to experiment further.

Where I make positive statements (not very often) I invite any doubters to come see, hear and examine; I hope they will present their evidence in rebuttal. Where I state that something has worked for me, I remind the reader that in a different community with a different type of population, adaptations may have to be made. Where I introduce material about which I am not yet sure and with which I am still inquiring and experimenting, I invite the reader to do some inquiring and experimenting on his own.

I hasten to add that I owe much of my knowledge and some of my procedures to a vast number of people. Some are listed here by name, but many more are nameless. I have gleaned significant information from such surprisingly unexpected sources as:

iv

a conversation with a chorister in Belgrade
a personal history told by a male alto in Addington Palace
a five-minute visit with a professional bass in a lay-over at an airport
a casual remark by a noted choral conductor
a demonstration at a convention
a suggestion from a classmate in a seminar
a volunteer letter from an unknown who comments on or corroborates
   or takes exception to something I have written in a magazine
   article
a comment from somebody who has tried one of my vocal arrangements
a passage in a work of fiction

These "incidents" have aroused questions and suggested fresh approaches to troublesome problems. Often I have had the use of special equipment and facilities in several universities. Many experts in the field have been gracious about giving me time and sharing their knowledge. Always I have had at hand a group of boys with co-operating parents who have allowed me to try out my hypotheses, who have allowed me to see and hear what is really there and what can work and what will not. I am also grateful to the several people who have raised their voices in anger or derision, who have taken exception to some of my statements and questioned my findings; these have caused me to examine and re-think most carefully to be sure of my data and of the conclusions I have drawn therefrom.

Frederick Swanson
Moline, Ill.
September 1977

Table of Contents

Section 1—Introduction

Section 2—The Boy Choir and the Boy Singer

Section 3—Voice Mutation in the Adolescent Male

THE APPENDIX

Table of Examples

Appendix

ACKNOWLEDGEMENTS

I am grateful to these directors of boy choirs who have contributed information and advice for Chapters VII and IX, as well as Appendix C.

Robert Buchanan—director of Brownsville, Texas, Boy Choir
Douglas Nesslund—director of California Boy Choir in Los Angeles
Robert McSpadden—director of Cincinnati, Ohio, All-City Boy Choir
Jerome Wright—founder of Northwest Boy Choir, Seattle, Washington and former director
Dr. William Ballard—director of San Francisco, California, Boy Choir
Dr. Steve Stevens—former director of Texas Boy Choir, presently director of Northwest Boy Choir, Seattle, Washington
Dr. Jeffrey Haskell—former director of the Tucson, Arizona, Boy Choir, director of jazz studio, University of Arizona at Tucson
Dr. D. C. Rhoden—director of Oconee County Boys' Choir, Athens, Georgia
Kermit Wells—director of Moline, Illinois, Boys' Choir

I also express gratitude to these people who have provided me with background information, practical advice and expert opinion for the material in Chapters XXII and XXIII.
Dr. Thomas Shipp—Speech Research Laboratory, Veteran's Administration Hospital, San Francisco, California
Prof. Morris Hayes—director of choral music, University of Wisconsin at Eau Claire, Wisconsin
Prof. Robert Eckert—Head of Voice Department and Director of Opera University of Iowa, Iowa City, Iowa
Dr. David Kuehn—Associate Research Scientist, Department of Otolaryngology and Maxillofacial Surgery, University of Iowa
Ronald Scherer—Doctoral candidate, Department of Speech Pathology and Antiology, University of Iowa
Prof. Edward Kottick—director of Collegicum Musicum, University of Iowa
Vlatislav Vinicky—bass with the Prague, Czechoslovakia, Madrigal Group
and also countertenors:
Jiri Kos—member of the Smetana Choir of Prague, Czechoslovakia
Simon Halsey—member of the Louis Halsey Singers of London, England and choral scholar at King's College, Cambridge University, England

Craig Broers—graduate student at the University of Iowa
Paul Forsmo—graduate student at the University of Iowa.

I am also deeply grateful to a host of classroom teachers, administrators, professional singers, choral directors and fellow workers who have been generous with comments, information and practical advice. Especially I am grateful to the young students, boy singers who have provided the actual data and recorded observations during the past forty years of study and research.

Frederick Swanson, Ph.D.
Moline, Illinois, September 1977

SCHEME OF INDICATING PITCHES

Because there are many schemes for indicating pitches, I have arbitrarily adopted one that will be used throughout this book. Note that from second ledger line below treble clef, the pitches are indicated by lower case letters; from fourth space bass clef downward pitches are indicated by upper case letters. The prime (′) and second (″) indicate the first and second octaves respectively.

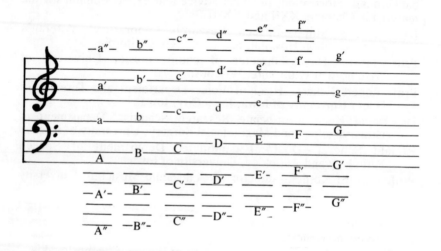

Chapter I

THE PURPOSE OF THIS BOOK

The male singing voice between the ages of eight and eighteen is:
fascinating to those who follow its maturation
challenging to those who seek to train and use it
frustrating to those who do not understand its erratic patterns
of development
highly rewarding to those who know how to use it properly.

It can also be a source of wonder, amusement, and pride to the boy's family as parents and siblings listen to the constantly changing sounds coming from the throat of the growing male child.

At no other time of vocal growth is development so extensive, so rapid or so erratic. There is no correspondingly great change in the female voice at any time, nor does much growth occur in the male voice after the second decade of life is past.

Eight to twelve is the period of the boy treble when high, clear, resonant tones can be developed. This boy-voice is most amenable to training for use both in choral ensemble and in solo singing. At its best, the boy treble has a distinctive and unique timbre that is almost universally liked and to which many people respond with strong emotion.

When the boy reaches puberty, usually between ages thirteen and fifteen, the voice changes noticeably in pitch and timbre. There is at this time a very rapid growth and hardening of cartilage throughout the body. As the larynx, which is cartilaginous, increases rapidly in size and alters in shape, the vocal bands increase correspondingly in length and thickness. The result is a radical drop in vocal pitch, anywhere from one to two-and-one-half octaves; the volume of sound produced is greater; the quality or timbre of that sound is dramatically different from the high clear treble of boyhood.

Since this laryngeal growth is quite fast, the fine adjustments and the established control of voice acquired by the boy treble singer are thrown awry, and only with careful training and practice are they brought back under control. The period of voice mutation can be one of discouragement, embarrassment, and frustration for the adolescent singer as well as for his parents and even his vocal coach or choir director. Yet when properly used and developed, the boy-voice during this period of rapid change often develops a very agreeable timbre, a warmly sympathetic sound capable of great expressiveness.

There is no need for the boy to stop singing at this time. Quite the contrary is true. Properly supervised and guided vocalising during this period can do much to ease the passage from treble to bass clef singing and to make this transition an adventure and a challenge. Within certain limitations, the boy can sing quite successfully both in ensemble and as a soloist to the satisfaction of all concerned.

In the third stage, approximately from ages sixteen to eighteen, after the rapidly growing larynx has attained its adult size and shape,

1

the male voice emerges as a deep bass or a medium baritone or a high tenor. This is the time when the young man is ready to learn how to hold, follow, and read the quite different vocal lines assigned to men singers. His fuller, richer, deeper masculine tones will complement the higher feminine voices of his girl classmates in singing the choral literature written for mixed voices. He is also ready to begin exploring the vast body of solo songs written for the male voice as well as the choral works written for men's voices only.

Unfortunately, the boy singer, in this rapidly shifting vocal development, can be exposed to more faulty use, more bad teaching and more emotional strain than is the case with his female counter-part. Not all of those who are responsible for the training of the boy voice during these ten years have the specific knowledge nor the techniques needed to train their boy students properly, nor do all adults have the appreaciation for or sympathetic understanding of both the boy's voice and boy himself as a person.

This is why in America we lose so many boy singers along the way. It is no secret that there is a chronic shortage of men singers in the United States. It is almost a scandal that there are so many high schools that enroll five girls to each boy in choral music classes. Worse yet, there is a sizeable number of schools that have no boy singers at all. Quite usually community choruses and church choirs have no difficulty in finding enough sopranos and altos, but are hard put to it to muster capable tenors and basses in sufficient quantity to attain a satisfactory balance of parts.

The fault is obvious. The young male singer needs a different training, a more specialized type of teaching than does the female singer. Those who are responsible for the development of boy singers need special techniques and special knowledge, and far too many do not know those techniques nor have that knowledge.

My purpose in this book is to impart these items of knowledge, and to describe some of the special techniques that work best in the training of the male singer in his various stages of vocal maturation. I will also attempt to develop in the reader an attitude of sympathetic understanding and appreciation of the peculiar hazards to be met and overcome by the boy singer with the aid of his teacher. Most important of all, I will try to describe the special rewards and satisfactions that can come to both student and teacher as they together seek to develop and train these growing voices properly from boyhood to late adolescence.

Chapter II
THE HAZARDS AND CHALLENGES
FACING THE BOY SINGER

The hazards that the potential male singer must overcome begin to beset him in early childhood. The normal boy is full of spirit, so he moves fast and plays hard. In the moving and playing he often yells, screams, or makes other loud noises. If left to his own devices and enthusiasms he tends to speak and sing exuberantly, and frequently pushes his voice up to such a level of volume that the voice is strained. The result can be a roughening and thickening of the vocal bands, sometimes to the point of producing inflammation. As a result, speaking and singing tones are hoarse in quality and limited in range, quite unsuitable for either solo or ensemble singing.

This hazard, not in the teacher's control, is common enough, but occasionally a would-be choral director, long on enthusiasm but short on musical taste and training, increases the hazard by demanding those very same over-loud, over-pushed tones in the music class. Somehow this misguided director equates loudness with quality, and raucousness with enthusiasm. Given a few years of this type of singing and noise-making, and our first casualties have appeared. Nobody wants to hear the hoarse, umpleasant voice, so these rough-toned boys that cannot blend with the class are labelled non-singers or undesirable singers, and shunted off to one side.

It is also a personal observation of mine that boys are slower in finding their singing voices than are girls. For over 25 years it was one of my duties to visit and observe the music classes in the primary grades in twenty elementary schools. It was a common practice then to seat the first and second grade classes with the strong, clear, well-in-tune voices in the back row, while those who were deficient in ability to match pitch or to sing in the desired light head voice always were seated in the front. Year after year, in class after class, I noticed that the singers in the front row always included more boys than girls, and this imbalance persisted into the second grade. Yet by grade three these out-of-tuners, mostly boys, had found their "singing voices," and often these very boys would be strong leaders both in singing and in reading music. I often wonder what would have happened to these boys if the first and second grade teachers had not been conscientious about working with them. What if these teachers had simply labelled these students as non-singers and let them drift? I daresay quite a few more boys would have been lost, along with the raucous-voiced lads mentioned above. Could there be cities and villages where just that may be happening?

At the other end of the spectrum there is the hazard faced by the boy who is so blessed with talent and who is so carefully trained that he is over-used and exploited. The member of a fine boy choir may be endowed with a naturally pleasing voice; being a talented and willing student he may have developed a fine vocal technique and an attractive stage presence. He then may become such an audience-pleaser that he is asked to sing often, much too often. He is rehearsed so many hours for so many years that singing becomes a chore and he comes to feel deprived of the chances to enjoy other activities that boys are fond of. It is something of a scandal that many a graduate from a top concert boy choir does not develop into a capable adult singer because he has had to meet too rigorous a rehearsal and concert schedule in his immature years. He may be "sung out before his time."

At puberty the boy meets a very great hazard-challenge. After six or more years of singing with success and pleasure, there comes a time when the young boy finds all the habits, the reflexes, the muscular adjustments acquired in those boyhood years thrown out of kilter. He discovers that his voice is not "going where it is supposed to go." Sometimes, to his embarrassment, it cracks or squeaks and sometimes it shifts abruptly into a much deeper sound than expected. Quite understandably he may become so thwarted and discouraged that he no longer enjoys singing, especially if nobody takes the time and trouble to explain to him what is happening. I have heard many a mature man say, a bit sheepishly, "Oh no, I don't sing any more. When I was a boy I had a really fine voice, but then something happened, and now my voice isn't good for much."

The onset of voice mutation can be especially traumatic for a boy who has won some success as a treble soloist or who has been a leading, enthusiastic member of a very prestigious choir. There comes a time when he receives the news that his days as a choirboy or soloist are at an end. Unless he is fortunate enough to find a teacher-director who knows how to guide him through the transition from treble to bass clef singing, the shock and discouragement may be great enough to cause him to give up singing altogether.* What should be an adventure and challenge becomes a discouragement and frustration.

This hazard of not adjusting to the voice change in the proper way is made more risky if our adolescent boy receives improper teaching. Bad or faulty teaching may be due to lack of knowledge about the phenomenon of voice change, for some teachers profess to be qualified to teach junior high or middle school music who have no clear idea of how a boy's voice changes: they cannot know what to do to properly guide it through the period of mutation. Worse than

---

*For two examples of gifted musicians who suffered just such a traumatic experience, see the biographies of Haydn and Schubert (1,2). In both cases the boys ceased their singing careers, but because of superior talent, became master composers. Important for our discussion here, neither continued to develop his singing techniques. We have to wonder how many other ex-choirboys simply gave up any further participation in musical endeavors who might have, with proper guidance and encouragement, continued their singing careers successfully.

1. Griesinger, G.A. & Gothwals, V: JOSEPH HAYDN, Madison, University of Wisconsin Press, 1963, pg. 11.
2. Schauffler, Robert H.: FRANZ SCHUBERT, New York, P.G. Putnam's Sons, 1949 pg. 52 ff.

this (since there is a chance that an uninformed teacher may accidentally hit upon a correct technique), there is bad teaching because of the erroneous beliefs some teachers hold about this phenomenon of voice change. There are, unfortunately, hypotheses rather widely taught and accepted which are actually in opposition to factual data. Teachers who insist on using procedures based on these faulty hypotheses may do actual harm to the voices of the boys in their charge. If a boy falls into the hands of teachers who are ill-prepared or who hold erroneous beliefs, that boy will be fortunate if he somehow survives this bad teaching.

We cannot blame the teachers entirely in these situations. Sometimes that blame can be attributed to some very deplorable practices in assigning teachers to junior high school music posts. The terms "junior high" and "junior choir director" carry a connotation of inferiority or lack of prestige in some people's minds. Because of this vague but prevalent connotation, the junior high music job is considered a good place to start a young, inexperienced teacher. Similarly, the minister of music or senior (adult) choir director in a church may look for some willing young person to relieve him of that not so prestigious and (in his eyes) less rewarding junior choir burden.

Often would-be music teachers take the junior high assignment merely to gain experience and to win a foothold in the teaching profession, thinking that in due time they will be "promoted" to a senior high post; or they may plan to remain in the job only long enough to earn enough money so they can return to graduate school for an advanced degree; eventually they hope they can find something "worthy of their talents and abilities." I have even heard some young ladies state frankly that "this junior high job will do for a few years" as they plan to be married and want to earn enough money without too much strain and hard work until they have put by enough money so they can help their husband-to-be buy a suitable home and adequate furnishings before they start to raise a family.

There are administrators who unwittingly reflect this feeling that "junior" means "less experienced, and less capable teachers" as they assign some mediocre teacher, who is not inefficient enough to be fired nor yet old enough to be retired, to the junior high school where he/she will not "do much harm" or where the public will be more apt to accept mediocrity without complaint. I have never heard of a failing junior high teacher being moved to the "easier" senior high where he will work with more accomplished students who register for music on a volunteer basis, and where voices are more settled, and music skills more developed.

All too often when a senior high school directorship or a city—wide administrative post is available, the capable, promising junior high teacher is "promoted" so that his competency can be duly recognized and rewarded, while he/she is replaced by a beginning, inexperienced teacher.

There is also the hazard of a boy getting a teacher who is not congenial to the adolescent male age 13 to 15. The "male animal" in his early adolescence is notoriously awkward, loud and apt to be obstreperous. Boys in their early teens are mature enough to detect

5

mediocrity or lack of confidence or unfriendliness, and are resourceful in finding ways to display their objections to this mediocrity. Not so often do people mention that the opposite is also true, that the junior high boy can be loyal, respectful and very amenable to direction when he recognizes a sincere, knowledgeable, congenial leader and will give a teacher he respects enthusiastic, unwavering support and cooperation. Alas, it sometimes happens that a teacher with an excellent music background does not succeed in controlling and inspiring junior high school music students. Equally unfortunately, we find an administrator hiring a teacher because he *is* a "strong disciplinarian," a teacher who is able to win the obedience of his students although he is really deficient in his music training. Rare is the junior high teacher who is both a thoroughly fine musician and a teacher who can win over his students. There are such, and they stand out in the profession. May the day come when many more junior high specialists will dedicate their professional careers to that challenging, fascinating time of boys'-voice-change and will be properly rewarded and respected for doing so. Might it ever come about that the neophyte, the young and inexperienced, will begin by teaching in the senior high school and then be "promoted" to handle the much more demanding, challenging junior high post?

If a boy survives the vicissitudes of voice change and persists in his musical training, he has yet another hurdle to clear. At the same time that he is trying to gain control of his "new voice" he must learn to sing in a new idiom. He must become skilled in singing a new harmonic part, quite different from the treble vocal line he has been singing as a boy. This new part lies in a different range and must be read from a different staff; in fact he really must become skilled in reading his vocal part from either of TWO staffs as they appear with either of two clef signs.

In the prevailing voicing for soprano-alto-tenor-bass ensemble, the tenor does not sing the melody, so the "new tenor" finds himself in the middle, with a much less obvious vocal line to follow. The new bass now finds himself at the bottom of the choral ensemble; not only is he producing a very different sound, but he is performing quite a different function in the harmonic scheme as he furnishes the support, the base for the vocal structure.

The bass-baritone finds his part written in the F-clef in ensemble writing, although quite often as a soloist he finds his part written in the treble clef to be sung an octave lower than written. The tenor may see his part written in the treble clef with instructions to sing an octave lower than written, but in hymn-books and song collections the tenor and bass may share the same bass-clef, so the tenor must follow notation written in the upper part of the F-clef. An adult, well-trained pianist may look at these various ways of indicating pitch and be not at all confused; an inexperienced boy with no instrumental background who has been finding his pitches by their location on the staff may take some patient, carefully planned practice in adjusting to this "new way" of writing music. How long does it take a "new tenor" to discover that the first ledger line above the staff may be a high-A requiring care to produce in the upper register, but in another book it may be a tone "right in the middle of his voice" and quite

6

comfortable? How long is it until a bass who used to sing alto realizes that the tones below the staff where he used to sing most comfortably now indicate pitches he cannot produce without much vocalising, while the note written on the first ledger lines above the staff which he, as alto, never had to sing, now is a rather frequently appearing note which he is expected to reach with some ease and comfort?

If the high school choral director understands why a young tenor or bass needs some special training in extending his note-reading skills (that the girls do not need), the shift to the new clefs and vocal lines can usually be made in a semester or less. A clever director may even "manufacture" music so the tenor lines are obvious and easy, while the arrangement challenges the female singers with parts much more difficult and demanding. But if the director assumes that "somebody" should have taught his budding tenors and basses to read music in the new idiom and expects them to sing standard SATB arrangements right off, he is quite apt to be disappointed as he finds uncertainity, bewilderment and then discouragement among his boys.

If then the director gets impatient, so he scolds and ridicules his "stupid boys," the discouragement turns to resentment and resistance. As he picks away at the boys, trying to teach them the difficult, slightly bewildering, often (to the boys) uninteresting parts while the girls look on with visible boredom or derision, he has set the stage for a general lack of enthusiasm in these boys. Likely an exodus begins and his supply of tenors and basses dwindles alarmingly. It is small wonder that with such treatment boys leave never to return.

Let us add one more hazard, the high school choral director who is more interested in the music HE wants his choir to sing than he is in the careful, proper development of singing skills in his young students. He may yearn to perform works of the old masters or prestigious compositions of the modern school. He may be fond of staging a big musical show intended originally for the professional stage. Since such works were originally written for adult, professional singers, we find adolescent tenors and basses (and the girls too) straining to sing notes too high for their young voices. So that the listeners in a very large auditorium may hear, this director may urge boys to sing and speak at a volume their not-quite-mature larynxes cannot sustain. If, in their eagerness to please, some of these young people force and strain, they may end up with vocal damage that takes a long time to repair. Or what is more likely, they may give up on trying to sing such difficult music which makes for vocal discomfort.

The individual high school director is not always the guilty one here. We can point an accusing finger at the committee that chooses music for a festival or contest that will involve many high school choirs. This committee may be more concerned with what will be impressive and showy than in what will be of most benefit to young singers. The committee may have selected a guest conductor, not necessarily a man who has worked with adolescent voices, quite possibly one who is unaware of their limitations. This guest director may feel that he must bedazzle the participating choral conductors, the students and the general public. To add to his "professional reputation" he may want to impress those who will read the reports in the music journals and trade magazines. So he selects something quite ambitious, prestigious and a bit unusual, with scant regard for its suitability for young singers and their inablility to sustain the long rehearsals and great strain of performing this difficult work.

With so many hazards to be overcome, why bother with our boy singers? Why not take the easy course? If our boys do not fit our desired, pre-conceived patterns, or if their voices do not develop on schedule as we want them to, or if these boys are restless or resistant to what WE ask them to do, why not simply dismiss them from our classes or label them as deficient singers and hopeless material and shunt them off to one side?

Why not indeed? That is what many of our music teachers *are* doing. This is why we find high school after high school where girl singers outnumber boys as much as five to one, or six to one. This is why we have such a chronic shortage of tenors. This is why many girls never have the desirable experience of singing the standard repertoire of soprano-alto-tenor-bass choral literature. This is why many junior high schools maintain a fine girl's chorus but have no boys' chorus at all. Most deplorable of all, this is why many a potentially fine tenor or bass walks down the corridors of our schools undiscovered, undeveloped and never used. Unfortunately, in this giving up, we help develop even more hazards. We allow the spread of some very fallacious and morale-damaging beliefs.

Music directors are very human. They often try to explain this sex-biased imbalance by rationalization. Being unwilling to admit that they, the teachers, could be to blame, they state "The boys in our school are not as musically gifted as the girls." On the surface this sounds rather persuasive, so persuasive that the boys themselves believe it, their parents accept it and even some administrators, who should be quick to detect the fallacy of this statement, are willing to go along with it.

Closer examination reveals no support for such an alibi. Twenty-five years of constant searching, using the facilities of several large universities, have failed to turn up any evidence that musical talent in general and singing ability in particular are sex-linked attributes. Anybody who maintains that boys are less capable in 1) pitch discrimination, 2) rhythmic awareness, 3) sensitivity to changes in harmonic structure, or 4) variations in melodic progressions than the girls are, has a great deal of proving to do. Not only will that person find no shred of evidence to substantiate his claims, but he will have to explain away some evidences to the contrary.

There are two musical endeavors that demand the greatest amount of musical talent, the composition of musical works and the conducting of professional ensembles — orchestras, bands, choruses. If you list the major composers from the days of Bach and Handel up to the present, composers whose works are performed perennially as standard items in the repertoire, you will find that they are all men. Similarly if you list the composers of enduring works for the musical comedy, operetta and stage-play-with-music, you again find these are almost exclusively men. Those who provide the music for commercial

8

cinema and television are men. Yet there is no reason why a woman, if she is talented, cannot, working in her own home or studio, produce and have performed musical compositions as successfully as these men.

The conductors of our major symphony orchestras and concert bands are men, as are the directors of the "name bands" in the popular music field. The one woman who has directed an opera at the Metropolitan Opera in a hundred years, when compared to the many male conductors, does little to counteract the perponderance of male conductors. How explain this preponderance of men if women are "more musical" than their male counterparts?

I am thinking of a junior high school (it could be one of several I know well) where, for several years, this statement that "the boys are just not as capable as the girls" was heard. Then a musically able and personally dedicated teacher was appointed and suddenly the choirs and glee clubs grew in size, boys as well as girls thronged to enroll and the general public as well as fond parents came to fill the auditorium at the various concerts during the school year. There were no remarks about boys being less talented, for basses and tenors seemed quite plentiful. Then this teacher was "promoted" and there followed a succession of less successful music directors. Within a year, we began to hear again that "the boys are less talented."

The second alibi often uttered is "In our community it is not considered a desirable activity for boys to sing. Boys who join the choir are considered less masculine, somewhat effeminate. People in our town just do not go for male singers."

It is easy to discover how such a rumor gets started. If five or six boys have been ignored, derided, scolded or expelled from music class because of undesirable responses and behavior it is not likely that they will admit that THEY are at fault. Quite typically they will say "Aw who wants to be in music class anyway. That's for sissies. I'm GLAD I'm out of there." The next step is for these boys to deride those who are still in music class, until they succeed in getting some of their classmates to join in the anti-music behavior. The more docile of their boy friends may not actually resist overtly, but may wait until the earliest opportunity to cease any singing activities so that they will no longer be looked upon as effeminate. I have even known of cases where a very fine boy singer has actually been physically abused because he was winning some fame as an accomplished soloist. Under such circumstances, it takes a very determined, dedicated and independent-minded boy to withstand the social pressures of his classmates.

Many parents will go right along with their sons in this "music is not for boys" attitude. In lower-middle class America most fathers are disappointed if their sons cannot bounce, throw, hit, catch, toss or propel a ball with great skill and precision, for somehow such skill is (to them) a sign of masculinity. If their sons display interest in science, or are clever with their hands in mechanical matters, or if they go in for fishing, hunting, boating or swimming, many a father can take satisfaction in his boys' prowess as "a regular he-man." But somehow if a boy is inclined to cultivate any of the fine arts where physical strength or large muscular activity are not of primary

9

importance, these fathers are less sure. Then if a son says he does not want to sing (or paint or write poetry) because such stuff is "for sissies" the father makes little protest. Should a mother attempt to apply pressure or encourage her son to persist, the effect may be other than good; it may be further proof that singing is effeminate.

Is this an extreme or distorted picture? Not at all in most school systems in most parts of our United States. But it need not be so. There are a few high schools where there are excellent mixed choirs with both boys and girls participating. There are some rare junior high schools where the boys do participate and where an able, dedicated teacher gets his/her boys through the transition from treble to bass clef with no losses. There are exceptional cities which maintain fine boy choirs, where the whole town is proud to give support and where membership is considered an honor. There are enterprising churches that maintain boys' and men's choirs of admirable reputation. There are large cities where most of the high schools have choirs that are woefully lacking in basses and tenors, but in that same community with the same type of population throughout there is one high school where choral music flourishes and where students, male and female, vie for admission to the choral classes. Yes, there are a few directors that prove that boys can sing as well as girls and where all the students are equally well-taught. The preceding paragraph is not distorted, but there are a few places that show that it need not be like that.

On this encouraging note, let me close this seemingly discouraging chapter and proceed to its opposite, a chapter where we will discuss the satisfactions, benefits and rewards that come when a knowledgeable teacher and a sympathetic community come to grips with these hazards their boy singers must face, and manage to change hazards into challenges and victories.

Chapter III

THE SATISFACTIONS AND REWARDS OF DEVELOPING FINE MALE SINGERS

In the preceding chapter, we asked "why bother, if boys face so many hazards in their vocal development?" Is it worth the time and effort required to guide our male singers through their difficulties and over their hurdles?

The answer is yes, very definitely yes, for some very good reasons. Here are four to consider. When we develop our male singers:

A. The musical results are eminently rewarding.

B. The enthusiastic responses of the listening public are uniformly reassuring and satisfying.

C.We teachers are making a realistic approach to preparing our students for adult life.

D. The democratic principle of equal opportunity for all is properly applied.

Part A.

The musical responsiveness of the boy voice has been known since earliest history. We all know the story of David, the boy shepherd, whose singing and playing calmed the troubled spirit of King Saul. What David sang, we can only guess 2500 years later, but we can safely assume that his songs were not stirring battle tunes nor passionate love songs. He had not yet fought Goliath nor wooed Bathsheba. It seems safer to assume that these were simple tunes matching the limited range of the seven-stringed harp, so it was the pure, naive timbre of the boy-voice itself that soothed and quieted Saul, not any highly emotional texts. Who coached David? We do not know, but since David was a shepherd lad he certainly got no extended, sophisticated instruction. Whoever taught David his songs found an apt, responsive voice, in the throat of an intelligent student.

Was David a boy treble, or was his voice in that very fascinating, quickly-come-quickly-change stage of adolescence when the male singing voice develops a timbre unique and esoteric? The latter seems more likely, for soon after David's debut at court we read that he met and conquered the giant, hardly likely if he was not yet in his teens.

David may have the distinction of being the first boy singer to be identified by name in history, but he certainly was not the first lad who charmed his hearers with the beauty of his fresh, responsive voice. What is more, he has been followed through the centuries by literally millions of minstrels, young lads, named or anonymous, who have produced the same aesthetic effect. For the singing voice of the young male is most amenable to proper training and capable of producing favorable responses in the hearer. Given a group of boys with only ordinary responsiveness, and musical awareness, a knowledgeable teacher can often develop a musical sound that is most pleasing.* Given a group of boys of above average musical responsiveness*, the same knowledgeable director will have at his command a highly rewarding musical organization, capable of great expressiveness.

The male voice during mutation may not seem as amenable to training as the young boy's voice, and not so well suited for choral performance, but those who have worked with boys during this period of rapid change have found that the voice of the adolescent male, when properly produced and when given appropriate music to sing, posssesses a warm, sympathetic timbre of peculiar beauty. There is a tremendous satisfaction for voice coaches who specialize in training boys in their early teens as they discover the unique vocal sound and, on occasion, even startling musical effects these voices can produce. To the suprise of the uninititated, these voices are not limited, but actually are capable of producing a wider range of musical sounds than either the young boy singer or the adult man.

The responsiveness of the adult male voice is well known. Anyone who has heard some of the touring male choruses from Europe, e.g. the Don Cossacks from Russia, or the Männerchoir of Germany or Austria have heard the tremendous range and wide variety of tonal colors available to well-trained choruses of men. When boys' and men's voices are combined, as happens so commonly in the cathedrals of the Catholic church on the European continent or in the Anglican cathedrals in the British Isles and far-flung countries of the former British Empire, the range of tone colors and musical effects is even greater. Many a conducted tour is planned to include the hearing of one or more of these fine male choruses.

Most important to Americans where the schools are co-educational and where churches and synagogues tend more and more to emphasize mixed choral singing there is great satisfaction in performing some of the tremendous body of musical literature composed for the soprano-alto-tenor-bass distribution of voices. Since the day of the madrigal and especially since the days of Bach and Handel where both church services and secular stage productions have combined the voices of men and women, there has grown a tremendous storehouse of musical compositions available to express every emotion and mood experienced by humans. This SATB chorus is the one organization that every high school should have so its students can become acquainted with the tremendous resources available to this combination of voices.

Fortunate are the students where membersuip in a good mixed chorus is available. Happy is the director who finds BOTH girl and boy singers in sufficient number and balance to perform SATB music satisfactorily.

---

*For our purposes here, let us define "some awareness and responsiveness to music" as the ability to sing in tune a major and minor scale and to repeat correctly any given rhythm pattern involving half, quarter and eighth notes. For a description of "above average responsiveness" see Appendix C.

Limited and deprived are the students in schools where a girls' glee club is the only choral organization. Not much better is the school where we find fifty girls and ten boys in the mixed chorus. A satisfactory performance is almost impossible to achieve with so few male voices. Of course it would be equally deplorable if there were fifty boys to ten girls if there could be found anywhere in America a coeducational high school with that enrollment!

It is not really satisfactory if there is only one well-balanced choir for soprano-alto-tenor-bass, supplemented by two or three all-girls' choruses for the "overflow". Too many girls are being deprived of the very valuable experience of singing the mixed chorus literature, We must also wonder how many potentially good boy singers there must be who are not being reached at all.

Ideally, in any high school of over 200 students, there should be at least one mixed chorus of from 40 to 60 students, for one student out of four enrolled in vocal music is not an unrealistic figure. We mean, of course, that there should be an almost equal balance of numbers in each voice part, for there must be enough deep bass voices and high tenors to achieve proper balance. It is my contention that where the boys have been trained properly in elementary school and guided properly through the period of voice change, the senior high choral conductor will have a very responsive body of male singers, capable of performing many types of choral works.

It would be highly desirable to supplement this mixed voice choir with an all-male glee club and an all-girl chorus where the literature composed for those voicings can be explored and experienced.

Part B
The Popular Appeal of the Male Singing Voice

It is a demonstrable fact that a fine boy choir will attract audiences and win community support more readily than will a girls' choir. That is why concert managers sponsor some of our present boy choirs on extended concert tours at sizeable fees; these entrepreneurs know that the concert-going public will pay to listen.

Similarly, a boy choir that functions more modestly within the confines of its home territory can expect to find plenty of opportunities to sing for appreciative audiences and through its modest concert fees even in this restricted scope of activity can often produce enough income to sustain itself.

Some of our largest, well-established churches have, for years, maintained fine boy choirs, ostensibly to add to the beauty of the worship services, but often with the added motivation of attracting non-church-goers into their sanctuary and, in some cases, actually inviting, through advertisements, out-of-town tourists.

Some of our most pretentious boy choirs are heavily endowed by wealthy individuals who are so deeply moved by the boys' singing that they consider it worth their financial support to underwrite the expense of maintaining such a choir. These boy choirs are able to afford competent directors and adult assistants, and are well-housed and well-supplied with music and costumes. Even smaller-scale boy choirs sometimes find their rehearsal hall provided, or music and costumes bought, or staff salaries partially paid for by local patrons.

Even in America we find that boy choirs are flourishing, not only in the cathedrals for religious services, but also on tour about the country singing as concert organizations, some with spectacular success. The Vienna Choir Boys, the Little Singers of Paris, the boy choirs of Stockholm, Oslo, Munich are matched by our American Texas Boy Choir, Columbus Boy Choir, and the choirs from Tucson, San Francisco and Los Angeles, et al. In contrast, there are virtually no girl choirs of equal reputation or public appeal. The reason cannot be a coincidence. It must be that the boy voice, when properly trained, has a color, a timbre, a vitality and thrust that few girl voices can match — and audiences all over the concert world subconsciously react favorably to the boy treble voice, and are happy to listen and applaud — and pay.

From all of the above, we can assume quite justifiably that the sound and sight of boys singing together arouses warm emotional responses, hence generous support from the general public. Small wonder that we now have over 600 boy choirs functioning in the United States and 600 directors actively engaged in training these boy singers.*

It would seem to the casual observer that during the voice-mutation period where voices are in a stage of rapid change, there would be no interest or support on the part of an audience. Very early in my teaching days at the junior high school level I found quite the opposite to be the case. The boys' bass clef chorus always received a more enthusiastic response than did the girls' glee club. The girls were always capable of singing more challenging music in grades seven and eight. Their voices remained nearly constant in range, so the singers were not constantly shifting parts. They were usually amenable to rehearsing. Musically speaking, they always did a creditable job, often with rather challenging music. The boys perforce had to sing within the limits of their changing voice capabilities, so music was always simple and never could be as finely polished. Yet year after year, the response to the girls' singing was politely appreciative and a bit restrained, while the applause for the boys was more spontaneous and noticeably louder. My experience was not unique; other experienced and successful teachers in junior high school and middle school have found it so as well.

At the high school level, the same is true to a lesser degree. If a high school is able to attract enough boys to form a male chorus or even a quartet, and they sing passably well, the public will be more than ready to hear them. This is not to denigrate the girls' ensemble, for by middle adolescence the maturing voices of the girls have gained in timbre, tone quality and power so they too can do some very emotionally satisfying singing.

Usually at the high school level, it is the *a capella* or concert choir that wins the most enthusiastic support from the citizen-taxpayers

---

*As chairman of the committee for boys' and children's choirs for the American Choral Directors' Association, I have access to a mailing list of over 600 boy choirs in the United States, plus another 50 in Canada and Mexico.

14

and establishes the reputation of the choir director. If this "top group" sings well and is available when called upon to sing for important occasions, the director has in his control the potential means for satisfying both students and himself, the school administrators and the general public. But I repeat, it must be a balanced choir, with enough basses and tenors to match sopranos and altos so the ensemble can satisfactorily meet the requirements the composer has made. Given such a balance it is quite possible to develop without fear of vocal damage or strain, a choir capable of a four-octave range (C′ in bass to c″ in soprano), and any director able to train the voices within that range has an organization capable of producing highly satisfying musical sounds.

If he can supplement this fine mixed choir with a capable male chorus and a full-voiced female chorus, he and his school can be highly satisfied indeed.

Part C.
The Great Demand for Male Singers

The chances for a man to make a successful career as a professional singer are about three times as great as for a woman. This is simply a case of supply and demand (as will be demonstrated in Appendix B).

Paradoxically, while there are more jobs available to male singers, there are fewer male than female singers moving from our high schools into the music schools and conservatories, to prepare themselves for these jobs.

The result is that any woman entering the professional field must compete with many other women for a relatively few jobs. In contrast, good tenors are scarce, the demand for them is great, so a competent tenor can often choose his assignments and name his price. Deep basses are in almost as short supply as tenors, so they too can expect to establish themselves as professional singers, if they are properly trained. Baritones, we hear, are comparatively more plentiful, but chances for gainful employment are much better for them, too, in comparison to the chances for sopranos and altos.

This is important for every professionally dedicated high school choral conductor to realize. One very valid goal set for us music educators is preparing our students for adult performance and enjoyment. Hence anybody concerned with teaching music to young people should be seeking out potential tenors and basses and encouraging them to develop their voices; chances for these tenors and basses for gainful employment are good if they choose to become professional singers, and a high school director does well if he finds and encourages his male singers.

The chances for male singers to participate in amateur vocal ensembles are superb, for in every community there are choirs and glee clubs and the appeal for men singers in notoriously urgent. Frequently there are part-time jobs to be had, e.g. serving as a paid soloist in a large church choir, or as a needed reinforcement for an amateur chorus that cannot recruit adequate volunteer men singers for a well-balanced choir.

Surely music teachers, of all educators, should be conscious of the vast opportunities for leisure time enjoyment and part-time employment in future years available to their students and be actively concerned in encouraging those students who will be best able to participate in such leisure time activities-and that means finding and training basses and tenors!

Part D.
The Democratic Ideal:
Equal Opportunity for All Regardless of Race, Creed or Sex

Democracy in education is one of the salient principles of American public school education. "Music for every child and every child for music" has been the slogan of the Music Educators' National Conference for many years.

If the music teaching profession, whether in public or parochial schools, accepts this slogan as valid, we music teachers are committed to try to reach every child enrolled in the institutions in which we teach.

Realistically, we know that this goal cannot be achieved solely through choral singing. Not every child has the vocal endowment or musical aptitude to develop into a successful ensemble singer, and fewer can hope to be outstanding soloists. Moreover, many potential music students are moved to choose non-musical outlets for their talents and ambitions, and must perforce pass up the opportunities for training in choral music. If in a high school of 1000 students there are only 500 or 300 enrolled in the various choral music organizations, nobody can justifiably point an accusing finger at the choral director. If in a junior high or middle school, vocal music is an elective subject in grade eight, not many educators can justifiably be concerned if only half the students register for choir or glee club. We surely can add to the slogan, "Every child for music — but not every child for CHORAL music."

But if, year after year, we were to find about 250 boys registering for choir, chorus and glee clubs, but only about 50 girls, there would very properly be searching questions asked. Musical talent is not sex-linked; we find the distribution of musical aptitude quite consistent for ALL humans. If, in a high school of 1000 students, there are approximately 500 boys and 500 girls, we can expect to find just as many boys as girls endowed with musical talent and potential ability. In other words, if enrollment in choral music is to correspond to the musical aptitudes and endowments of registrants, we can expect that there will be just about as many girls as boys enrolled in choral music.

If we find, year after year, that there are five boys for every girl actively participating in choral music, we can charge the choral director with a strong anti-female bias and accuse him of discriminating according to sex. Those individuals or groups that are concerned about equal rights for both women and men could

16

certainly find grounds for lodging complaint.*

The illustration chosen is, of course, quite unrealistic. There is no senior high school in the United States where the ratio of boy singers to girl singers is five to one. It would be difficult to find very many where the enrollment is close to one boy for one girl. But there *are* schools where the ratio is five girls to one boy, many such schools. As proof I refer to a survey made in 1957 and another in 1976 (Appendix A).*

Why is there such an imbalance endemic in our secondary schools? If we agree that boys are as well endowed as girls in musical aptitude and vocal endowment, there must be some factor that causes large numbers of girls to enroll in vocal music classes, but only a few boys.

It is my belief that many boys, talented and well endowed with promising voices, drop out of vocal music classes because:

1. There are certain built-in hazards that a boy must overcome that a girl does not encounter.
2. Too many music teachers are not sufficiently aware of those hazards, so do not adapt their methods and materials to the special needs of their boy singers.
3. Some music teachers are erroneously informed about how voices change and actually do harmful teaching, by asking boys to sing what they cannot sing without great strain.
4. Teachers as well as the general public tend to adopt false ideas about the appropriateness of musical participation by boys, so social pressures are put upon these boys to drop out of musical activities.

It is also my belief that the hazards facing a male singer can be changed into challenges. These hazards that are "built into" the maturing and growing up of all boys can be regarded as natural characteristics, therefore challenges to be studied, mastered and enjoyed. Those that are caused by uninformed or ill-informed teachers can be minimized as information is disseminated and teachers are better prepared to deal with the problems. Then those hazards caused by the frailty of man — the false excuses and incorrect explanations given for failures, the irrational, silly prejudices created by people trying to rationalize away their own weaknesses — will disappear as success is attained.

I hope that this book will have a part in bringing about this improvement. As more and more teachers take the positive attitude of meeting challenges head-on rather than the negative attitude of dreading difficult hurdles, I hope that more and more vocal coaches will open eyes and ears to learn what their students CAN do, as well as what they cannot do. I look forward to the time when in schools, churches and communities, ALL students will have the chance to experience the aesthetic enjoyment and social benefits of making fine music together.

---

*From evidence here presented, it would seem that many choral music directors in our junior and senior high schools ARE sex-biased and vulnerable to the charge that they are discriminating-*against males.*

SECTION 2
THE BOY CHOIR AND THE
BOY SINGER AGE 8 TO 12

Chapter IV

THE BOY TREBLE SINGER

By the time most boys are eight years old they are ready physically and psychologically for some formal training in singing. Of course boys can sing at a younger age. Many do, quite pleasantly and happily. Even before kindergarten, some can sing on pitch with correct rhythm; they may have a sizeable repertoire of nursery tunes, simple hymns, rhythm and game songs, even television and radio commercials. A rather precocious lad may be quite able to entertain informally a group of relatives and family friends to the delight of his sympathetic audience.

This can be quite beneficial, both musically and pedagogically speaking, if the songs are limited in range, and if the child sings spontaneously rather than under duress, in a light, unforced tone. But there is chance for harm if over-eager parents urge the little fellow to "Sing out so we can hear you", or if he is encouraged to continue singing to the point of vocal fatigue. Even more deplorable is the situation where a six or seven-year old is put on a stage as a featured performer. If there have been long rehearsals and the singing is forced and unnatural, permanent damage to the vocal apparatus may result.

More desirable than formal singing lessons in the nursery school and kindergarten years are the ear-training and rhythm-response activities engaged in as a group activity. Many children need help and guidance in finding the "up and down" and the "long and short" of music. When they are aware of pitch changes and rhythm patterns singing will come easily, but not before.

It has been my personal experience in over 25 years of elementary school supervision that boys as a group tend to mature more slowly than girls in acquiring this ability to discriminate pitch and to match tones. As I think back over the first and second grade classes I have observed, there were always more boys than girls in the group needing tone-matching exercises in the first and second grades, and there were always more boys than girls who could not "find their singing voices" until the end of the second grade year.

I remember cases where boys were labeled "out-of-tune singers" in those first two grades who became very capable, dependable members of my boy choir several years later. Had these boys not been allowed to mature at their own pace in the unpressured surroundings of an elementary school class, but had been subjected to the pressures of singing for public performance or derided for being so poor at singing, some very fine singers could have been lost. They would have been excluded from the singing group, labeled as deficient singers and would have lost any desire to join in singing activities. Just as there comes a time when a baby is ready to start

19

walking or talking, there is a time of readiness for singing, and that time varies greatly among individuals.

By the time he is eight years old a boy is usually in the third grade of elementary school. By this time he can read English independently, he is accustomed to working in class groups, he is able to do some work and practice on his own at home. He has probably developed a liking for some subject areas and found others less to his taste. If he sings on pitch in correct rhythm and he displays a fondness for singing he is probably ready to begin some specialized vocal training.

It is my belief, based on experience as well as observation, that there is much merit in beginning vocal training in a *group situation* when boys are age 8 or 9. For that reason I will begin this section dealing with the boy treble singer by discussing the boy choir and recommending that participation in a boy choir is the best way to begin formal vocal training, leaving a discussion of training the boy soloist to a later chapter.

Chapter V
REASONS FOR ORGANIZING A BOY CHOIR

Part A.

Vocal Development Reasons: Boy Centered

A most effective way to develop boy singers is to organize a boy choir. There are several reasons for this.

1. It is more efficient and more economical to teach young boys in a group in several sessions per week than to teach each boy in one private session each week.
   a. Fifty boys, each getting a half-hour of private instruction would require 25 hours of teaching time while three sixty-minute sessions per week will suffice for the same number of boys in a group.
   b. In these group sessions the young boy is under the direct surveillance of the master director; he will be vocalizing correctly and regularly in his important first lessons.
2. Competition is a powerful motivation for a boy to do his best. If he must pass an entrance try-out, he must strive to be better than his competitors.
   a. If he fails to win a place on the first trial, he will be impelled to try harder on the second chance, and prize his acceptance all the more if he passes.
   b. Once in the training class, he must strive to do good work in order to be promoted to the more advanced choirs.
3. Most boys have a strong desire to be accepted into an organization to which many of their age-mates belong, especially if membership carries the implication of excellence.
4. Younger boys tend to imitate other boys who are slightly older. As each new boy moves into an organized choral group he will tend to learn from the older boys with whom he will be singing.
5. In a group situation, there are desirable musical experiences not available to solo singers, e.g. singing two and three-part music, studying and performing choral works, singing in public without the strain of performing alone.
6. There is opportunity to supplement the musical experiences with highly attractive and enjoyable extra-curricular activities that add to the pleasure of being in a choir, e.g. summer camps, tours to other parts of the country, meeting and forming friendships with boys of similar tastes and talents, enjoying contests and tournaments.
7. Not many voice teachers are available to teach juveniles in private sessions and not many parents are inclined to pay for expensive private coaching for young children.

Part B.

Supplementary Reasons, Community and Director Oriented

While the primary purpose of organizing a boy choir is to train the singing voices of the choristers, there are other reasons for organizing and maintaining a boy choir. Here are some examples of motives that may impel you, the reader, to organize a boy choir.

1. You are an organist preparing to become the minister of music in a large parish

21

church or cathedral. Your assignment will include directing several choirs, including a boy choir. However you feel about it personally, if you want the appointment you must organize and maintain such a boy choir.

2. The Sons of Hibernia have begun a campaign to involve the youngest generation in the activities of their lodge. Besides attracting many boys into their organization by some organized activity, they would like to have a group sing the traditional songs of their ancestral Ireland. They advertise for a choir director. You want a job. You apply.

3. In a ghetto area there are social workers who want to organize a worth-while activity that will counteract the evil influences of boy gangs. It is proposed that a boy choir might serve the purpose. You have training as a choral director. You apply for the appointment.

In these examples the motivating force is obvious. You are preparing to be a professional choir director, you want a job and you want an opportunity to gain experience and recognition as a choral director. YOUR EMPLOYERS WANT TO USE THE CHOIR TO BRING BOYS INTO THEIR SPHERE OF INFLUENCE IN AN HONORABLE, ATTRACTIVE ENDEAVOR. Here are some situations where the motive is not so obvious.

4. You have always admired a certain noted European boy choir. You have a secret ambition to develop such a choir yourself. You seek an opportunity to develop such a choir.

5. Your former college friend has made a reputation for himself as a boy choir director in a neighboring community. Being competitive by nature and a bit envious of his success you decide to equal his accomplishment.

6. You are dismayed because there are so few good male singers in your community, so you plan a long-range campaign to improve the situation. A big part of that campaign is to start the boys in their most formative years on the road to becoming capable, interested singers. You hope, through a boy choir to "sell" the boys on developing their singing voices and the community on the charms of boy voices raised in song.

7. Your community theater group is staging a production that requires a group of boy singers (e.g. THE MAN WHO CAME TO DINNER by Moss Hart). You are an experienced choral singer so you recruit a few boys from families and friends of the cast and crew. The experience is so pleasant for you and the boys that you decide to continue and expand the singing group.

8. You are a recent graduate with a degree in choral conducting. Jobs are scarce and you have to take a temporary job in some non-musical field. In order to keep your conducting skills in practice and to display your talents to others, you decide to organize a community boy choir.

9. The boy scout regional council is seeking suggestions for summer recreational projects to supplement the usual sports programs and camping trips. You suggest that a good boy choir is a worthy, attractive enterprise that may bring more boys into the scouting program in large numbers with minimum of expense.

All of the above situations are quite honorable and legitimate. In fact, as I read the histories of various boy choirs in America, or talk with the directors of well-established boy choirs, I find that every one of the above situations has had a part in the formation of one or several choirs that are flourishing today. Nor are they the only motivating forces that have led to the formation of boys choirs, for there are many ways in which a boy choir can bring about desirable results other than purely providing musical training for young singers.

22

As I pointed out in chapter III, the almost universal appeal of boy voices raised in song and the pleasure that such singing gives to both the boy singers and their hearers is so great that many objectives other than those purely musical can be attained through the formation of a boy choir.

Chapter VI

THE QUALIFICATIONS OF A
GOOD BOY CHOIR DIRECTOR

If we accept the idea that establishing a boy choir is a good way to provide for the first formal training of male singers, it becomes desirable to find a good director for the choir. It is going to be the director who will work directly with the boy students in rehearsal and eventually in concert. Everybody concerned will look to him for guidance and leadership. IF YOU are thinking of being that director, or if you are responsible for finding that director, you will want some criteria for determining what the qualifications of such a director are.

Consider the case where a would-be director is enthusiastic but inept. He may not understand the limitations or the potentialities of the boy treble voice; he may be of the "louder, louder" school so tones are forced and are harsh and off-pitch. He may pitch the songs improperly, asking altos to sing too low or sopranos to strain for notes too high for their vocal resources.

I have heard a choir where the sopranos sang a half-tone flat with no correction by the conductor; where the altos, who should have been singing in parallel thirds with the sopranos, were actually singing at the interval of an augmented fourth while the director seemed totally unaware that anything was amiss. A well-known song involving a succession of dotted eighths followed by sixteenths came out as a succession of even eighth notes, and in a canon the sopranos entered a full beat late and so continued. Small wonder that nobody cared to hear this choir except some loyal parents and the most obtuse of patrons.

Ask yourself then, "Am I musically competent?" Do you know how to build the singing voices of young boys so the result is that clear, bright unforced sound so much beloved the world over? Will you be developing a solid, correct technique of voice production that will allow your boys to grow and progress into fine adult singers? Do you know how to achieve clean part-singing and clear diction? Will you be happy to work within the limitations of what children's voices can do, and will you enjoy that vocal result?

Secondly, along with musical competence, have you empathy for little boys? To you, are boys below twelve years of age "little monsters" or "precious little darlings" or "grubby little animals" or "little puppets to be manipulated and maneuvered by a martinet?" Or do you look on children as human beings with rights and hopes and special talents of their own? Can you find that fine line that separates the strict disciplinarian from the jovial good fellow and straddle it so you can at once command respect and obedience while winning affection and loyalty?

Consider the case where the director feels he must be a rigid drill

24

master, so he demands such intense concentration and undeviating obedience that little boys cannot stand the strain of a full hour rehearsal, especially if he scowls, scolds, uses sarcasm or even physical pain. There have been cases, I hear, where boys have refused to go back to another rehearsal or where parents have removed their boys because they have been too harshly dealt with.

Just as much a cause for failure is over-permissiveness, where the director is so eager to be considered a good fellow that he jollies his boys along and lets anything go for fear that if he reprimands he will be disliked; or worries that if he sets high standards he will lose the affection of his little lads. This director speaks, but the boys do not listen; he gives directions which the boys do not follow. The caretaker complains of broken furniture and unnecessary litter. Parents who come to observe are dismayed at the bedlam that prevails and withdraw their boys, or the better boys themselves quit in disgust because their time is being wasted.

Thirdly, can you communicate with the younger generation? This is not a matter of how old you are. I have observed a seventy-year-old priest getting his points across to his choirboys efficiently and economically, and I have watched a recent college graduate getting only stifled yawns and restless shuffling as he spoke. I have seen a middle-aged, motherly woman who had her boy singers responding to her every signal while an attractive, vivacious young miss found it necessary to scold, to harangue, to pound and to stamp while her students became resentful, resistant and even defiant.

How can you tell if you have the musicality, the empathy, the presentation skills mentioned above? If you are not sure in your own mind, I pose these questions to help to clarify your thinking.

Have you had any success in coaching one or more singers yourself? Have you taught any kind of music, instrumental, vocal or theoretical, with success? Can you play the piano, or any other instruments, fairly well? Do you know a reputable source book that outlines methods for developing the singing voice? Have you ever taken voice lessons from a reputable teacher and did you analyze what that teacher had you do, so you could discover his method for building a singing voice? Have you had much opportunity to watch other choral directors as they rehearsed their groups or voice coaches as they taught their students?

Have you had a good experience working with boys in groups, e.g., led a boy scout troup, coached a Little League baseball team, taught a church school class? When you see boys playing at some game are you apt to stop to watch them and do you feel an urge to join them, or do you pass them by? In your own childhood, did you get along well with boys your own age?

The music director is not the only leader needed, for there is much more to organizing and maintaining a boy choir than just directing music. You will want some organized assistance. You need a thoroughly competent piano-accompanist. There should be somebody in charge of equipment so music is filed and kept in repair or so costumes (if there are any) are properly fitted. You can well use a prefect to handle such matters as helping with discipline and morale; taking care of personal problems; handling emergencies; checking stage and properties; keeping attendance records.

True, in a small choir of twenty-five or less, you can be a one-man director for there are such versatile directors who succeed year after year. An inept pianist can be a detriment rather than a help, so you may feel you have to play the accompaniments yourself as YOU want them played. But for best performance, anything which takes your full attention away from the all-important matter of teaching the boys how to sing and how to present music excellently penalizes the choir and its performance. Before and during a concert or rehearsal the director should be concerned with musical matters only and your full attention should be focused on the performance of the music; a missing button, a lost choir robe, a fainting boy, a misplaced piece of equipment — these are items better handled by an assistant. During rehearsals there may be a knock at the door, a telephone ringing, a mischievous trouble-maker to keep in line or trouble in the parking lot to be straightened out; attendance taking, having music in repair and ready for quick distribution, straightening up the room before and after practice sessions — these should not be distractions for the director. Best of all, if this assistant can take a section of the choir into another room to work out a troublesome passage, or to coach a soloist for correct notes and words, how much more can be accomplished in limited time!

This is an aspect of leadership that will be worth developing — the knack for finding and keeping capable assistants. Happy is the director whose helpers are competent but not obtrusive; Unfortunate is he who gets embroiled with adult assistants. Hard is the lot of a director who must take care of all things himself, for the quality of his musical results must suffer as his attention is constantly distracted. Equally hard is the lot of the director where his assistants get in his way, where the pianist wants to set the tempo or dynamics, the prefector intrudes on rehearsal time as he handles routine matters, or a parent becomes bossy or is tactless so that feuds develop and the director must be a peacemaker.

Chapter VII
THE RECRUITMENT OF BOY
SINGERS FOR A CHOIR

To maintain a boy choir there must be boy singers. In order to get good boy singers you will have to plan a good recruitment campaign. In ideal situations you will have enough prospective singers applying for membership so that you can try them out to determine which boys are most likely to become satisfactory singers, and you would like to eliminate in advance boys who have little talent or qualifications. It may take several years of functioning before a choir attains the prestige that will attract candidates in sufficient number for that situation to prevail. For the first few years, you will have to find your boys as best you can, and work with the talent that is available.

If you are being sponsored, if you are working in a certain church or have been hired by a civic of fraternal organization, you can expect some help. The priest or minister or rabbi will introduce you to members of the congregation, there can be announcements in the church bulletins or lodge newsletters; quite possibly you will be supplied with a list of boys of the proper age for you to call on personally. If the park board or police department is sponsoring the choir as a civic project, the word will go out via notices to social workers or settlement houses, and newspapers can be persuaded to inform the general public. If the local symphony orchestra wants some boy singers for a special performance, e.g. the Prelude to Boito's "Mefistofele", you can expect the announcement to be disseminated through the musical community.

That assistance will be valuable, but if you wait complacently for a large response to published announcements you are apt to be disappointed. The first turnout may be meager as boys are hesitant about appearing in something new or cautious parents wait to hear how things are working out. You will do well to do some active recruiting on your own, via the telephone or even by house calls.

If you have decided to organize a boy choir quite on your own, the problem is even more difficult. Suppose there is no sponsoring organization and you have no indication from anybody at all that there is a desire for a boy choir. How then do you gather your boy singers?

One of the tried and true ways is for you to gather a small group of boys, e.g. relatives, sons of family friends, children of known musicians in the community, and to start informally and modestly. As the boys speak enthusiastically about their pleasant experiences, you hope they will attract their friends and acquaintances to come join the group. If the boys are heard by people in the community, you hope your singers will captivate the audiences with their delightful singing so other boys will be motivated to join you. If all goes well and the

27

fame of the choir spreads, membership will increase and competition to be chosen will become keener. The auditions can become more exacting and discriminating. Eventually you hope you can require a period of pre-training or cadet-ship when you can give instruction in voice production, notation-reading, practice in part-singing. Also important, you can, in this period of cadetship, discover which boys are amenable to the routine of rehearsal and working in groups.

This method, uncertain in its beginnings, has one advantage. Should things not work out well or if you discover that you are not going to be happy directing boy singers, you are free at any time to stop the enterprise. If you find you cannot develop singing of the quality you want, or if nobody seems to enjoy your results, you are not committed in any way to continue the project.

The disadvantage to the method just described is that you must find singers as best you can, with no good source of contacts. A quicker method for initiating a boy choir is to find or contrive a special occasion. If the city or county is celebrating its centennial with a pageant, or if the local lodge is to host a district convention, or if there is to be a community Christmas tree in the park, or if the bishop is due for a visit to the local church, you have a reason to put out a call for boys to form a special choir for the occasion. We have already mentioned the situation where a play or an opera is planned by a community organization and there is a need for boy singers. The public appeal for interested boys can go out, the plans for the choir to sing can be explained, the rehearsal schedule announced, the date of the planned performance posted, and the music selected. If the first turnout is disappointingly small, the boys who do come can be asked to recommend good boy singers or dependable friends. You, as director, can supplement their persuasion with a telephone call to the parents.

Often you can find a recruiting committee who will do your canvassing for you, this committee being made up of the adults concerned, some friendly parents, one or two of the most enthusiastic boys.

Chapter VIII
AUDITION PROCEDURES

Fortunate is the choir director who can select the boys by tryouts, who can find the most apt and eliminate the incapable and untalented. Even the director of a church or community or ethnic choir will hope for the right to choose his singers; hard is the lot of the director who must accept *any* boy who belongs to his church or synagogue, or who must work with an unmusical boy from a ghetto area "because he needs the social benefits the choir can give him;" or who finds the "master of the lodge" insisting that his three untalented sons must be included in the choir program.

To find out what procedures experienced directors follow in auditioning their prospective choir members, I have asked eleven "experts" to outline what they do when new boys come to try out. Understandably not all of these eleven were willing to be precise, but a gratifying number did go quite into detail. From these responses I have worked out a composite audition procedure that can serve as a model for anybody setting up an audition plan for the first time.

The first response I asked for was a listing, in order or preference, of the attributes each director considers most significant in predicting probable success of a boy candidate. Making a composite order of preference, these are the items.

1. Music aptness, i.e. keen pitch discrimination, ready response to rhythm patterns, display of good tonal memory.
2. General intelligence: revealed by quickness at understanding and responding to directions supplemented by background inquiries from school teachers and administrators.
3. Pleasant quality of voice, quite free from faults.
4. A poised, assured manner, rather than a hesitant, bashful appearance or a brash, aggressive type of behavior.
5. Good family background, i.e., one or both parents obviously interested and eager to co-operate.
6. Good study habits and self-discipline as noted by school teachers, clergymen and group-leaders.
7. Attractive looks, i.e. not so much physical handsomeness as being well-groomed and neatly dressed.
8. A voice of sizeable range, either high or low, and of some volume and power.
9. Evidence of a stable family background, with interested parents; a family having reputation as responsible, upright citizens in the community. Some family member with musical background either at professional or amateur level is an added strength.
10. Ability to play some musical instrument, preferably piano or an orchestral instrument.

It is important to note that for the first four items there was almost uniform agreement. It may come as a surprise that these experienced directors have found that the combination of musical aptness and high general intelligence are more important than a beautiful voice for indicating a good potential boy choir singer. Apparently the voice need not be particularly good as long as there are no faults (hoarseness, extreme nasality, coarseness) that would require therapy or much individual training. Add to this the straightforward manner rather than an obnoxious forwardness or a withdrawing, hesitant manner and the chances are very good that the boy will develop very well.

On items 5 to 9 there was considerable variation; item 9 was particularly controversial, ranging from "very important" to "not to be considered." Likewise number 8 aroused such comments as "may be a mixed blessing; too hard to blend." Number 10 was volunteered by two directors as being helpful, the others did not mention instrumental playing at all.

In your announcements of tryouts you will want to include some important information. The location where the auditions will be held should be clearly mentioned as often as possible. A variety of times should be scheduled, since family situations vary widely. There should be one or more "after dinner" evening times as well as several late afternoon "before dinner" periods; at least one Saturday morning and a late Saturday afternoon take care of situations where choir membership is open to boys in rural areas outside the city limits or when fathers are "on the road" during the week; some directors find a Sunday afternoon accomodates people with unusual situations. A rule of thumb suggested by one director is that 12 to 15 boys can be handled at a single session; so, if 60 boys are expected to try out, at least five different audition times should be available.

Each boy candidate must be accompanied by at least one parent, preferably the father for psychological and sociological reasons. If there is no parent a responsible adult should be substitute.

Each boy is asked to bring a simple nursery tune, a Sabbath Day School hymn or a song learned in school.

Since you are going to be checking on items 4, 5, 7 as well as 2 along with the items strictly musical (numbers 1, 3, 8, 10) you may find the following advance preparations suggested by our experienced directors worth considering:

1. Several veteran choirboys should be on hand to act as greeters and ushers while being used as "assistants" at one point in the audition. If this is a new venture, so there are no experienced choirboys, several personable adults who sing well can be pressed into service. These ushers take turns in greeting the candidates, showing them and their parents to a waiting place, handing them the audition sheet and number, and being a "friendly adviser" through the whole procedure.

2. Several comfortable chairs are placed at the far end of the audition room, for parents' convenience. Several songbooks with very familiar songs, especially one with "America," should be in the audition room. If the accompanist does not transpose readily, the accompaniment for "America" should be written out in at least five keys — e.g., F, G, B-flat, C, and E-flat.

3. Individual blanks, numbered in sequence, are ready so each boy can provide desired information to hand to the auditioner.

As each candidate arrives, he and his parent are greeted politely by one usher who introduces himself, tries to put the boy at his ease, hands him a numbered audition sheet (see Appendix D), shows him to a place where he can fill it out, and hovers about until the boy's number is called. The usher has been coached to observe many things, e.g. item #2, if the young boy fills out the information independently and quickly, if he responds readily, sits quietly or fidgets or moves about, making a nuisance of himself.

As the candidate is ushered into the audition room, the director makes mental notes on appearance and attitude of the boy; as the adult is shown to a seat at the far end of the room, mental notes are made of the parent's appearance and attitude too. A few casual comments or questions may be made to put boy and father at ease, while getting clues as to what the religious affiliation is (if that is going to be important), where the parent works, whether or not he is active in any civic organizations, or whether the boy or the parent is acquainted with present choir boys in that school and part of town.

When the boy candidate is somewhat at ease, he sings the song of his choice, the director maintaining a pleasant but impassive expression no matter what the quality of performance. If there is a lapse or hesitation, the tester may casually say "I liked that. Now I'd like to hear you again, but from across the room. Would you stand over there and sing it again?" Opinion is divided about the auditioner writing notations or comments during the performance, with most agreeing that it is better not to write at all, or at least to be unobtrusive with encoded jottings (e.g. sh= shrill, br= bright, th= throaty) to be made quickly and casually while boy and father are present.

From here on, each director may want to proceed on his own as his particular training and experience dictate. For those who would like some specific test-items, I refer you to Appendix D.

Whatever the procedure, it is agreed that 100% prediction for success is never achieved. There are other characteristics that cannot be measured. Besides the "challenges" suggested above, some choir directors have other vocal "tasks" that they highly recommend to determine a boy's readiness for choir membership or his likelihood for success.

Most are in agreement that there should also be a period of pre-choir training. The *declared* reason for this is to develop a good basic technique for singing — some vocalising to extend the range, working on tone quality until a uniformity of blend is achieved, and providing for experience in part-singing.

A second reason for this trial period is that there seems to be no test devised that foretells how a boy will adapt to the choir discipline, how he will work alongside other boy singers, or whether he will follow through on his homework and assigned vocalising.

No sure test can be given to predict if parents will be co-operative, will share in car pools, will help with committee work, will provide choir equipment or will help a young boy in caring for choir costumes or music.

A term of training lessons in late spring and summer is usually sufficient to eliminate the lazy, the careless, the undisciplined or the maladjusted that are not revealed in the first audition, and will usually discover where a boy's probable success is apt to be negated by a problem parent. During the same period you are discovering the boy whose eyes glow with eagerness, who responds readily and

31

participates happily and finding the parent who displays great interest and obvious support for what you are doing.

Chapter IX

THE IDEAL CHOIR TONE AND HOW TO ACHIEVE IT *

Since you are organizing a boy choir, you will want it to achieve the *sound* of a boy choir. There is a certain quality, a timbre, a distinctive sound that even the amateur, untrained listener is quick to recognize when young boys are singing correctly. (That is, when they are not urged to sing LOUD, to "give their all", to hit the highest and lowest tones with full force). There is a difference in the sound of an all-girl chorus or a mixed boy-and-girl children's chorus and an all-boy choir, and only the most obtuse of listeners would fail to differentiate between a chorus of adult women and a choir of young boys. Anyone who has heard the Vienna Boy Choir or the Westminster Cathedral Choir knows what I mean. Nor do you have to go to Europe to hear this sound; the Columbus Boy Choir, the Texas Boy Choir, the boys from Tucson or San Francisco or any other of our touring and recording American boy choirs display this distinctive tone quality superbly.

In my search to find a listing of the attributes of good boy choir sound, I have asked ten experienced, established**boy choir directors for their definitions. The resulting descriptions are points on which all, or at least most of these directors have agreed.

1. The tones are clear and resonant, with no harsh overtones or muffled sounds
2. The head tones are well developed and unforced.
3. The chest tones are full and rich, but not pushed and strident
4. The two regsiters are so smoothly blended that the passage from one to another cannot be easily detected.
5. Tones are so well focused that the voices are heard in the farthest reaches of a large auditorium
6. There is enough control so that the loudest tones are full and resonant with no trace of stridency or harshness, while the soft tones float effortlessly. The transition from soft to loud or loud to soft is so gradual there is no perceptible point of transition.
7. All the voices blend so that no individual voices can be singled out.

To find methods by which these seven points can be developed in boys at the immature ages of nine to twelve, I asked our ten "established directors" to share some of their methods.

---

*Much of the material included in this chapter appeared originally in THE CHORAL JOURNAL, the publication of The American Choral Directors' Association, the December 1975 issue, and is used here by the special permission of the editorial board of that magazine.

**Established in that their choirs have existed more than ten years; they have concertized and toured extensively, they enjoy the respect and admiration of other choral directors, and they are presently willing to be personally involved in sharing their knowledge and experiences with others.

I had expected that not all of those who were asked would tell very much, for it has been my experience that most directors have their own "secret devices" and "special procedures" to which they attribute their unique successes. To my pleased surprise, almost every one of those who were asked to contribute, gave some very meaningful suggestions and provocative devices designed to get the particular tone quality described above.

To these responses I added a great many more from people who responded to the questionnaire* in the May, 1975, issue of THE CHORAL JOURNAL, where persons unknown to me graciously took the time and effort to write extended descriptions of their methods, techniques, and devices.

From all of these contributions plus the procedures I have developed in my own twenty-five years of boy choir directing, I have endeavored to evolve a composite "procedure" which incorporates the points on which there is general agreement and to avoid any unique procedures that do not seem to agree with the general consensus.

Let us suppose that you have ten, sixteen, or twenty new boys, age nine or eight, assembled for their first lesson. They are understandably eager, expectant, and a bit tense as they await some sort of new and exciting experience.

It is recommended that you start with a high head tone, for you want to redirect the vocal apparatus from the low-pitched conversational register to the high, light, unforced head register. Let us not use the word "falsetto" for, although it is a commonly used term, it carries with it the implication that there is something false or fake about it. Instead of the Italian word, let us use the French derivative from the same Latin root "fossa" to get "faucette".

In both languages "fossa" (ditch) became "pipe" (windpipe?). Just as the water is diverted into a smaller pipe (It. falsett, Fr. faucette), so the air flow is re-directed so only the inner bands of the vocal bands function.

Group the boys in a semi-circle around the "tail" of the grand piano, or around your mini-piano so as you sit or stand at the keyboard you have each boy well within your line of vision (It is obvious that one of the big old-fashioned pianos backed up against a wall will not do).

1. Ask them to extend their arms high above their head in a big stretch while yawning uninhibitedly, uttering a very high pitched "Ha.a.a.a" that slides down in a rapid glissando. Repeat this several times, encouraging them to move their arms high and low, and to lift shoulders up and down as they stretch and yawn. Spot the boy whose yawn-sigh starts the highest and descends the lowest, and ask him to demonstrate so the others may imitate.

2. Ask your little boys to pretend they are country bumpkins seeing a city skyscraper for the first time. Direct them thus: "Let your mouth hang open in surprise, move your head slowly from side

---

*The Choral Journal is the official magazine of the American Choral Directors' Association. Its publication address has just recently been changed from Tampa, Florida, to Lawton, Oklahoma.

to side with eyes staring away up there at the top of the tall building. Make soft, high, sliding 'oh's' to express your amazement." Again spot the boy whose tones are the highest and freest so he can model for the others to imitate.

3. Ask the boys to imitate little puppy-dogs whining for attention.

4. Ask them to be good actor-pretenders. When you, the teacher, say accusingly "Did you break the glass?" they are to look very innocent, open their eyes wide, let their mouth hang open loosely as the say in a high, soft voice "Whoooo. . . me? Oh no.o.o.o.o."

All four of the above will go much better if you personally can demonstrate effectively. If you cannot, choose one of your older, more experienced choir boys who can serve as a model. If you have no experienced choirboys your first year, proceed as best you can with piano. It is NOT recommended that you bring in a woman or a girl to demonstrate, but if a tenor with a clear, light "faucette" can be found he will serve very well as a model.

When your little rookies have learned how to "turn on the faucet" to produce a high, light, unforced tone, they are ready to "direct the flow" of tone, i.e. to control the pitch.

5. You blow high f' and d' on your pitch pipe (if fianances permit, give each boy a chromatic pitch pipe for home practice) or strike f' and d' on the piano. In a high head tone you (or your boy-veteran) sing "yoo-hoo" asking the cadets to imitate. If there is reluctance, stiffness, tension, you can encourage them to yawn and stretch again.

Next try f#-d#, then g'-e', etc., taking them as high as they can go easily. Do not be amazed if one or two of your little boys approach high c' successfully after a few practice sessions! Of course you are alert for any signs of throat tension, over-eagerness, straining, reminding them always to keep the feeling of stretching and yawning.

6. Now try the descending scale. Tuning on f' you or your boy-veteran sing down the scale in quarter-notes, andante, using the word "too." Be sure the head tone is carried throughout the full octave, allowing no shifting into the heavier chest tone.

During the next several lessons, start the descending scale on e', on d', on c', encouraging the cadets to "keep it light," to carry the faucet-tone all the way down, for the very good reason that most American boys have over-developed their chest tones, even abused them. They have, in their outdoor play, in their raucous shouting, in their "tough talk" pushed their chest tones over-much and over-high, until there is almost certain to be a trace of roughness and of heaviness that you want to obliterate. Only until the habits and the reflexes of singing in the light head tone have been established do you begin to work on the chest tones.* (See example 1 for a song using the descending scale.)

Meanwhile, you are also working to attain homogeneity of tone quality. There is almost uniform agreement that the first vowel of choice here is the sound "oooh" as in "cool" or "moon." Certainly the English choirmasters have exploited this vowel sound for several

---

*I am well aware that the terms "head voice" and "chest voice" are not valid. The sound producing mechanism is in the larynx. But the two terms are widely used and *do* serve as an "image" for students, so they are used here, albeit reluctantly.

Example 1   WE MERRY MINSTRELS — Purcell

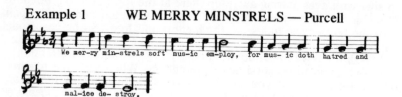

We mer-ry min-strels soft mus-ic em-ploy, for mus- ic doth hatred and

mal-ice de- stroy.

centuries, and none of our "commenters" have made a case for a different one. This vowel is high and back in the mouth, so it tends to direct the tone upward while opening the oral cavity "all the way back."

Go back to that first lesson in "innocence." Ask each boy to open his eyes wide, raise his eyebrows high, breathe deeply and say the words "Who.o.o.o. me?" and then "Who.o.o.o. yo.o.o.o?" as if utterly amazed that the teacher could say a thing like that!

If you prefer a more mechanical approach try this. Say "Open your mouth wide. Put your pointer finger all the way back into your mouth, as far back as you can without actually touching. Remember, your finger is probably dirty, so as you wrap your mouth around that finger, don't let any part of your mouth touch the finger. Now pull the finger out without changing the position of your mouth at all. Inhale, and matching pitch to this (sound f') sustain a surprised "ooooh." Don't let your mouth change position, open your throat as far back as you can, duck your head ever so slightly to keep that loose feeling in your neck." Spot the boy who comes the closest to the desired tone and have him demonstrate the sound as well as the sight of mouth and throat for the others to imitate.

The experienced director will recognize this vowel sound as the one the English choirmasters have used to achieve the distinctive tone quality known politely as "the cathedral tone", more derisively as "the hooty tone." Once the cadets get this sound, they sing down and up the scale, they sing arpeggios, short phrases, and complete songs on this neutral sound "oooh." For clean tongue articulation, "too" may be used; for a light "diaphragm bounce" in faster passages, the syllable "whooo" is good.

Some directors continue to use the ooh-vowel for a long time, beginning every vocalisation, every song with the boys using this neutral sound as they learn pitch and rhythm. Others prefer to counteract its hootiness with a very bright EEE as in the exclamation "Whee.ee.ee." This vowel is also high but it is far forward in the oral cavity; to use an old-fashioned phrase, it moves the voice "into the mask."

Care must be taken that the tongue, which HAS to be arched high, does not rise so high that it touches the roof of the mouth so the tone is pinched and scream-like. The admonition "Smile, but keep your teeth apart" will help here.

One director dropped the hint that he uses the French word for "summer," "été", where the vowel is halfway between ee and ay, and the "t" moves the tongue toward the alveolar ridge rather than to the roof of the mouth.

Another device hinted at by an experienced director is to ask each boy to pretend he is about to sneeze. As he lowers his head and wrinkles his nose, he gives a few preliminary gasps, then utters a strongly aspirated "heee."

Anybody old enough to remember the days of vaudeville, before the era of microphones and sound amplification, will recall that this was the over-bright sound exploited by singers of that day so their voices would cut through any orchestral accompaniment and ping up to the top balcony. Obviously if over-used, the tones will become white with a tendency to shrillness, not quite what is expected of a boy choir.

Midway between the hooty "ooh" and the cutting "eee" is the European "ah." This vowel can be difficult to focus properly if a director is working with boys from the midwest, the deep south or the western plains. The fundamental position of this vowel is low in the mouth, so it tends to be unfocused and to spread, especially when boys are accustomed to speak with a drawl or a twang.

A hint from one director is to use the French exclamation "ooh-la-la" or the American expression of derision "la-dee-dah" with the tip of the tongue touching the alveolar ridge lightly to direct the tone toward the front of the oral cavity ("into the mask," "toward the base of the nose," "into the moustache"). To avoid the complication of placing the tongue, have the boys say "A-ha!" as in "A-ha, I've caught you!" said with eyebrows lifted high and a smile of triumph.

Once these three vowels are properly formed and the desired tone-coloring of each is attained, the word of choice to combine them seems to be "Alleluia." The first syllable is the well-focused "ah"; the second syllable is the "almost ee" of "été"; the third syllable is the high back "ooh" and the fourth is the "ah" again. A descending scale from high f', with the word "alleluia" well formed on each tone at a medium fast tempo, if properly executed (formed with a "rubber mouth") can blend the desirable qualities of each of the three vowels into a remarkably resonant, free, clear singing tone. If all goes well, the voices are blending, none stick out, the boys sound like an ensemble instead of a group of individuals.

From these three vowels can be discovered all the other vowel colorings needed for singing in English, Latin or whatever. One good exercise suggested to get the boy singers to "get the feel" of these vowels as they seem to "move about in the mouth" is to say in succession on a given pitch "heed-hid-head-hade-had-hide-hod-hawed-hud-hood-who'd," feeling the focus of tone shift from high front to middle-low to high back.

Of course anybody who has ever worked with eight-or nine-year-olds knows that, with their short attention span, only a short amount of time can be spent on straight vocalisation at any one session. No matter how docile and tractable your cadets, five minutes of the above type of exercises at a stretch will be as much as they can take at first. So of course you will be teaching songs (Remember, they came to sing something and the family at home will want them to have something to sing!). But in the teaching you will start with either the too-too-too or the tee-tee-tee or the ta-ta-ta sound before words are attempted; later as certain consonants need improving it may be "koo-koo" or "ra-ra" or "ba-pa-ta," or whatever combination of consonants is needing attention at the time. As song words are learned, whenever the tones become undesirable, you select the corrective vowel of choice and vocalise the troublesome passage several times. Eventually the boys will be able to sharpen focus, lighten or darken the coloring as desired, and the voices will become homogenous and there will be no troublesome voices that "stick out."

All of the above is valid up to a point. Always the boys of any given city, state, region will have a distinctive tone quality. In the deep south the ubiquitous softness of "hi-ya, y'all" will never be entirely eradicated. The nasal "howdee-podner" of the western plains, the clipped, tight vowels of New England, the Chicago twang— all of these will still be there in just enough quantity to tinge the tone quality to give each boy choir its own unique tone quality.

Several of us smiled knowingly, a few years back, when a certain noted English choirmaster announced that he was going to work with a group of American boys until he had developed in them the desired ENGLISH choral tone. He came, he stayed awhile and then departed for England to be heard of no more. Anybody who has compared the drawled American "I dunno" to the tightly formed, crisp British "I don't know" understands why he was foredoomed to disappointment from the start.

Similarly it is not likely that an American boy choir can ever achieve the sound of the German-Austrian lads with their rolled r's and their peculiar umlaut vowels, or the French with their nasals, or the Russians with their heavy "nyet." If you, like several of our contributors, have said "I know what the tone is that I am trying to achieve, but I always have to settle for something less than the ideal," your frustration is understandable. After a boy has been speaking in a certain dialect for some seven years, he is not going to develop an entirely different method of producing vocal sounds in a few months or even years of spaced practices. Of course those who meet their boys four or five times a week will come closer to the sound the director wants than those who have only two or one sessions per week.

This is not necessarily cause for sorrow or dismay. In variety is interest. Who wants every fine concert singer to sound exactly like every other? How monotonous if we could not compare the sounds and style of the ten top symphony orchestras in the world, or the boy choirs of Austria, Italy, England and France. Half the fun of giving critiques would be gone.

As for me, in a quarter of a century of working with a boy choir, I have never ceased to marvel at how adept most young human males are at adjusting their vocal apparatuses. How often my boys have come off the playground or from the parking lot, talking vociferously, laughing boisterously, indulging in horseplay, with voices pitched high and loud. I strike a chord on the piano, and allow them a few moments to assume the proper stance. It is as if I had flicked an invisible switch inside the boy-mechanism, for out comes a soft, resonant, floating high tone, thoroughly satisfying, and entirely unlike the chattering sound of a few minutes earlier. If the English choirmaster shakes his head at our too "personal" American tone, and the French director is disappointed because our sound does not "cut through" I can match their disdain with a derisive smile when I hear the English lads attempting songs from "Oklahoma" with a British accent, or the Parisians attempting the spiritual "Deep River" in their bright nasal voices.

There comes a day when these rookies can carry the light clear head-tone down the full scale with never a break, no signs of tension, no roughness of sound, at least to a middle-C and even to a B-flat. Then the working up from the fuller, richer chest tones can begin.

One very good concept that has been suggested is that of "building a pyramid." As the boys assume a balanced but relaxed stance, they are to think of a pyramid (or a cone if you prefer) with a wide base that tapers to a sharp point at the top. Tuning on a high f′, they think "high and pointed." As they sing down the scale each tone is to be slightly broader and a bit more solid. By the time they reach "low-do" the tone should feel as big as the base of the pyramid (but not forced! At no time is the word "louder" used). Conversely, with the ascending scale the lowest tone is thought of as solid and firm, but each succeeding tone becomes slightly smaller as the scale tapers to a high, sharp point.

Nothing much has been said thus far about establishing proper breath support and control, since this is not a major factor in establishing a definite quality or color of tone. It is rather well agreed, however, that without proper breathing habits, there are apt to be tensions in the throat, shoulders and upper chest that may inhibit a free-flowing tone. So we will include here one very intriguing approach to having each boy discover the proper muscles to use in breathing and a suggestion of how to get him to use those muscles.

1. Ask the boys to pretend they are balancing on a diving board. With arms extended wide at shoulder height, they are to balance at the end of the board, rising on their toes then settling back lightly on their heels.

2. After several balances, when boys think they have found the "center of balance," they let their arms drop to their side, they close their eyes and hold the position for a slow count of ten. You can say to the rookies, "If you are in perfect balance, boys, you won't sway a bit, but if you are off-center you will find yourself falling forward or backward."

3. Eyes open, each boy presses his upper teeth firmly against his lower lip and sucks in his breath until his lungs are completely filled, pulling hard against the resistance provided by the teeth. Remind the boys to keep shoulders loose-and-low and to fill the lungs from the back and sides.

4. When each boy thinks he has reached full capacity, ask him to suck in a bit more. To his surprise and your satisfaction, he will feel the lower abdomen (about a hand's width below the navel) tipping inward.

Note well that because of the pressure of teeth on lip, the boy will have to pull hard to get the air in, so he feels the proper muscles as they exert their pull. But teacher had better be alert, for some little fellow, unused to the rich supply of oxygen and the pull of unused muscles may pitch forward in a faint! By all means, only one or at most two attempts are to be scheduled at a given practice for several weeks.

There is one important factor yet to discuss in this matter of choral tone—the director. Above all, he must have a very clear aural image of the tone quality he wants, and should be constantly seeking to add to his "pocketful of devices" to get his boy singers to achieve it.

Once he has attained a desired tone quality, for even the briefest moment, he must be consistent and persistent to repeat and maintain this ideal sound. It does little good if he vocalises his boys for ten minutes to establish proper concepts and techniques if he then, in his hurry to cover much ground as he drills parts or goes over a large number of songs, lets "anything" go. Transfer of training does NOT occur automatically, and little boys maintain only those standards insisted on by their teacher. It is better to develop only a few songs for the repertoire at first, and to choose no songs involving sophisticated harmonic or contraptal problems while the establishment of the ideal tone quality is going on.

Even when a particular quality and homogeneity of tone is achieved to the conductor's satisfaction, he can expect criticism. It is not at all an unusual happening that after a concert he may hear in succession such contradictory comments as 1) "tone was too straight and impersonal," vs. "too much vibrato and individuality," 2) "tone just heavenly," vs. "tone too forced," 3) "too intense, too adult," vs. "tone too pale and colorless," or 4) "admirable variations in tone coloring."

As we said in our introductory paragraphs, everybody has his own concept of what a boy choir should sound like, and look like, and while there is general agreement, individual listeners can vary in specifics. If you try too hard to model your boys after those Austrians or French or English choirs, your American audience may shake its collective head in distate; if you let the local dialect color the sound too much, the critics in other parts of the country may criticize adversely.

How can a director then be sure of himself, when he gets such a "bewildering variety of criticisms?" Let me suggest a few objective, observable signs that you are doing a satisfactory job.

1. Your boys can rehearse for a full sixty minutes without showing fatigue or loss of vibrant tone; they can present a full ninety minute program including music demanding some virtuosity and endurance, while remaining responsive and alert.

2. They sing songs of varying schools, periods, styles, with satisfactory gradations in dynamics, in shadings, in tempi, responding to director's demands readily.

3. Boy graduates are still singing well ten years after "graduation" from the choir, with comments made directly or by implication that the training received carried right on into adulthood.

4. The choir has little difficulty with pitch; the boys seldom sing flat or sharp because they are so much in control of their tone production that they can adjust quickly.

5. Many people like to hear your boys sing. Requests for appearance are frequent, and audience reaction is uniformly favorable.

Chapter X
INTRODUCING PART SINGING

There comes a time in the development of most boy choirs when they are ready for part-singing. Not that there is any reason to avoid singing in unison. A choir of boy trebles singing a soaring melody can produce a very pleasing musical effect. Many master composers have written for unison boy trebles. Most boy choirs have a collection of unison songs in their libraries to be used many time on many different occasions.

In some situations a small boy choir, rehearsing only once a week and singing a modest number of performances, may never attempt anything but unison singing. Most directors just starting a choir wisely begin with unison and work exclusively in that voicing until they have achieved the proper tone quality, the desired blend of voices and the responsiveness to directions, and several try-out public performances have been lived through.

Unison singing has some limitations, so before many months have gone by introduction of part-singing can begin even in a small choir. The storehouse of compositions arranged for two-part or three-part voices is immense and the list of "standard compositions" and "old favorites" that everybody expects a boy choir to sing at some time or other is extremely long. There may be occasions when the choir will have to sing without instrumental accompaniment when unison songs would sound rather thin and spare but a three part arrangement would sound quite complete, even without piano or organ support.

Let us suppose that your choir has been practicing for several months. The boys are acquiring the "sound" you want, they have established proper breathing habits, they sing on pitch and with precise rhythms, they respond well to your directions and are displaying a high level of enthusiasm and camaraderie. You know that some can soar up to high c″ and others can produce a solid, unforced G. They are certainly ready to begin singing in parts.

Part A.
Contrapuntal Singing

Many directors start with rounds, e.g. "Are You Sleeping" or "Row Row Your Boat". Personally I prefer starting with "simultaneous songs" for success comes rather quickly when each group is singing an entirely DIFFERENT tune and there is less temptation to "flip over to the other team".

Take for example the songs "Skip to My Lou" and "Bell in the Tower". When each has been learned thoroughly and each has been sung with assurance in unison, try dividing the choir in equal halves.

(See Example 2a & 2b)

Example 2A   SKIP TO MY LOU

Lost my part-ner, what shall I do? Lost my part-ner, what shall I do?
Skip.. skip... skip to my Lou! Skip.. skip;.. skip to my Lou!

Lost my part-ner, what shall I do? Skip to my Lou, my darl- ing.
Skip... skip.. skip to my Lou! Skip to my Lou my darl- ing.

Example 2B   THE BELLS IN THE TOWER

High in the tow-er rings the bell. Old Father Si-mon tolls the knell.
Hark how the tones so sweet-ly ring As they the welcome mes-sage bring

Tell-ing the peo-ple all is well, clear on an A-pril eve- ning.
Win-ter is o- ver, now it's spring clear on an A-pril eve- ning

To assure success, take these precautions

1. Separate the two teams by as great a distance as possible, putting each section in a shoulder-to-shoulder-circle so they can hear their own team-mates clearly, but the opposition rather faintly.
2. Caution them to follow YOUR beat so they stay together, and not to depend on their ears. Several boys will have to turn sideways so they can see you. A strong rhythmic accompaniment will help here.
3. As success is achieved, move the two teams closer together, gradually opening the circle into a semi-circle facing you, and eventually standing in close formation.
4. Allow individual boys to stop their ear nearest the "opposition" so they can hear their own voices clearly.
5. On successive days, shift various boys from one team to the other, noticing which boys sing either song with assurance, which boys seem to handle the higher tessitura of Skip-Lou well and which seem more comfortable in the lower Bell-Tower Bell Song.

When the two songs have been done in many combinations successfully, introduce the third song, "Silly Song" and proceed as before, sometimes with "Skip-Lou" and sometime with "Bell in the Tower". Eventually you will attempt a three-way rendition, and even try having a given section trade songs with another. (See figure 2c)

Example 2C   A SILLY SONG

Dai-sies bloom-ing in the dell. What is the reason they don't smell?
Sus-ie's kit- ten is quite pink. He was ply-ing in the ink.

That's the se- cret they wont tell. Oh what a sil-ly stor- y.
She shouldn't let him, I should think. Oh what a sil-ly stor- y

43

You, as director, will be constantly observing to discover which boys sound better on high or low, which sing with assurance no matter what song or in what group, planning for the day when there will be three sections.

Canons follow easily after several simultaneous songs have been learned. Once the complete song is learned it is easy to instruct each "team" to begin on signal and sing through the song any number of times desired. Sometimes a little "Coda-cadence" is added for teams one and two to sing as team three is finishing its last phrases. See Ex. 3, "Grace Before Meals" for a sample canon. Tallis' Canon is another well known work, available in many source books.

Example 3 GRACE BEFORE MEALS — Canon in 4 parts

A Descant is an ancient form of contrapuntal writing. Given a melody, a "cantus firmus", a counter-melody is composed which complements and enriches that melody. A descant is really a special type of simultaneous song, except that the descant is dependent on the given melody for its interest; independently it may be rather dull and uninteresting. In other words, in the simultaneous songs, either of the songs can be sung by itself, but a descant cannot always be used as a song in its own right.

See Example 4 for an example of a melody with descant.
1. Teach the melody if it is not already known.
2. Next teach the descant to everybody.
3. Select a small group of boys to sing the descant as the rest sing the melody. Since the descant is "subservient" to the melody, it is usually best to have a relatively small group of singers on the descant.
4. Since the descant does not necessarily lie above the melody, you may want to try having a group sing the descant an octave lower than written, perhaps pitching the song one or two steps higher than indicated so the descant does not lie too low for comfortable singing.

Example 4 ARE YOU SLEEPING? — with descant

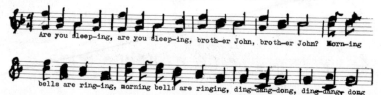

44

Part B.
Singing in Harmony

Singing in counterpoint is one matter, but singing in harmony is another. How does a boy choir director get his eight or nine year olds to sing in parallels and chords? Instead of asking his singers to sing in opposition, how does he get them to support a single melody, harmonizing in thirds, sixths, fourths, combining consonances and dissonances?

One best interval to start with is "the third". Literally thousands of choral passages and vocal duets consist of two voices moving in parallel thirds and such passages fall gratefully upon the ear, especially the immature ears of untrained children.

One recommended procedure that is usually successful with immature singers proceeds thus:

1. Instead of vocalising on a scale, the class vocalises on skips of a third (as in example 5a).
2. When, after several days, the choirboys can sing this easily with very little assistance, ask them to alternate. Half the choir sings the first note (stem down), the other half sings the second note (stem up) and they continue thus until they all join on high "do". In descending, the order is reversed: the second section sings the first note (stem up) and the first section sings the second note (stem down) and so they continue.
3. When #2 goes easily and successfully, ask the "altos" to hold their first note while the "sopranos" sing note 2; the altos hold the third note until the sopranos have completed their fourth note (see ex. 5b). Practice this until the two tones of each combination match in volume, and are in tune.
4. When #3 goes well, tune the altos on "do" aud the sopranos on "mi" and ask them to sing up and down the scale in parallel thirds. If one section falters:
    a. separate the two sections as far apart as the room permits
    b. suggest the "weaker" section put a finger in one ear
    c. enlarge the faltering section by adding members from the other team.

Singing in Thirds

Example 5a

Example 5b

Example 5c

Now try your choir on a two-part song that uses the parallel thirds through most of the song. (See Example 6, Schubert's "Slumber Song")

Example 6   SLUMBER SONG — Schubert

After your choir can sing in parallel thirds, begin to give the boys practice in singing in sixths. The procedure is much the same as for introducing thirds.

1. Have the whole choir sing downward in skips of a sixth (see example 7a)
2. Ask the sopranos to sing the first note, the altos the second, the sopranos the third, altos fourth etc. At mid-point reverse, asking altos to begin, sopranos to follow. (See example 7)
3. As in the example #3 for thirds, ask the sopranos to sustain their tone until the altos have entered, the sopranos hold the next tone until the altos have sounded theirs, etc. (See example 7b). At mid-point, reverse, asking altos to sound their tone first and sustain it until the sopranos enter.
4. When #3 goes well, ask the choir to sing the scale in sixths downward and upward as in example 7c.
5. Give the boys a song involving parallel sixths (see "The Bells of Bojolay", example 8. The boys may be able to sing it right off in two parts, but if they cannot, teach the altos their part first until it is thoroughly learned, then ask the sopranos to harmonize a sixth above.

The Interval of the Sixth

Example 7a

Example 7b

Example 7c

46

By way of review and to combine thirds and sixths ask the boys to sing example 9 where sixths alternate with thirds.

When the boys can sing in either thirds or sixths you can begin to sing three-part blocked chords. Divide the choir into three fairly equal teams, remembering which boys have been singing tones below the treble clef easily (altos) and those who "float" the tones in the upper reaches above the treble clef effortlessly (sopranos). The middle section can be called "mezzos" (Italian for "middle") rather than seconds, a title tnaι carries a faint connotation of "second best". Some directors, myself included, are of the opinion that the "mezzos" should be the most acute in pitch discrimination and ability to hear and sing the several tones of a chord easily. If a boy can sing comfortably both high and low and if he has just such a keen, discriminating ear he will probably be a competent "mezzo" singer. Thus to sing "mezzo" is an honor, not "second best".

Example 8   THE BELLS OF BOJOLAY
A Study in Sixths

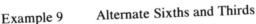

For the first excursion into three-part chordal progressions, example 10 is a good exercise. Put your altos in the center, mezzos on one side and sopranos on the other; the altos will be the "anchors" so the other two parts must hear the altos clearly.

Example 9   Alternate Sixths and Thirds

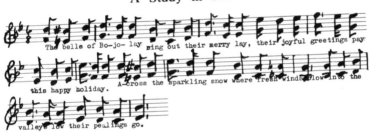

Example 10   Three-Part Faux Bourdon

1. As the altos tune on "ti" (notice, not on "do") they sing down the scale to low "ti" and back up agin, adding upper "do". Repeat on a neutral sound like "too" or "la"

2. Tune the mezzos on "re" and ask them to sing down and up the scale a third above the altos, adding a final high "mi. Presumably they have had enough practice in thirds so this goes well. Permit boys who feel uncertain to "stop the ear nearest the altos" so they can hear themselves clearly. Repeat on "too"

3. Tune sopranos on high "so" and ask them to sing down the octave and up again in sixths above the altos, holding the final high "so" until the altos have moved up to the final "do". Repeat on "too"

4. Now using the altos as "anchors" (that is why they are in the center) ask mezzos to sing the third above the altos and ask the sopranos to sing the sixth above the altos. If you have done the preliminaries well, this should "go along" quite easily.

The result is known as "faux bourdon" (false bass), for the root of the triad has been transposed to the top, thus avoiding the parallel fifths the classicists found so objectionable.

Now try the choral response in example 11 where the penultimate chord introduces the first non-parallel progression and a mild dissonance.

Example 11   A FOURFOLD AMEN

A- men,   A- men   A- men,   A . . . men

As a final step in your preparations for part singing, try combining voices in harmony and voices in counterpoint at the same time. Going back to the Purcell "We Merry Minstrels" in example 1, assign the melody to the MEZZOS. The sopranos will harmonize in parallel thirds ABOVE the mezzos, while the altos will develop a very interesting counter-melody "down below the melody". Noticing that the composer is Purcell, I sometimes wonder if this was a rather late (historically speaking) example of the choir "tenors" holding the melody (the cantus firmus) with the basses furnishing a contrabass, while the boys with unchanged voices sang the treble (the third) above the melody (Ex. 12).

Example 12   WE MERRY MINSTRELS — Purcell

Once the choir is singing in parts, the whole vast storehouse of musical compositions for two, three and even four part treble voices is available. A conservative director working in a community or church that prefers music of the traditional, familiar type, the "tried and true" so to speak, may do well to stay with compositions of the nineteenth and eighteenth century for his first two years. Once the choir has built up a "standard repertoire" and won a following of loyal listeners, a more adventurous spirit can lead the boys and their director to move into twentieth century works.* Composers like Bartok, Kodaly and Britten have written effectively for boy voices. It has been my experience that the boys take to singing in three different keys at the same time, or handle complex cross-rhythms or chords involving major sevenths and minor seconds surprisingly well. They are more at home with such "modern sounds" than their director who was trained half a century earlier!

---

*Not all music composed in the present decade is "twentieth century music"; much is music written in the style and idiom of a century ago.

Chapter XI
MUSIC TO BE SUNG

This topic may seem to have little to do with the success of the choir, yet many a music director gains quite a following because he knows what music his boys can sing competently and what songs will appeal to the audience the choir is singing for. The director who presents a complete Bach Cantata for a Saturday afternoon meeting of the local Women's Club need not be amazed if he is not asked back again: nor will the director who presents a program of light show tunes to a sophisticated audience of professional music directors win favorable comments.

A church-maintained choir must usually confine its repertoire to literature for the religious services of that particular church, just as the ethnic groups feature music of their own peoples. The campfire-jamboree type of boy choir will specialize in marching and hiking songs, stunt songs and similar light fare.

In contrast, the concert-touring choirs are free to range far and wide in repertoire, singing music from many musical periods, many genres, many composers. Music may be chosen strictly because of its popular appeal to a general audience, or music may be performed for its prestigious difficulty, in order to impress sophisticated critics; or the repertoire may be carefully chosen to give young students exposure to as many types of music as possible.

If you are limited in rehearsal time, or your singers are of less than superior ability, you will wisely confine your repertoire to tried-and-true compositions, mostly unison or two-part works with a good piano accompaniment to fill in and support.

A "good accompaniment" may be described thus for our purposes here: 1) The instrumental accompaniment should provide a firm, full bass since there are only treble voices which may sound thin. 2) The upper part of the accompaniment should be light and unobtrusive so it does not "cover" or interfere with the projection of the vocal part. 3) It should not double the voice parts unless the singers are quite uncertain about holding their parts. 4) Broken chords, arpeggios or lightly repeated chords are usually most satisfactory.

The choir that meets three or four times per week and for which the boys have been chosen after a year or two of cadetship can usually sing three - or four - part music effectively, often unaccompanied by instruments. The problem here is to find boy altos who have full (but not forced) low voices to support the harmonic structure of the composition.

If boys with changed or changing voices are used, it may be possible to use standard SATB choral arrangements, but more often the director may find it advisable to manufacture special arrangement to accomodate the peculiar limitations of voices in mutation.

A few boy choirs are expected to sing on occasion with adult men—usually in a church-connected situation. Here the standard SATB literature is usually satisfactory. If the director has a supply of counter-tenors, or is interested in developing such a group, he may decide to develop a S-CT-T-B repertoire, in the European style, with all the boys singing the soprano (treble) and the men divided into three-part. For most American groups, soprano and alto parts sung by boys, tenor and bass parts by men, are usually satisfactory—if men's sections are smaller in number.*

In one special area, all boy choirs seem to agree on repertoire. At Christmas time, the familiar songs of that season are always sung, the only variations between one choir and another being in the simplicity or elaborateness of the arrangement. Music of Holy Week and Easter also finds a certain amount of uniform repertoire. Where membership includes non-Christian boys, the emphasis tends to be on the more secular songs of the season, e.g. "Jingle Bells" rather than "Silent Night" in December, and the spiritual "Were You There" is replaced by Grieg's "Spring" in early April.

If any composers tend to be favored, they are Schubert, Handel, and Mozart, with Bach and Mendelssohn not far behind in frequency of appearance. Britten is the twentieth-century composer whose name appears rather frequently on programs sung by concert choirs. If the potential audiences are such that they will appreciate music of the Renaissance and Baroque, the works of Palestrina and Di Lassus or the English madrigals are most congenial to the boy treble voice.

On the lighter side, hiking songs from Austria, Swiss mountain tunes, or German folk melodies are very congenial, as are American folksongs, e.g. medleys of cowboy songs, songs of the sea, and white spirituals. Certain popular songs and selections from operas (Carmen's "Street Boys") or commercial operettas and musical comedies (Sound of Music, Mary Poppins, Oliver) fit boys' voices and are usually well-received.

Commercially arranged music for female voices is usually all right, but quite often it should be sung a whole tone higher than printed, since such music demands a lower and fuller alto sound from the adult singers than boys can match.

The experienced choir director has a number of "staples" that are sung year after year, that the boys know thoroughly, and that fit most situations. Some examples are 1) Patriotic songs (The Star Spangled Banner, in a three-part unaccompanied arrangement probably in the key of C; America the Beautiful; This is My Country; all singable out of-doors without accompaniment if necessary); 2) songs of certain seasons, 3) certain hymns and spirituals.

Quite often a choir identifies itself with certain songs that people come to expect. One choir is known as The Happy Wanderer group; one always closes its formal programs with The Lord's Prayer, another always has Schubert's Ave Maria available and another features Do-Re-Mi. As new boys enter the membership, they quickly

*Choirs at both Canterbury Cathedral and St. Paul's Cathedral have these distributions: 8 boy trebles, 2 countertenors, 2 tenors, 2 basses on each side of the chancel.

51

learn from the veterans surrounding them those certain songs, so the choir director knows that no matter what the sudden invitation he has songs that will be appropriate. As a result, people in the community know that they can call on the choir and find the boys ready for almost any situation.

Chapter XII
FINANCING THE BOY CHOIR

One reason frequently given when a boy choir languishes and ceases to function is the lack of financial support. I am always reluctant to accept that as a completely true reason for a choir's demise. There are two sides to this question of requiring and seeking a great deal of financial subsidizing of a choral group.

It is true that music has to be bought and a rehearsal room provided. If there is to be a distinctive costume somebody has to pay for robes, blazers, or uniforms. If the choir develops so it is ready to travel to other places to sing, the cost of transportation and lodging plus meals will have to be taken care of. You, as the director putting in much time and effort, would like to be paid and you may want the support of a professional accompanist with perhaps an assistant director or prefector-chaperone. Yet I must report that there are boy choirs functioning very effectively, if a bit modestly, on a budget of less than $100 per year.

Consider the case of the small parish church where the wife of the minister (a music major in college) has gathered a group of boys from the church membership to sing occasionally at religious services. The first songs she finds are arrangements for treble voices already in the library, and she personally pays for an inexpensive collection of standard choruses. Several women in the congregation who are capable seamstresses sew black cassocks (rather simple) and white surplices (more complicated). The church has a music room available for practices, there are no salaries, music purchases over the year are very modest. At the end of each season the boy choir is responsible for a song service with an offering taken so cassocks and surplices are paid for; any surplus is used for more music. As younger boys come along and an occasional boy from outside the church asks to join the group, the choir increases in size and improves in its singing to the admiration and respect of all who hear it. The Boy Choir of Church X is, within its modest scope, a very successful boy choir.

Consider the case of a music supervisor in a medium size school system who forms an all-city boy choir. Each Tuesday before school and each Thursday in the late afternoon the boy singers meet in the central junior high music room. Music is selected from the many songbooks and octavo arrangements which have accumulated in various school buildings over the years. Parents from each section of town take their turns in providing transportation. For costumes each boy is asked to buy a plain white skirt (wearable on other occasions), a clip-on red bow tie (bought wholesale in five dozen lots at a discount) and each family agrees that the next pair of trousers bought will be dark blue. Each December and April there is a sixty-minute concert for which tickets are sold. During the season there are requests for the boys to sing for civic groups, service clubs, parent-teacher meetings, and, while no set fees are ever charged, a hint is dropped that a donation to the choir treasury will be accepted. The supervisor and one of the music specialists share conducting responsibilities and a capable high school pianist furnishes accompaniments, backed up by another music teacher when technical demands are greater than the student can meet.

In neither of these examples is success or failure of the choir's enduring worth dependent on financial support. Yet these examples are not fictional, nor are they atypical; there are a significant number of just such boy choirs, singing very well and providing boy singers with valuable experiences, that have been flourishing for many years. In such cases, success is the result of finding a group of boys equipped with normal vocal apparatuses and music aptitudes, plus a dedicated, knowledgeable director. With the addition of a place to rehearse and some suitable music to sing, all the ingredients for a successful, if not grandiose, boy choir are present.

We read that the lack of a sponsor is the cause for the demise of some boy choirs. I suggest that the *opposite* is more likely to cause difficulties and even be cause for failure. That may come as a surprising statement to some choir director who is getting along with little or no financial backing. It certainly is tempting to look at one of these handsomely endowed boy choirs and wish for a similar organization. Certainly it is a great luxury to have ample money for equipment, for music, for travel. You, the director, would like to have sufficient salary so you can devote most of your attention to the boy choir. You would like to have an assistant director, several professional accompanists and any other paid assistant you need to help in the functioning of the choir. Yet there is in the memory of some of us who go back more than two decades the case of a very fine director who started modestly in a small parish church and built an estimable boy choir. He was offered the financial backing of a very well-funded foundation. The choir began to function at the professional level—and then suddenly he was dismissed and the choir he had so unselfishly developed was given to somebody else. Nor do we have to go back so far to hear of boy choir directors resigning in mid-season, of sudden dismissals, and of announced searches for a different director.

The reasons may be varied and complex in detail, but they all can be summarized in the old adage "He who pays the piper calls the tune." The wealthy benefactor, not always musically sensitive, may dictate what music is to be sung, what concerts are to be scheduled, what boys may be accepted. When the director finds that he cannot adapt to these restrictions, he can object and be dismissed or he can resign, or he can remain and become a director in name only.

Finances may not seem to be much of a problem if you are being hired by some organization. Just as a church certainly has a place to rehearse, the lodge or civic group has its own quarters. Along with your salary, if you are to get any, you can ask for a budgeted amount to be spent for music. There may be robes already available, and the lodge may have a distinctive uniform they will provide. It would seem then that you will have everything you want to function well.

Unfortunately this is not always the case. All too often persons responsible for expenditures are reluctant to grant any but the most necessary funds. I have personally seen the situation where the director is expected to train his boy singers, find the music for an effective presentation and contrive an attractive stage appearance including uniform dress. Meanwhile the sponsors are sitting back, waiting to be shown that the choir is going to do well, saying "Let's wait and see if this is going to amount to anything. If it is, then I'll be willing to support it." In such a situation, only the most imaginative and resourceful of directors can hope to succeed—and there are such directors.

As pointed out in the earlier part of this exposition, there is no such thing as a "typical American Boy Choir," but of those that are well enough established to have continued for as many as ten years, this may be a fairly typical description of financing that works. The choir has no financial endowment, no permanent or guaranteed funds. The boys pay their way through self-assessed "dues" and handle the sale of tickets for concerts, with sometimes a modest list of patrons being solicited for small donations. Quite frequently there is a sale of candy or fruit or magazines to make up a deficiency in the budget or to pay for some unusual venture.

There may be a board of directors made up of elected parents who serve only as long as their sons are in the choir. Hence there is a constantly shifting personnel. If recordings are made, they are contracted for privately and sold to choir patrons and families; not always does this sale cover the full cost. If a tour is taken, it is seldom financially self-supporting; the deficit incurred is thought justifiable as the tour serves as a "reward" for the boys and their director. The choir director, if paid at all, gets just enough to justify his giving up several hours per week after he has done his regular day's work. The accompanist, if there is one, is paid even more modestly; often the choir has to depend on a volunteer of uncertain talent and ability. Any other help is either paid a mere token amount, or is entirely volunteer. Yet working under these less than ideal conditions, these choirs continue to flourish year after year, often with a very high spirit of loyalty and devotion in spite of, or maybe because of, their meager resources and the extra effort all must make to carry on the traditions of those who have gone before. They set their own goals, choose their own methods, and are constrained by nobody.

Chapter XIII

THE BOY TREBLE AND PRIVATE VOICE LESSONS

Are there circumstances when a young boy should take private lessons? In Chapter IV I presented some strong reasons why the boy will do better in a group situation. Now let us discuss cases where the boy will do better with a special teacher working in a studio set-up.

The most obvious case is where there is no boy choir within reasonable commuting distance and no likelihood of there being one. In thinly settled areas there may not be a central location which can serve as a base of operations. Competent and motivated directors are rather rare, and even in a densely populated city there may be nobody to attract and train young boys effectively. There are school systems where music is not included in the curriculum or where it is badly taught and there are cities where there is no church or synagogue with an organized program to develop singing skills in their young children.

If in such a community there is a boy blessed with a naturally pleasant voice and a strong desire to sing, especially if he comes from a family in which singing is considered a desirable accomplishment, private instruction is the only recourse. Alas, such talented and highly motivated boys are rare. There are, luckily, other reasons why a boy may seek the services of a private voice coach. Consider these examples.

There is the lad who tried out for a boy choir and was rejected because of poor voice quality; he wants help in correcting his faults. There may be a boy who has his heart set on being a member of one of the nationally famous choir schools and wants to attain the best technique of singing that is possible before traveling across the continent for his audition.

A member of a boy choir may have aspirations of being a featured soloist and may, with the approval of his director, seek outside coaching to develop a repertoire of songs suitable for boy treble soloists.

There are twentieth century composers who write stage works that require boy singers. A prime example is the part of Amahl in Menotti's *Amahl and the Night Visitors*. If there is an organization that presents such works, certain boys in the community may aspire to play the role and seek out a teacher to prepare them for such a presentation. Likewise in the rapid proliferation of opera companies, there are occasional calls for boys to serve in special choruses* (the chorus of street boys in *Carmen* or the choirboys in *Tosca,* for

---

*Morris, Rebecca: WHO GETS TO WEAR THE BLUE COSTUMS TONIGHT?" New York Sunday News, Jan. 19, 1975, pp. 22-26; describes the New York City Opera Children's Chorus, Mildred Hohner, conductor; New York State Theater, Lincoln Center, New York, N.Y.

example); such calls are not frequent enough to warrant organizing a permanent boys' chorus, but the opera company keeps a list of boys with enough vocal training to qualify them for occasional use.

Occasionally a church may not be able to maintain a boy choir, but may want a boy soloist. I can remember one of my own choirboys who had quite a steady demand for his services for weddings and even funerals; the fees he earned were modest but much appreciated by a twelve-year-old boy.

Where does a boy find a teacher who will train his singing voice so he can secure such training?

There is usually in a community either a teacher of adult singers or somebody who has had a thorough course of vocal training in college or conservatory. Quite often such a person can train a boy treble to sing correctly as a boy while building a good foundation for future vocal development after voice mutation.

There is one hazard. Such a person may use exactly the same methods of teaching he/she would use with an adult, and apply the same standards. It is true that this may not be entirely bad. For example the basic principles of breathing are the same for all singers. Problems of diction must be solved in like manner by people of all ages. Such matters as phrasing and interpretation of text are common to all singers.

It is in the aspects of range and tessitura, tone quality and volume that the boy voice must be developed with special care. The voice coach must not only be aware of the limitations immaturity places on the boy voice, but he must also know the unique beauties and resources inherent in that very immaturity. Anybody who tries to make a boy treble, age ten, sound like a mature woman soprano of thirty is not only doomed to disappointment, but he is also apt to hamper the boy's vocal development and at the same time miss the opportunity to produce sounds of peculiar beauty and charm.

How can you, the reader, prepare yourself to be a teacher of boy treble soloists? There are, I regret to say, few schools which offer formal courses in methods for teaching boy soloists. This need not deter a would-be vocal coach from preparing himself for such teaching.

A good way to start is to get a well-established concept of what a fine boy singer sounds like. There are available recordings of superb boy choirs and their soloists. A planned regime of listening will help any discerning teacher to realize what a boy voice can sound like and what material that boy can sing.

Another resource is to travel to where established boy choirs are located. There are some 600 boy choirs in our own United States. Any determined student can find a way to travel to where some of them are located. If finances permit and the opportunity presents itself, a few weeks of traveling about Europe can enable a person to hear a significant number of excellent boy choirs. To attend a concert or church service in which a boy choir is featured is certainly possible. A politely persistent student may get permission to observe several directors as they rehearse their boys.

I can assure you from personal experience that the fraternity of boy choir directors is a very friendly one. Most directors welcome visitors, especially if these visitors send a letter well in advance asking permision and identifying the purpose of the visit. In my own experience, a letter sent has been sufficient to get me two days with the director of the Stockholm Goss Kor and a long session with the Munich Boy Choir. Permission to observe a rehearsal and song service at St. Paul's in London was readily granted, and there was no difficulty in attending Evensong at Canterbury Cathedral. Permission to attend a two-week session at the Royal School of Church Music at Addington Palace near Croydon in England took a bit longer to secure, since I am not a member of the Anglican church and certain restrictions had to be waived, but once admitted, I was accepted whole-heartedly.

Our American boy choir directors are for the most part a very cordial group. Many of the statements, the methods, the concepts and teaching devices included in this section have come from one or more of some very knowledgeable and successful trainers of boy singers. A would-be teacher of boys need have no hesitation about asking permission to visit and observe; if the time is convenient the welcome will probably be warm and sincere.

Before you, as a novice, go seeking an appointment as a boy choir director you may do well to try your wings by coaching a few boys individually. If you have had a solid foundation in voice production yourself, and have found and read some good method books on vocal pedagogy and have had experience singing as a soloist as well as in a choir, you will do well to find one or two willing boys to "practice teach", if we may borrow the phrase that medical doctors use when they speak of "practicing medicine" and "having a large practice" instead of "serving clients" or "dealing with customers". Perhaps the sons of some friends and neighbors, or a few boys from a nearby church or synagogue, or a YMCA or boy scout group may provide you with some students to "practice on". By the fourth lesson, YOU will have learned much, perhaps more than the students, as you discover what works or does not work for you, how you must phrase your explanations and present your illustrations so a young boy will respond.

If you have some success as the boys attain a good "sound" and if you can communicate with them to your effectiveness and their enjoyment, you may discover that you can build a class of private students as the word gets about the "boy community". You may even have the boys to form a nucleus around which to start a boy choir!

Chapter-XIV
TEACHING THE BOY TREBLE SOLOIST

In previous passages in this book, I have recommended that students in music schools spend some time in studying the boy treble voice and how to train it properly. I repeat this recommendation here. The field of senior high and college voice teachers is well filled, and competition is keen for the few positions available. In contrast, here is a field that is not crowded, where a would-be voice teacher or choral director can "break into the profession" and be welcomed.

I have said there are three aspects of singing where the boy treble needs training different from that of adult sopranos or altos. While much of the best approaches and techniques to these aspects of singing have already been described in Chapter VII, it is desirable to again describe these differences here, from the standpoint of a single student learning from a teacher in a series of private lessons.

Part A.

Range

I find almost universal agreement among boy choir directors with whom I have discussed the matter that it is better to "find the head tone" and carry it downward, than to work from the lower tones upward. There are several implications that follow.

1. Once a boy has found the light head tone, well-supported by the breath and free from all tension, the voice will tend to soar upward. It can be expected that the boy will find that he can sing above the treble clef to a high a″, b″, even a c″ with ease. I have had a sizable number of boys in my 25 years of directing who could sing up to high e″ and f″, with recordings available to verify this. In fact, a "rule of thumb" for each season was that no boy was in the high soprano section of the choir unless he could sing a high c″ easily.

2. There were always boy altos, fellows who could sing below middle-c down to a G or F comfortably and happily, but these boys could also soar up above the treble staff on occasion. It is significant that the tones differed from those of the female contralto in that they were not as rich, full and "covered" in quality.

3. Music written and arranged for adult female voices could usually be sung by the boy-choir, but it was often advisable to RAISE the pitch, sometimes as much as a minor third.

The teacher of a boy soloist need not restrict the boy's singing to a limited "middle range", but can let him soar above and dive below the treble clef—in fact should encourage such soaring and diving—as long as it is not forced.

59

Part B.
Quality of Tone

Sometimes a well-meaning but ill-advised adult, wanting to compliment, will say "You boys certainly can sing high. You sound just like girls". Over the seasons my boys acquired a stock answer. "Thank you, but there isn't a girl in this city who can sing as high as we can nor who *sounds* like us." They have been quite justified. No girls' glee club nor woman's chorus, singing the same vocal arrangements, can produce the same type of sound that a boy choir does. It does not require a very knowledgeable, sophisticated, discriminating listener to determine quite soon, by sound only, when the singer is a boy-treble rather than a woman. That is no doubt why Menotti specified that the part of Amahl must ALWAYS be sung by a boy, never by a woman. That is why the three genii in "The Magic Flute" of Mozart sound more "genuine" when sung by boys as specified rather than by women as is sometimes done for expediency.

For a more precise description of the ideal boy-treble tone, I suggest you review Chapter IX. There is one feature not discussed there that deserves special mention. The boy treble voice is quite free from tremolo or marked vibrato. Yet the tone is not "straight" and without "give".

A simple example may effectively explain what I mean. If you hold your arm out full length you may think you are holding it steady. Close inspection will reveal that there is a slight wavering up and down, so slight only close observation can determine it. To hold the arm absolutely still, great rigidity of the muscles is required, with resultant fatigue. It is this same slight "give" to a tone when the throat muscles are quite relaxed that distinguishes a good boy-treble tone.

If the extended arm should be holding a heavy weight, or if the arm muscles should be fatigued or weak, instead of a slight "give" there would be a noticeable tremble. Similarly, if the voice is subject to too much straining, or if with advancing age the throat muscles become weaker, the "wobble" in the voice becomes very pronounced, sometimes to the point that it is difficult to determine what pitch the singer is attempting to sing. A pronounced tremolo may be tolerated in an adult singer, even preferred (just as some organists seem to like a great use of the tremolo and some "gypsy violinists" cultivate an overwide vibrato), but few are the people who expect to hear an eleven-year-old boy soprano with a wobbly voice.

The young boy singer is not capable of producing a sound of great volume for any length of time, without vocal impairment (one of the hazards mentioned in Chapter II for the young boy is the tendency to yell and shout at play, with resulting vocal damage.)

How then is it possible for a young boy to sing with orchestra accompaniment as in *Amahl and the Night Visitors*, or even above a pipe organ and still be heard? How can twenty-two young lads fill a large auditorium with sound so that people in the furthest reaches of the upper balcony can hear with no difficulty?

60

The answer must not be the command, "Sing louder, raise your voice so we can hear you!" We hear stories of the young boy who, after playing the part of the boy in *The Music Man* for a season, lost his voice completely, and even after a period of rest will probably never be able to sing or speak effectively again. We hear of a certain boy choir which emphasizes the LOUD TONE, and we are uncomfortable as we hear these lads singing off-pitch and with unpleasant, raspy tone quality.

The answer is to work on "projection," on reinforcing the normal voice by finding and using certain "resonant areas" in the body.

Everybody knows how, by using a megaphone, a cheerleader can increase the carrying power of his/her voice; even cupping the hands around the mouth will achieve the same result.

Anybody who has called out in a natural cave knows that the sound of his voice echoes back and forth as the sound waves are reflected off the various walls. There is in St. Paul's Cathedral a "whispering gallery" where even the smallest sound can be heard in the opposite gallery because of the fortuitous configuration of the rounded wall.

There are in the human body certain built-in reinforcement areas which can be used to increase the carrying power of the voice without increasing the pressure in the throat to produce a shout.

The largest resonance chamber is the chest cavity. If the size of the chest cavity is increased by expanding the rib cage to the utmost (back and sides as well as front) the voice, because of the reinforcement of the hollow cavity, will gain greatly in carrying power. When you hear a director say "Pull the tone up out of your hips" or "Dig your toe-nails into the rug and suck deep" you can be sure he is trying to get full chest-rib expansion from his boy-singer, hence more resonance.

The second largest resonance chamber is the mouth, the oral cavity. When the mouth is opened "all the way back" the oral cavity assumes the shape of a parabola. Just as the parabola-shaped automobile headlight focuses the beam of light to the maximum intensity, so a parabola-shaped oral cavity focuses the tone so it carries forward across the room to reach the ear of the listener in the back row. I have heard a director/vocal coach say, half seriously, "All you have to do to develop a singer is to get him to take a deep breath and open his mouth." Not quite true. Not really that simple! But he was making a point, a very important point.

If you have ever examined a human skull, you know that it is not perfectly round, nor is it smooth and regular of surface. There are the hollows of the sockets; there are "gulleys" or hollow spaces around the cheek bones; even the temples are shallow parabolas. If the singer can somehow use these hollows to reinforce his tone, the "parabolas" and hollows will add to the carrying power of his voice without exerting any added force or pressure on his sound producing vocal apparatus.

When a coach says "Sing into the mask," or "Raise your eyebrows and feel the tone above your eye-balls!" he may sound ridiculous to the uninitiated layman, but any well-taught singer knows what that coach is trying to accomplish.

If you walk into a rehearsal room and see the choirboys with the right thumb aud forefinger ALMOST pinching the nose while the left thumb and forefinger are straddling the bridge of the nose, you can be assured those boys are attempting to "find the points of resonance." If you see each boy with a forefinger touching each temple and his eyes open wide, you are not viewing the pantomime of a mass suicide but one director's pet device for getting a bit of added resonance from the shallow hollows of the temples. Here is where the private teacher has it over the choral director, for he can discover what his one student already does well and devote his attention to working on the deficiencies. It is often amazing to the layman to hear how a boy with a pleasant but not very large voice can grow and develop vocally in a relatively short time until his voice attains a brilliance and "thrust" that wins admiration from his hearers.

This all sounds rather simple to achieve, this getting the maximum reinforcement of tone. Alas, it is not always so. There is the natural inertia of little boys who do not stretch the muscles to the full or who do not stand erect without slouching, or who "forget" to open the mouth to the full. It takes a persistent mentor to get these basic habits firmly established. In a large choral group a boy may "get by" unnoticed. The private teacher catches on quickly and lazy habits are worked on.

In the problem of attaining good diction, the private teacher can achieve much better results. Vowels are extremely different in their formation; some are easy to shape with open mouth, and not difficult to focus; others are "closed", lie far back in the mouth or low in the oral cavity and so are hard to focus. It is extremely difficult, for example, to sing a pure "ee" on a highpitch; short-i in hit and midwestern a in hat are often hard to control; the broad aw in "call" drops low in the mouth, so tends to be "swallowed." To form each of the many vowels, yet keep the tone focused and resonant, requires much practice. Again, the private teacher can spot the troublesome vowels and concentrate on them.

Here is one of the distinguishing marks of a competent trainer of boy treble singers. When a little eleven-year-old, a slender 80 pounds in weight and barely five feet in height, fills the big church with pure, silvery, resonant tones you can be sure somebody has taught him to reinforce his small voice to best advantage. When the sixteen little boys of Canterbury Cathedral or the twenty-two lads from Vienna sing a full service or concert program with no signs of tiring and with ample sound to echo into the highest arches of the cathedral or the last row of the balcony of the huge auditorium, this is not a miracle but the result of many hours of patient and knowledgeable coaching and rehearsing.

Part C.

Volume

In light of the preceding exposition on tone quality, the problem of achieving control of loudness and softness of tone becomes simpler of solution. In fact, the trainer of a boy singer will do well never to use the words "Loud" or "Soft," for these words tend to cause tenseness or slackness.

If a boy (or an adult for that matter) hears the command "Sing louder! Sing out!" he will tend to tense his muscles, to push and to force with the result that he will actually constrict or close in on the tone, with less volume rather than more, and with badly distorted vowel formation and less than agreeable tone quality.

Likewise the command "Sing softer! Shush down!" is apt to cause the boy to relax his breathing muscles, to sag, to let his mouth close. The tone will be soft, of course, but will also lose resonance, and carrying power, while words become indistinct and lose vitality.

It is fascinating to discover how experienced successful boy choir directors achieve increase or decrease in the volume of sound. Such commands as "Think big, as if you were twenty pounds heavier" or "Dig your toenails into the rug and spread those lower chest muscles" or "Brighten your sound, fill your head with tone, sharpen up the pronunciation of your words" or "Open your throat" seem to be typical, when more volume is desired. In contrast, for pianissimos such phrases as "Think small," or "You've got a secret that you want ME to hear but nobody else" or "Lean forward, crisp up your words and almost whisper" or "Tell it to the people in the back row without letting the people in the front row know what your secret is" give indications of how some directors get the proper results.

Part D.
Repertoire

One problem that a coach or teacher of boy trebles must face is "What kind of music can a boy age 8 to 12 sing?" Especially in communities where boys do not often sing in solo, and some ill-informed people may tend to say "Well, you sound just like a girl," an astute vocal coach chooses songs that are masculine in text.

Songs with a religious connotation are always acceptable, especially if sung in a church/cathedral/synagogue setting, with the boy in cassock and surplice or choir robe or whatever costume takes the singer out of an every-day connotation. In the secular world, matters are a bit more touchy. Songs dealing with the great outdoors ("I Love to Go A-Wandering"), with the joy of living ("I Have a Song in My Heart") or songs from "boy-shows" like *Oliver, Tom Sawyer, or Amahl* all suggest masculinity, with texts that are not usable for a girl. Songs of patriotism ("This Land is Your Land"), of world unity ("Let There Be Peace"), and of brotherhood ("One World") are themes worth exploring. Certain spirituals (white or negro) are very usable.

Conversely, anything having to do with "LOVE," with "daintiness," with childish themes, or with sticky sentiment should be avoided. Likewise it is a bit ridiculous to give a boy of ten a very "masculine song" more appropriate for an adult baritone or tenor ("Give a Man a Horse He Can Ride" or "Tramp, Tramp, Tramp, the Boys are Marching").

Some boys in certain communities can carry off a bit of costuming to emphasize the "masculinity" of their songs. Dressed in chaps and ten-gallon hat, a cowboy medley ("All Day on the Prairie," "Whoopee-Ti-Yi-Yo") may give the boy a chance to sing with no

63

hint of "You sound like a girl"; likewise a group of sea-songs, traditional chanteys or composed numbers, sung by a boy dressed in sailor outfit, can introduce a boy treble to a community not yet ready to accept a boy singer on purely musical terms.

If the above suggestions sound a bit light-weight, be assured they are made to help solve the problem of having a boy singer accepted. There is much music of more enduring worth available to the young boy singer. Out of the hundreds of Schubert songs, there are some fifty that will challenge yet be suitable in text ("Wohin," for example). Schumann, Mozart, Scarlatti, Grieg, Dvorak are suggested composers. Unfortunately, for us who like to include our own American composers' works on our programs, there are not many modern American composers that seem to write for the boy treble voice, but there *are* some, if an enterprising teacher chooses to search.

How advanced a technique can a boy soloist hope to acquire? I have ceased to be amazed at how far a boy soloist can progress in two or three years of disciplined practicing. Because of the lightness of the boy treble it is particularly amenable to singing crisp, high, rapid passages. Songs with a bit of coloratura are very possible. I have heard young lads sing Mozart's "Alleluia," the Liebling variations on "Carnival of Venice," and Handel's "Oh Had I Jubal's Lyre" not only convincingly, but with considerable elan. The high lyric line of Cesar Franck's "Panis Angelicus" can certainly be sung by any serious student within two years of private study—even less. Similarly for the boy alto, the lyric, flowing lines are best, with an occasional bit of coloratura.

The one type of song that is best avoided is the highly dramatic work. Songs with a broad sweep building to a big climax are not often for the boy trebles.

The question always arises: "Is popular music acceptable?" If a boy is asked to sing in a musical revue or where only music of the lightest type is expected, can he sing a song that is currently popular? If we rule out the songs dealing with themes of ardent love and passion (themes of unrequited love, or broken hearts, or lyrics that are quite frankly erotic) and if we stay away from the "rock and roll" shoutings the answer is a qualified affirmative. There are many songs with a catchy rhythm and witty lyrics available from time to time, and there are usually smoothly flowing, melodious ballads which are congenial to a light, fresh boy treble voice. Under no circumstances should a young boy be allowed to "belt out" a popular tune in the style of our more raucous-voiced "pop singers".

All of the above discussion leads to some words of caution. The voice teacher should be concerned not only with the proper development of the boy's singing voice, but should also demand the right to approve or disapprove the appearances of that boy in public performance. Young lads, and often their parents too, do not always use good judgment in such matters; they are often naive enough to be flattered at being asked to sing and are eager to show off their vocal accomplishments. They do not usually know how to be sure that the auditorium or room will be suitable for a young voice or that the master of ceremonies will present him properly, or that the audience will be respectfully attentive. This is where the voice teacher will do well to make sure that his pupil will be presented in the most favorable setting possible.

Chapter XV
THE POSITIVE APPROACH

The most formidable hazard a boy must overcome in his singing career is voice mutation.

Yet it should not be a hazard, for voice change is a natural phenomenon, a part of growing up that every male child experiences. Hence it is better thought of as a challenge, an intriguing development, an adventure into a newer vocal world.

A more mature voice is about to emerge, richer in quality, more powerful in volume, lower in pitch. There is an element of mystery as the boy and his family and friends wonder if he will become a lyric tenor, a rugged baritone, a deep resonant bass. There is hope that the lad with a mediocre singing voice will develop a far better "new-voice", more pleasing in quality so people will want to hear and enjoy it.

Every descending tone that is added in the bass clef is an event of interest; a change in quality in the treble range is fascinating; each quirk that develops in the erratic descent is not so much a nuisance as it is a curiosity.

This is what voice change *can* mean to an adolescent boy as well as to his choral director, his family and friends. But far too often it is not that way at all. One day the boy singer finds that his voice is incapable of doing what it has been doing for some six or seven years. The boy is frustrated and dismayed. Members of his family glance at each other significantly as he speaks; they make veiled remarks and whisper humorous comments. People laugh and tease because his voice falters and breaks at unexpected times.

Most devastating of all to a boy who has been a capable singer is the change that comes over his vocal-music teacher. His smiles are a bit less friendly, there is even an expression of annoyance. Where last year this much-admired voice coach was warmly complimentary, he now actually suggests that his former favorite boy sit off to one side with the request that he sing softly, or just pretend to move his mouth. One day he assigns his former soprano to a new voice part, something called alto-tenor or baritone, where the notes are in a strange new clef and the voice part drones along on a dull voice-line that he can hardly maintain, instead of letting his voice soar in an interesting melody. Last year's star has been betrayed; he has been relegated to obscurity. He is crushed.

Is this description an exaggeration? Not in many schools, not for many boy singers. It takes a very determined fellow, one with an unusually great love for music and with a deeply rooted ambition, to hold his own against the resistances and shocks he must contend with when his voice changes.

There are exceptions. A few dedicated choral directors and junior

66

high school music teachers are not only well-trained musicians, but are also sensitive to the physical and mental workings of that outwardly brash and ebullient, but inwardly sensitive and bewildered human being, the adolescent boy. These rare teachers and directors have made the effort to learn about the phenomenon of voice change and how to exploit it to proper development. They do not dread it as something catastrophic, but look on it as something fascinating.

Year after year these outstanding mentors have classes with plenty of eager boy singers; there is no lack of tenors and basses in embryo; each year a new group of parents is intrigued by the deep voices of their sons who only a year ago were singing in a piping treble. The senior high director is grateful for the steady supply of tenors and basses which arrives each September. The school administrators prize this strong leader of youths who develops such dedicated loyalty in the student body. In the community, the choral music directors can rely on an ample number of male singers and the private voice teachers find young men with promising voices asking for a term of lessons.

These outstanding directors and teachers may seem to be touched by a magic fire from heaven. They are not, nor are they endowed with supernatural abilities that lesser mortals cannot hope to acquire. Rather, these are dedicated teachers who have decided to specialize in the field of junior high school music and who seek to become master teachers. They supplement their musical training with study, experimentation, and innovation. They compare notes with other workers in the field to find out what is successful elsewhere and to incorporate these procedures into their own classrooms.

Fortunate is the boy who has such a knowledgeable and sympathetic teacher in junior high or middle school. His chances for progressing through the voice-change happily, easily, and properly are great. If he is so fortunate, I hope the boy and his parents express their appreciation and gratitude to that teacher and, more important, to the principal and other administrators who have it in their power to keep that teacher in the school and community!

Chapter XVI
THE PHYSICAL ASPECTS OF VOICE MUTATION

Sometime in the second decade of his life, a boy's primary sex glands, the testicles, increase noticeably in size. Where for the first ten or more years of the boy's life, these glands were relatively small and not very active, now they begin to secrete, among other things, certain hormones which produce marked changes in his physical appearance.

Most noticeable to the casual observer is the rapid increase in physical size. Some pubescent boys grow rapidly in height, even in extreme cases as much as twelve inches within one year. Others gain in weight at an amazing rate. The case of Jim who entered seventh grade a mere 85 pounds and graduated from ninth grade two and three-fourths years later at 170 pounds may be unusual, but it is not incredible.

Often the boy does not grow evenly. He may shoot up, tall and thin as a beanpole, or he may become a roly-poly fat boy. Feet and hands may grow faster than the rest of his body, so he moves in an ungainly manner; he is in "the awkward age". When last year's jacket is donned, the sleeves may reach only half-way down the forearm, and trousers may be "high water" because pants-legs do not cover ankles.

The skin on face and upper chest roughens and pimples appear; if the boy carelessly scratches, the skin may become scarred and pitted. The cartilaginous appendages grow apace so we see jug-ears and bulbous noses.

Most startling and significant is the appearance of hair in areas that for twelve or more years have been smooth and hairless. Fuzz appears in the pubic area, across the upper lip, along the cheeks and across the chin, under the arms, and eventually across the chest. This fuzz, scarcely noticeable at first, rapidly increases in quantity. Adults may tease the adolescent about "the new whiskers" and his need to shave. Over-protective relatives have even been known to sigh and weep as they see their "darling little boy" becoming a man about to leave their sheltering influence.

Such growth does not appear at any one specific age. Puberty may begin as early as age 12 or as late as age 15 (in unusual cases even earlier or later). It is not unusual to see a group of eighth grade boys (age 13-14) walking along, with one tall and skinny, one short and fat, and another striding along like a full-grown man, with a "little boy" trotting along at his side.

Of most immediate concern to teachers of vocal music is the rapid growth of the larynx. We have mentioned the effect the male sex hormones have on the cartilaginous areas of the body; the larynx being cartilaginous, like the ears and nose-tip, grows rapidly, changing in shape and sometimes doubling in size. Of course the vocal cords (or vocal folds) increase in length and thickness with a corresponding rapid change in vocal pitch and timbre.

In light of succeeding discussion, it should be pointed out that just as growth in height and weight is erratic, and sometimes extremely rapid, so is the growth of the larynx as evidenced by the sudden appearance of the "Adam's Apple"*

The story of Sam who bade his teacher good-bye and "Happy Holidays!" in December in a high piping treble, and wished him a "Happy New Year" in early January in a deep, husky bass is by no means unusual. As we will see later, a boy leaving school in June singing a high treble may return in September, ready for singing in the deepest ranges of the bass clef.

The teacher of vocal music who is not well-versed in what is going on in the larynxes of his rapidly developing pubescent boys may be quite at a loss as to how to proceed in their vocal training. In contrast, the music teacher who is aware of the many ramifications a voice in mutation can display and who has a repertoire of techniques and devices to help and hasten the maturation of the changing voice will be fascinated and challenged by what is going on. For the former, the bewildered, voice change is a nuisance and a trial; for the latter, the aware one, voice change is an intriguing phenomenon.

One important point must be made in this discussion of the physical basis for voice change. The onset of rapid mutation can be predicted; it can be anticipated and put on an almost exact time schedule. In a situation where a teacher can make provision for giving his boys with changing voices some special attention, it is sometimes possible to guide a boy into his newly emerging bass-clef voice before or just as voice mutation is about to begin. Often a boy is able to sing happily and comfortably during the entire time of rapid change, with a minimum of difficulty and embarrassment, with a maximum of interest and enthusiasm.

My discovery of this predictability was a happy accident. During a year of residency at the University of Wisconsin I mentioned, in my discussion group, my eagerness to find some objective method of predicting onset of voice change. A visitor in the group, not previously known to me and never to be seen again, referred me to Shuttleworth's Pictorial Atlas**. In this little book there is published a series of five photographs provided by William Greulich, in connection with his definition of the five stages of sexual development among boys. I learned that the one dependable, readily observable measure of a boy's advancement into puberty is the amount of pubic hair he has acquired, and these photographs can

---

*Some boys rather enjoy the observation (made with obvious tongue-in-cheek) that "Nobody ever talks about the Eve-Apple. It looks like only Adam has to take the consequences for eating that forbidden apple in the Garden of Eden. Eve too tasted of the forbidden fruit but carried no sign of it in her throat".

**Shuttleworth, Frank K. THE ADOLESCENT PERIOD, A PICTORIAL ATLAS, a monograph of the Society for Research in Child Development, Vol. XIV 50, No. 2, 1949, published by Child Development Publications, the University of Chicago Press, 5801 - Ellis Ave., Chicago Ill. 60637; 1949 pp. 31-33. Obtainable from Kraus Reprint Co., Rt. #100, Millbrook, N.Y. 10546.

serve as objective standards for rating that advancement.

When it was arranged that I could have all eighty-two boys of the eighth grade in one junior high school for observation for one school year, and I could group them *in advance* according to whatever scheme I desired, I asked if the boys could be assigned to me on the basis of sexual maturity. In May I handed the Shuttleworth book to the man teaching the physical education classes and asked him to rate the boys in the future eighth grade according to stages 1 through 5 in the Greulich series. Within a week he had prepared such a list. When the 82 boys came in September as eighth graders, they had been assigned to music class according to the Greulich-Shuttleworth scale, with no administrative difficulty at all.

During the school year, as we checked not only vocal ranges but various aspects of physical maturation (increase in height, weight), we discovered that quite without exception, boys in stages 1 and 2 of pubic hair development showed no signs of losing their treble tones nor of producing tones in the bass clef, but at stage 3 the first signs of vocal change occurred, and by stage 4 the lower, fuller tones of the emerging adult voice were clearly audible and measurable.

In the twenty years that have since elapsed, this useful, informative correlation has proved to be almost perfect and reliable. As I have worked with summer music groups, spot (one-time) checks have invariably showed stage 3 to be the time when first signs of voice change have been audible. As I have guided boys as private or small-group students through voice-change, no boy has ever shown signs of singing anything but treble tones if he was in stages 1 and 2, and always a boy showed change in quality and deepening of pitch at stage 3.

Because of social mores that prevail in some communities, this measure of sexual maturity must be used with discretion. In the situation where a entire class of boys is to be rated, it has always worked satisfactorily to ask the co-operation of the physical education department, where inspections can be made quite unobtrusively, if necessary even without the knowledge of the boys being examined (of course it is highly recommended that the building principal and/or the dean of boys know what is going on with full permission granted). In the case of private (studio) voice lessons, I have found that such inspections can be best made by the boy's father (or other responsible male member of the family) after a full explanation of why it is desirable and what is involved. The result is two-fold: much very useful information is forthcoming and a father becomes involved in the progress of his son, which usually adds re-enforcement to the regime of developing the "new voice". I have even had fathers thank me for giving them the opportunity to establish some very desirable and desired communications with their sons.

If there is any need of proof that voice change occurs as a result of testicular growth and increased function, the reader has only to refer to the subject "Castrati" in any reputable reference book, e.g. Grove's *Dictionary of Music and Musicians.*

For many centuries it was the practice to preserve the high treble voice of males by castration (removing the testicles by surgery). If a boy was the possessor of a voice of great beauty he might be castrated before he became pubescent. The voice never "changed," i.e. the high treble continued throughout the entire adult life. It might drop from high soprano to mezzo or contralto as some of the female voices in adulthood do, but there never occurred an abrupt "break" or rapid deepening of the voice into the bass clef ranges.*

While this practice began in the earlier centuries, it was after the "invention" of opera in the early seventeenth century that castrati became famous, sometimes attaining the same hysterical adulation that present day Americans accord "pop singers" or stars of the cinema. Because training could begin in childhood and continue uninterruptedly, these castrati (de-masculinized males) could develop voices of great power and technical proficiency along with a timbre of peculiar beauty, attractive to the opera fans of the 150 years between Monteverdi and Handel. Composers wrote solo passages demanding great virtuosity to display the prodigious expressiveness and vocal technique of these unnaturally-voiced singers. We read of such idols of the opera stage as Bernacchi, "The King of Singers;" Farinelli, "The Most Beautiful Voice Ever Heard;" and Nicolini, the rage of the London opera world.

We must wonder what the voices of these fabulous castrati sounded like, but we cannot know. In the mid-eighteenth century there was a reaction to this admiration and a rejection of these artificial, de-masculinized singers. To deprive a man of his sexuality seemed too great a price to pay for beautiful sounds and spectacular vocal display for the post-Baroque public. To hear such heroic figures as Hercules, Jupiter, Perseus singing in high, feminine-like voices might be acceptable in the highly artificial, stylized world of the Baroque, but it seemed not only ridiculous but was actually repugnant to the people of the post-Handelian era. With the operas of Gluck and Mozart which dealt with real-life characters, not god and heroes of antiquity, the use of the castrati with their "artificial voices" went out of fashion. One reason the operas of Handel and his contemporaries are seldom performed nowadays is that present day singers cannot cope with some of more florid roles written for castrati. Even if tenors or baritones develop the technique to sing the highly florid music in *their* range, it never quite comes off; it is as if a flute solo were to be played by a bassoon, where the notes are heard but in the wrong tessitura. For a woman to dress in a man's costume and to attempt a castrati role is equally unsatisfactory; there may be coloraturas with the technique for the bravura style, but the sight of a female trying to be a Hercules or Jupiter is simply ludicrous.

The practice of using castrati in certain monasteries and cathedral choirs continued for some time, into the nineteenth century. In religions where celibacy was considered a virtue of the highest order, it was deemed a noble, saintly act for a boy to give up his sexuality to live a life of monastic asceticism for the glory of his church. As late as 1922, the choir of the Sistine Chapel toured America and I, as a

---

*For a fictional account of such proposed castration and the various reactions the proposition brought about, see Kingsley Amis' THE ALTERATION, New York, The Viking Press, 1976.

71

young boy, heard men sopranos who, I suspect in retrospect, were castrati.

But now, in the last quarter of the twentieth century I will venture to state that nowhere in America, and in very few places anywhere else in the world, are boys castrated in order to prevent voice mutation and to preserve the high treble voice ranges of young boys throughout the whole life-span.

Suggested Readings

1. Graulich, W.W. et. al., *Somatic and Endocrine Studies of Pubertal and Adolescent Boys*, Monograph, Society for Research in Child Development, 1942.
2. *Grove's Dictionary of Music and Musicians*, Third Edition: New York, MacMillan Co., 1935.
3. Shuttleworth, Frank K., *The Adolescent Period, A Pictorial Atlas*, a monograph of the Society for Research in Child Development, Vol. XIV number 50, #2, published by Child Development Publications, The University of Chicago Press, 5801-Ellis Ave. Chicago, Ill. 60637 1941, pages 31-33. Obtainable from Krause Reprint Co., Rt. #100, Millbrook, N.Y. 10546.
4. Stolz, H.R. and Stolz, L.M.: *Somatic Development of Boys*, New York, MacMillan 1950.
5. Swanson, Frederick J.: *Music Teaching in Junior High and Middle School*, Englewood Cliffs, N.J., Prentice-Hall 1973.

Chapter XVII
FAULTY METHODS FOR GUIDING THE BOY DURING VOICE MUTATION

By far the most prevalent and least successful method for handling the problem of the boy's changing voice is to ignore it, or to avoid it, or to eliminate the problem entirely by removing the boy. The teacher often says, not always consciously, "I am not competent to handle this problem. I will either just pretend it is not there, and close my mind to it, or else I will pay as little attention to the problem as possible". He dismisses boys from his choir when their voices are changing if he can arrange it. Otherwise he ignores them, puts them off to one side.

This is bad enough but other teachers do what is worse. They decide what music these boys should sing and insist that the boys sing it somehow, no matter how they must strain and force. Let us discuss these two faulty practices at length.

Part A.

Removing the Boy from Singing Activities

Some teachers solve the problem of what to do with the boys whose voices are changing by getting rid of the boys.

The European choirmasters have followed this procedure for centuries as any reader of the biographies of Haydn and Schubert knows. When a voice breaks (deplorable term!) the boy is dismissed from the choir and usually the departure is final. After some months have gone by and the voice has settled, he may be one of the few permitted to resume his singing with the basses and tenors—if the choir has a use for changed voices and the boy has not drifted off into other activities.

As an illustration of this, consider the boy choir in Europe that has for many years been regarded as the model for other boy choirs to emulate. In fierce competition the boys in this choir are carefully chosen for their natural talent as well as their beautiful voices. For five or more years they are given the most intense and thorough musical training possible.

The rewards for this heavy regime of practice and drill are great. These boys have the aesthetic satisfaction of singing fine music superbly. They experience the thrill of winning applause from large audiences and of adulation from numerous admirers. They have the opportunity to travel to many parts of the world. They form close associations with boys of like talent and ability. With such exceptional background and training for an advance start it would seem likely that the graduates of this choir would be far to the front in the professional fields of concert, oratorio, and opera singing. Yet in reading the trade magazines dealing with musical performers the world over, we find almost no distinguished male singers who claim as part of their background membership in this famous boy choir school.

Where are these hundreds of graduates? What lasting use has been made of the superior musical training they have had? I suggest that these shocks—the abrupt dismissal when the voice "breaks", the transfer from an environment of glamour and adulation, of singing in many countries before large audiences to a style of life that could be called living in obscurity; the implication that now that the voice has broken, a singing career has come to an end; the lack of any school ready to accept these graduates and carry on with their vocal development, the lack of financial means for independent study, all of these are too much of a hurdle for a fourteen or fifteen-year-old boy to surmount.

Part B.

Ignoring Boys with Changing Voices

We Americans are quick to claim that this type of treatment could not happen here. Our public schools boast that music is a standard part of the curriculum through the eighth grade, so we reach all of our thirteen and fourteen-year-old boys in our required music classes. This is true in many places, but it is also true that a boy can be physically present in a class, yet he may have been dismissed from singing activities just as definitely and abruptly as if he had been sent from the room. Let me cite some examples.

Come with me to visit a junior high vocal music class. Most of the students are singing, but over in one corner of the room there are four boys sitting around a table. The teacher explains in a very audible voice that these boys aren't able to sing right now, their voices are changing, so they are working on a special project. The boys look up, half shame-facedly, half defiantly, then return to their cutting and pasting, "busy work."

In a second class there are a few boys sitting glumly at the side, slouched over and barely moving their mouths. We are about to walk over that way when the teacher stops us. "These boys are non-singers. They just can't match the tones of the rest of the class." There are a few titters from some of the girls and the boys look embarrassed.

Less obvious is the unintentional change in attitude many teacher-directors display toward their teen-age boys. Consider the lad who has been an enthusiastic, loyal singer in the treble choir, and who has been treated most warmly and appreciatively by his teacher. One year he is met with a less than enthusiastic greeting and he gets the news, "I'm sorry Tom, but you will have to graduate from the choir. Your voice is changing and we have no place to put you." Tom

74

is crushed. He is shut off from the exciting world he has been enjoying; he is dismissed for no good reason; he certainly has not done anything bad. The teacher of whom he has been so fond obviously is not interested in him any longer. So he drifts away to find some other type of activity.

Or take the example of the minister of music in a large church. He speaks glowingly of his large children's choirs, one for kindergartners, one for primary grade boys and girls, one for those in the intermediate grades. He displays to us the programs of impressive song services his adult choir has sung. When we ask about the teen-age singers, his enthusiastic smile fades a bit. He has had to rely on his girl singers here, he admits; he has given up on the boys. They are so busy, their voices are changing, he can't seem to get them to come out on choir night.

Small wonder the boys lose their enthusiasm for singing in situations like this. Yet such teachers and directors cannot be summarily condemned as incompetent or selfish or malicious. Certainly the professional boy choir director cannot keep a boy who has lost his treble tones. It takes a very good junior high school music teacher, very knowledgeable of methods and very strong of personality—yes, and very dedicated to his profession—to provide for the boys with changing voices in a heterogeneous class. There is, I fear, just as much waste of talent and potential vocal resources in our American schools and choirs as there is in the European situations described above.

Part C

Requiring Boys to Conform to Pre-Conceived Notions of What They Should Sing

One of the most frustrating and even harmful ways of guiding boy singers through voice-mutation is for the teacher to decide ahead of time exactly what pattern the boy's voice will take during its drop from treble to bass clef ranges. Consider three such "pre-conceived" notions some teachers hold:

1. The belief that vocal growth is gradual, so change is slow, regular and constant throughout adolescence.
2. The theory that voices change exactly within definitely defined limits in orderly stages. These limits are exactly located and boys are assigned to voice parts within these precise pitch demarcations.
3. The belief that song materials written for adult voices or that conform to the above described limitations are quite appropriate for boys with changing voices to sing. Boys who do not sing this material comfortably or willingly are to be labeled deficient singers.

The fault in all three of the above is that voices do NOT change uniformly.Each boy's voice goes its own way, often in a most erratic, unexpected way. This is quickly discovered by anybody who has observed and recorded the patterns of change displayed by boys in stages 3 and 4 of puberty. Since there will surely be many boys who will NOT fit any pre-determined pattern of development, teachers who demand that their students conform to their pre-determined voice labels and range-limitations will either discourage boys from a desire to sing or may do actual vocal damage to those boys who strive and strain to conform to the demands of their teachers.

Chapter XVIII

ORGANIZATION OF CLASS GROUPS FOR BOYS WITH CHANGING VOICES

Let us examine some alternative procedures that will improve the teaching of boy singers during voice change.

Part A.

Segregated Boys' Classes

One plan is to segregate these boys with changing voices from the rest of their classmates for awhile. There are some very good reasons for this.

1. First, there is a negative but urgent reason. The girls and less mature boys can perform and appreciate some very challenging music by the time they have reached grades seven and eight. The uncertain voices of the maturing boys are apt to be a detriment or at least a disturbance in a heterogeneous class. If the capable singers have to wait while the teacher works with these faltering, unsure voices, the majority of the class may be penalized. They may become bored, they may begin to make disparaging remarks. Yet if the teacher pushes these developing boys to one side, telling them to sing softly so as not to spoil things, or, worst of all, not allowing them to sing at all, this teacher may be solving a musical problem but may be producing a strongly negative social and psychological reaction that will be almost irreparable.

2. A second, very positive reason for segregating these maturing boys is that they can be prepared psychologically for this important change in their singing apparatus; they can be told that this is a boys-only situation, a part of growing up, and that a new, different, more mature singing voice is going to develop that will give them more power and popular appeal once they learn how to handle this new voice and the music it will be expected to sing.

   We can tell them about the other things that are happening right now. They are growing very fast, getting tall, to the delight of the basketball coach. They are gaining weight to the joy of the football coach and the dismay of mom as she tries to satisfy this ravenous appetite. We can make jokes about the high-water pants and the sleeves of last year's jacket that barely cover the elbows, and about the over-large feet that are so clumsy. We can talk about the acne, the pimples appearing on faces and chests. We can console them as we state that ALL normal boys have this trouble, and the consolation will be welcome. We can tell them about the hair that is appearing in many new places and how the term "puberty" comes from this phenomenon. We can warn them jokingly about the teasing they will get when the moustache first appears, about the first shave, about the sideburns and beards that they can sprout in a few years. You can be sure that the class will be very attentive here, for this is of great interest to these young colts eager to grow up.

Most important in this preparatory talk, we tell them about the Adam's apple. the voice box that contains the vocal bands; we show them the protuberance about a half-inch below the chin that indicates the increase in size of this voice box. We explain that as the larynx grows rapidly the voice will go out of control for awhile; just as last year's coat looks comical as it barely covers the elbows, the voice will sound quite funny at times as it drops deeper, sounds fuller, maybe cracks or squeaks so that everybody laughs.

Next we can explain that we are going to leave the girls and younger boys for a time and go about the business of learning how to handle this new man-voice. If we sound pretty awful at first, it will not matter; the doors will be closed and nobody will hear. Some day, maybe in a month or so, we'll rejoin the girls and give them a big surprise as we sing out with our new tenor and bass voices. We may choose to give a hint that the boy with the little pip-squeak voice that nobody ever seemed to admire may develop a full, rich man's voice that people *will* like to hear. He may even develop into a very popular soloist. This is a fascinating and powerful motivation for any boy who, thus far in his school career, has not had much success as a singer.

Within a half-hour any teacher who has prepared his talk in advance and who speaks with sincerity can have most of the boys on his side, as he reassures them that to sing now is going to be an exciting adventure. If there is any uncertainty about saying some of these things convincingly there is much to be said for asking for assistance; a member of the medical profession, a dean of boys, one of the physical education staff (whom you want to have on your side anyway) can add to the authenticity and importance of what you are presenting.

Some caution is needed here. We must be careful never to betray these boys. If Sam sings badly off key, there must be no wincing, no frowning or indication of disapproval; if Ron's voice breaks into one of those silly squeaks there must be no sign of laughter. We will get a more favorable reaction if we make a few encouraging quips like, "You're missing your shots pretty badly today, Sam. Concentrate on your aim," or "So it's your turn today, is it, Sam? Last week it was Chuck. Wonder who it will be next week." Always you call attention to progress, to new developments and interesting quirks that appear.

3. A third reason for segregating boys with changing voices is very practical and pedagogical. The music to be sung must be

very carefully chosen; it must fit the voices present in the group at any given time. At this stage, more than any other, we should ask a boy to sing only what is comfortable and what produces no feeling of strain whatsoever. Anyone who has been sold on the idea that boys' voices change neatly, regularly, according to a definite pattern is destined to be surprised. I have found that in the more than 500 changing voices which I have observed and charted in the past two decades almost never have any two voices matched in their pattern of making the transition from treble to bass-clef voice. General patterns there are, but within those broad, rather blurred routes of making the transition, the individual differences abound.

Part B.

Segregating Classes with Team Teaching

There is nothing unusual nor improper about segregating students from their classmates for awhile. All sorts of remedial and enrichment work goes on in special groups throughout the modern educational system. If very bright boys can be excused from standard reading class, or if gifted and interested mathematics students are put into an honor class to do more challenging work, then a music teacher can ask that more mature boys be put into a special group to meet and solve vocal problems unique to themselves.

When there are two teachers of music in a large junior high school or middle school, team teaching is possible. If two home rooms or class sections are scheduled at the same time and there are two music rooms available, the boys ready for special attention can be separated from the rest of the class for as many minutes and days as desired. The advantage here is that the boys need not be separated for an entire period or for a whole semester; since there are many desirable activities other than singing in the general music curriculum, boys may be separated for only a part of the period and then can rejoin classmates and be re-grouped for other activities. As soon as voices have developed so they produce a fairly solid bass and tenor section, mixed chorus singing can be introduced gradually.

Part C.

Specially Organized Class Groups

In many junior high and middle schools there is only one vocal music teacher. In this case the administrator should be approached to see if there is some way to schedule certain boys away from their classmates. If the administrator shakes his head and says there is no way he can upset the rigid groupings worked out for the school year, there are still some workable schemes to consider. There is the possibility of alternating music with physical education or shop classes, putting, for example, boys with changing voices on Monday and Wednesday with Physical Education on Tuesday and Thursday, and the other boys in Physical Education on Monday and Wednesday, with Vocal Music on Tuesday and Thursday.

Part D.
The Bass Clef Chorus

In some schools there are what are called activity periods or administrative periods; these are used for such non-academic activities as taking attendance, issuing bulletins, scheduling all-school assemblies, arranging for guidance and counseling sessions. Quite often some of these periods are for clubs or enrichment classes or remedial work. Here it is quite feasible to schedule a bass-clef chorus once a week. As the teacher goes through his class lists he can spot the boys who are due for special attention and can ask everybody concerned if these boys may have the honor and privilege of coming to the music room that day.

If there is no such activity period, or if more than one meeting per week is desired, there is always the possibility of meeting before school, or, once football and basketball schedules have been worked out, after school. It is, of course, a sacrifice for teacher and boys to rise an hour early to attend "bass clef chorus" rehearsals, but one benefit is that the teacher will be compelled to motivate, to plan carefully, to make each rehearsal exciting so that the boys will be eager to come.

A second benefit is that the chronically lethargic, indifferent, lazy boys will just not make it, leaving the alert, ambitious, co-operative boys to enjoy the experiences—or, even better, that such lazy boys will change their ways as they are motivated to put forth extra effort.

It may be that even in the team-teaching situation an all-school bass-clef chorus will be desirable. One lesson I learned very early in my junior high teaching days was that if I could present twenty or thirty young men, dressed neatly in white shirt and bright tie, standing straight and tall, singing music with spirit and obvious enjoyment, the audience response was always warm and enthusiastic. It seemed not to matter if they sang only in unison, if the tones were more fuzzy, less robust than those of the senior high boys glee club, or if the music was not very pretentious; the sight and sound of young lads in their early teens doing a creditable job never failed to impress audiences.

Part E.
The Church-Related Chorus

Of course in a church situation a choir director will have no great problem with forming a training group for boys with changing voices. If there is a choirmaster or minister of music responsible for the total music program, a time and a place can easily be scheduled for this special group. He has been working with his singers since they were little children, so he should know which boys are ready for the transition to bass clef ranges. He has the backing of the minister or

80

priest; communication lines to parents are well established. In many churches there is a confirmation class or pastor's class already organized for young teen-agers. There is an adult choir with mature tenors and basses; a demonstration by these men is quite feasible; when the occasion arises, the new basses and tenors can stand next to their adult counterparts to experience the sound and feel of singing the new voice parts. With a girls' choir functioning, combining boys with girls for SATB singing with their own age-mates is easily arranged, when the boys are ready for mixed chorus singing.

Part F.

Individual Coaching

A desirable auxiliary for training boy singers during the time of voice change is to find in the community a teacher who can give individual lessons. Boys who have a strong desire to continue their singing career into adulthood can then get the individual teaching needed to take care of the unique problems their individual voices develop.

Take, for example, the case of a boy who has just graduated from a boy choir because of voice change. He has had five or six years of intense vocal training. He has acquired a good basic technique of voice production. He has had the valuable experience of performing music of artistic worth. He has had the satisfaction of being applauded and praised. There have been enriching experiences; e.g. being drilled in stage deportment, traveling to other communities, associating with boys of similar talents and interests, learning to adapt to difficult schedules and concert conditions, singing music of artistic worth and technical difficulty.

It seems opportune, efficient and economical to give training to this boy, still eager to sing and with a firm foundation on which to build. Now is the time to see that the newly emerging tones are produced correctly, without forcing or straining; now is the time to keep the treble tones functioning so they can become a usable faucette register. Rather than to let the voice break, with all the emotional and psychological hazards resulting from the worry and embarrassment at finding a part of the vocal range that is undependable, this is the time to help the boy ease into the lower register so the passage from head tone to chest tone is smooth and unobtrusive. If this can be done in the privacy of a studio, rather than with classmates present, under the guidance of a knowledgeable teacher, such a youth can continue singing through the period of rapid change without losing all the valuable skills he has acquired during his boy-choir, treble-voice years.

Of course such a private voice coach must accept the idea that a boy should and can continue his singing activities while the voice is in mutation. He must agree that nothing is being added to or subtracted from the vocal mechanism; the larynx may be growing rapidly in size so the vocal bands may be becoming longer and thicker, but the vocal bands are not losing their power to function.

81

The difficulty with making such an individual coaching opportunity available is that such one-to-one sessions take a great deal of time. It cannot be expected that the director of a professional or very active amateur boy choir should be available for coaching his graduates. This director's responsibility is to train the next generation of treble singers and to meet the performance requirements of the coming season.

The very busy music teacher of the junior or senior high choral department has to meet all his school assignments plus his schedule of extra-curricular activities. To ask him to make time for private, individual sessions is unrealistic and unfair.

Part G.

Co-operating with Private Teachers in the Community

An obvious way to provide for private, individual instruction is to work with an established voice teacher in the community. Unfortunately it is not easy to find a competent teacher who will have the time to give to these youths, or who has the inclination to work with these boys whose voices are changing. It is much more challenging and satisfying to most private teachers to work with mature voices, to prepare recitals and to coach songs of some technical advancement.

Another difficulty in finding a person to give individual lessons to these boys is that many admit quite frankly that they do not know how to develop the singing voice during mutation. Others may not admit their deficiency but will proceed to teach these boys as if they were adults, using the same techniques and procedures they use with mature students.

How then can a teacher for boys with changing voices be found? Here is where college councilors can be of assistance, as can established voice coaches and those in contact with the voice majors and future public school music teachers presently enrolled in college or conservatory. There is, we understand, a scarcity of teaching positions available to our college graduates these days. There are not many colleges or high schools looking for choral directors. Many potentially good voice teachers and choir directors are having to take jobs outside the field of music to "mark time" until they can find a place to practice their chosen profession.

Suppose some of these voice majors were encouraged to prepare themselves to work with these adolescent boys' voices during the period of voice change. Suppose an eager young graduate were to take some routine, non-music job as a stop-gap until he could get established? This recent graduate could make his services available in off-hours as a private voice coach. Working in co-operation with the choral directors in junior and senior high, and in church and community, he could very possibly become known as a competent

82

voice teacher. Being in the community when a vacancy does occur in the school, he would be known and available to take over any permanent teaching position that might open up.

Obviously, the individual student would pay for his own lessons, just as we find band and orchestra students paying for private coaching. If there are students who cannot afford such lessons, there are such things as music scholarships; it is quite possible that various music clubs, commercial music stores and private individuals can be persuaded to provide funds for a term of voice lessons to recommended students.

Chapter XIX

WHAT LEARNING EXPERIENCES TO INCLUDE IN THE BOYS' CHANGING VOICE CLASS

Segregating boys from their classmates when voices are changing will not automatically solve any problems. Getting them interested in what can happen as their voices change will be a powerful motivation, but motivation alone will not accomplish results. It is what learning experiences we provide that determine our success in guiding these boys through the period of rapid voice change easily, economically and efficiently.

Let us consider what new material we will want to present in the light of the problems we are attempting to solve and the goals we are trying to achieve.

1. We will be very much concerned with how to ease these adolescents into the bass clef ranges and with how to develop the new low tones gradually. At the same time we will want to keep control of the boyish treble tones so they do not atrophy.
2. When the boys are ready, they will need an explanation of the bass clef and of the ranges usually assigned to bass, baritone and tenor. Along with these explanations we will want to give them practice in the reading of bass and tenor parts from the score.
3. We will be acquainting these boys with song materials written for male voices and will be building a library of songs young fellows can sing for their own enjoyment and will also be able to use as adult singers.

Part A.

Song Material (Introductory)

As we plan to give boys these three types of learning activities, we can start with an activity already familiar and probably enjoyed in previous years—the singing of songs. First in importance is that the music be limited in range, well within the compass of an octave and readily adaptable to quick transposition to any key at any time. Second in importance is that the first songs be obvious of melody and characterized by a marked, simple rhythm pattern. The full attention of these boys has to be focused on getting their voices under control, and not on solving complicated rhythm patterns or following difficult melodic lines. For a time, handling these rapidly changing voices will be quite difficult, or at least unfamiliar and frustrating, so it will be desirable to have no other problems.

Since we have a limited amount of time and we want a large, varied repertoire of songs to keep up the interest, songs of the A-A-B-A or A-B-A type are recommended, as are songs with short verses and recurring chorus; texts should be the kind that boys of this age can identify with. The experienced teacher will observe the responses of each class for positive reactions to discover what appeals to boys of this particular school in light of their community background and current tastes.

On the first day, we start with a very well-known song, e.g. a school song, a familiar patriotic tune or a well-known hymn. For purposes of illustration here let's choose "Joyful, Joyful, We Adore Thee," with the option of using secular words if more appropriate; we sound a G, key of E-flat, and ask the boys to sing. Suppose it does not work out well; we drop to the key of C, starting on E. It comes out somewhat closer to being recognizable. We try the key of A-flat, starting on C, and this time all goes passably well; the song is recognizable, the voices match. We discover that the boys are singing in octaves, some singing down in the lower reaches of the bass-clef, the others in what would usually be called either the tenor range, or the very low alto range. We make a note that a range of a fifth, from A-flat to E-flat, works with this group. We ask the boys to sit tall, fill their lungs with air and to sing easily, with plenty of bounce.

Managing to produce a smile of pleasure, we ask the boys if they enjoyed these new low tones they are producing. A second song follows, still in that particular range, e.g., "He's Got the Whole World in His Hands." The boys have had experience with producing finger snaps, light hand claps and gestures in previous years, so these are added until the goup has lost any self-consciousness or stiffness. If these adolescents get over-boisterous, they can be cautioned (in a calm voice) not to force these newly developing voices which are not yet strong and firm.

Part B.

Voice Graphs and Songs with Special Ranges

This very superficial method of determining best ranges for songs described above should be made more exact. One very effective way to do this is to make a voice graph for each student, thereby having in plain sight what is possible for each boy to do.

The general plan of a voice graph is quite simple. On two music staves (treble and bass) you sketch a column graph to include all the tones a boy can sing comfortable and audibly, i.e. with no signs of throat tension or strain and no loss of vocal control. Care must be taken that ALL singable tones are shown, both those in the head-voice (faucette-falsetto) and in the modal (full, chest) voice.

VOICE GRAPHS OF FIVE STUDENTS

Example 13

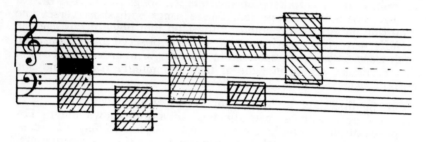

The graphs for five boys might look like this, where a slant from high left to low right indicates the treble tones and a slant from low left to high right shows the tones sung in the modal voice. Solid black is used to indicate tones where there is overlapping, i.e. where the boy can sing either lightly in the faucette register or in full voice in the modal register. Where there is a break in the continuity of the column, there is an "area of silence" where the boy cannot produce a sound at all, or only with great effort and strain.

Here is one detailed, step-by-step procedure, used in an actual classroom situation to determine the voice ranges of students.

1. As each boy came, he was asked his name and the teacher (referred to as "T") matched the speaking pitch with the proper tone on the piano. For example, if the first boy said "My name is Bill" and his speaking voice approximated F, the teacher sounded this F on the piano.

2. The direction was given "Sing for me the first part of 'My Country 'Tis of Thee'."

3. When it was established that this was a comfortable singing range, T struck an E-flat, a whole tone lower, and Bill was asked to sing the first phrase again; the D-flat was struck, followed by C, B-flat, etc. until Bill could sing no lower, i.e. his voice either stopped or became so soft it was scarcely audible. .

4. Returning to the first F, the procedure was repeated but this time the given pitch was raised to G, then to a, to b, to c, until Bill could sing no higher in modal voice without noticeable strain or until his voice stopped, or his voice "broke".

5. This was duly recorded on the double-staff, and a column graph was filled in with blue pencil to show the extent of his modal (chest) voice.

6. T. then said "Bill, pretend you are a little fellow, let's say in the third grade. I want you to say 'Good morning' in a high, little-boy voice". If Bill did not succeed, T. illustrated in a high faucette (head) tone. If Bill succeeded, T found the pitch on the piano and Bill was asked to sing "My Country 'Tis of Thee" in this high, thin voice. If he still could not find his faucette voice, the audition stopped.

7. As in steps 3 and 4, the starting pitch was lowered by whole steps until the lowest faucette-tone was found and recorded.
   a. Bill's voice became so soft it faded into silence.
   b. Bill's voice "switched over" into the fuller tones of the modal voice, quite abruptly and obviously.
   c. Bill's voice suddenly dropped a complete octave.
   d. Bill lost vocal control and produced an unmusical sound of no definite pitch.
8. The starting pitch was raised, step-by-step, until Bill could go no higher in the faucette voice.
9. The highest and lowest tones in the faucette-voice were then indicated by a column graph in red.

Part C.
Using the Voice Graphs

In a class situation, you will next make a composite graph (see ex. 14) on which the voice ranges of all the boys are sketched. Suppose, for example you have sixteen boys and when you put their individual graphs in sequence (lowest to highest) you get something like this:

Example 14   VOICE GRAPHS OF 16 STUDENTS

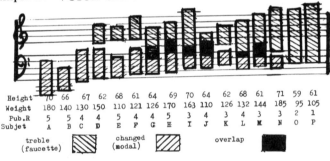

It immediately becomes obvious that there is no song nor vocal exercise where all sixteen can sing in unison. The inexperienced teacher may declare in despair that he does not know how to handle a class with such disparate voice ranges. The teacher indoctrinated with some "method" or pre-determined scheme for classifying voices may stare in disbelief and say this is impossible, that such a situation is not supposed to happen.

On the surface this does seem impossible. Note that height or weight do not indicate voice change. Students A, I and N are of almost equal height, but by no means of comparable voices; nor do the three "shorties" F, M and P match. In weight we notice students A, N and H are heavy, but voices do not match; nor do the voices of the lightweights E, J and P.

The teacher who is a realist wastes little time in questioning or despairing. Instead he inspects the graphs and begins to plan his classroom procedures. He looks at these graphs and discovers that it is possible for all the boys to sing in unison-octave if he can find songs that lie within the range of a fifth or sixth. Subjects A through E will be comfortable between G' and D, while subjects F and G can match them if the lowest G' is sung very softly. Students H through P can sing from G to D safely, with N being cautioned to sing lightly on the low G.

Are there any songs that lie within the restricted range of a fifth that are usable, interesting, appealing to adolescent boys? Surprisingly there are quite a few. I personally have collected a repertoire of over a dozen that are ryhthmic, tuneful and that such boys have enjoyed singing together; for special occasions or situations I have even managed to compose a few with the help of the boys themselves. Some hardy old favorites, very much in the public domain hence reproducible legally, are the hymns "Praise the Lord Ye Heavens Adore Him," and "When I Survey the Wondrous Cross"; there is a very swingy spiritual "O Sinner Man" and another "Climbing Up the Mountain, Children"; there is the dance tune "Skip to My Lou" that lies within a range of a minor sixth (We made up our own humorous lyrics to this!); the all-time favorite lying within a fourth is "Now the Day Is Over".

As you graph many boys' voices over several years you will discover that the only generalization that can be safely made about the manner in which boys change from treble to bass clef singing is that each boy will develop in his own peculiar way.

As you chart the tones a pubescent boy can sing comfortably from week to week, you will find that he adds tones to his singable range, and loses tones formerly singable, all according to patterns quite unique to himself and different from any other boy.

This was true in 1956 when I first began to graph the voices of adolescent boys individually. It was true when I charted the voice ranges in large class groups over a whole school year. It has been true as I have checked the voice-ranges of teen-age boys in summer choruses, in workshops and demonstration groups. It is still true today as I work with individuals in private voice-coaching sessions.

This uniqueness of vocal change is important to understand for several reasons:

There is the negative reason that teachers of adolescent boys must beware of any method that is developed according to some arbitrary classification of voices. There have appeared from time to time, "experts" who have proclaimed that they have the one perfect method for classifying and developing boys' voices during the time of mutation.

Some of these people are very precise in describing what boys can sing, yes even MUST sing, during voice change. Adolescent "baritones" they say, can sing pitches between exact limits; likewise "tenors" are expected to sing tones within carefully defined ranges. Sometimes artificial labels are applied to these voices, rather than the traditional tenor and bass titles. Should anybody question these absolute limitations or claim to have boys who fall into other range demarcations, the veracity of such people is immediately questioned. Boys in the choirs of such people are urged, harangued, forced to somehow conform to the patterns prescribed. Alas, boys, I have found (and you will find it so too) do not fall readily into classifications neatly and precisely defined. If you or I insist that our boys MUST conform, we will either urge them to strain and force to the point of vocal damage, or "turn them off" so they leave us either frustrated or despairing, to sing no more.

A positive reason, most important to teachers of adolescent boys, is that at this time, more than any other, much provision has to be made to find and accommodate the vocal capabilities of ALL the boys in a class or choir. Where a teacher is very aware of what each of his boy singers CAN do, he can proceed to find music and materials that are appropriate.

This may seem like a very difficult, almost impossible task. It is not! Assuming that the music teacher has had a standard background of musical training and that he is willing to experiment and adapt, the musical results are so gratifying it is well worth the effort expended.

I refer you to Chapter XX in Section IV when we discuss methods of making or finding musical arrangements to fit certain types and limitations of young voices.

Part D.

Rote Songs

You will note that I have been careful to use only tried-and-true tunes as illustrations. I have done so for the very good reason that any song on which the copyright is still in effect cannot be reproduced, or even written, words only, on a chalkboard. But it is quite legal to teach such a song by rote, i.e. by hearing it sung over and over until it is learned by ear. This means that some of the current popular tunes, if not too trivial or overly-sentimental, can be used. There are ballads sung by country folk singers that are not hopelessly cheap and trashy. A collection of cowboy songs will reveal several possible tunes to use, some of them copyrighted; and so will a book of sea-chanteys. Folk song collections will provide tunes not always well known but easily taught, and sometimes these "folk songs" are composed and copyrighted. Negro spirituals are a ready source for rhythmic, appealing material, and there are spirituals that lie within the range of a fifth, both white and black.

If any junior high school music teacher or junior choir director is a bit disappointed at the thought of regressing to unison-octave singing of an elementary type song, let me point out that this is not to be the repertoire for the whole year but only for a limited amount of time. Since voice change is not a disaster but a temporary period of rapid change, within four to six weeks the boys in most groups will achieve a relative homogeneity of tone and will have extended their potential range so songs of an octave compass will be possible, and part-singing can begin.

In fact, I have, on occasion, heard bass choruses other than my own sing compositions of considerable difficulty and established artistic worth most effectively. Handel's "Where'er You Walk" and Schubert's "The Trout" are two songs highly effective (if put into proper key) when sung by adolescent basses or tenors in unison, certainly highly reputable and worthy "learning songs".

It is important that we notice that the use of such songs of limited range would not work in a mixed class. Keys and ranges suitable for these boys would not be suitable for girls or boys with unchanged voices. You might find that the key of G-flat is the only one appropriate for your boys at a particular time, but G-flat would be highly inappropriate for the girls!

A comment about accompaniments and appropriate keys is in order here. Songs used in the changing-voice class should be rather simple in accompaniment and readily transposed at a moment's notice. Hence songs in the standard I-IV-V chordal sequences are most desirable, since even a very inept accompanist can usually sketch out those chords for every possible key. One enterprising teacher who had very little facility on the piano purchased a bass ukulele and learned the three basic chords. By the simple expedient of raising or lowering the tuning of his four strings, he could easily adjust his accompaniment to fit any of the twelve major keys desired. As I recall, he mastered the chords for the keys of A, C and E-flat, so he needed to tune the strings, at most, a minor third higher or lower. For example, raising the tuning to B-flat, or B, lowering it to G or G-flat makes the same fingering work for five keys.

Part E.

Vocalising to Improve Voices

Along with the singing of songs, there can be vocalising to develop the newly emerging low tones. Adolescent boys are usually quite amenable to vocalising IF they see a purpose for doing so. American boys are accustomed to spending much time swinging on the putting green, shooting baskets in the back yard, balancing on the diving board or throwing a ball back and forth, patiently working to perfect their skills in order to become better performers, even hoping to become champions. Once convinced that singers too must work to perfect their form and to increase their control, boys are usually willing to work, especially if the drills are short and the purpose of such vocalises seems worthwhile. The need for exercises to achieve proper breath support and good diction, to increase resonance, or to enlarge the range is no different for teen-agers than for singers at any other age. A boy who sees a hope of becoming a good singer will take to a regime of "working out" quite readily.

It should be emphasized that vocalises to find the best ranges and to extend those ranges need special attention during voice change. Since the voices are moving downward in pitch, vocalises that work the voice in descending passages seem to be much more valuable and

90

productive at this time than are ascending exercises. Thus a descending five-tone scale (see ex.15) on so-fa-mi-re-do, or on "no", or "ya", or "win" will ease the voices down to find and develop the newly emerging lowest tones. A descending tonic chord "do-so-mi-do" with the five vowels on the lowest "do" (see ex. 16) as well as a descending octave-scale on various vowels and consonant combinations (see ex. 17) are also effective. Songs that include descending scale passages can follow and strengthen these vocalises, e.g. "We Merry Tooters" (see Chapter IX, ex. 1) or "The Streets of Laredo" or "Joy to the World".

Example 15   Descending Five-Tone Scale

Example 16   Descending Tonic Chord

Example 17   Descending Scale

By all means these descending passages should be begun in the high treble and gradually dropped down until the "passagio" from treble to bass voice can be negotiated smoothly. It is not at all unusual for many of the boys in these segregated classes to achieve a descending scale of over two octaves with no noticeable transition from treble (faucette) to bass (full voice), if the voice change is anticipated and the boy continues to use his treble voice, not allowing it to atrophy. In many cases a boy can move smoothly from boy-voice to deeper tones in the bass clef keeping in his control as much as three octaves. Voice mutation need not be a period of limitations but actually a time for great resources!

Part F.
First Part-Songs

Once unison octave singing is going well, part singing can be begun, tenor-bass preferred. Two-part music is quite possible in this changing voice class; the recommended idiom is melody in bass, and harmony in sixths in tenor. (see ex. 18) A good way to begin part singing is to use a simultaneous-song combination. For example, have the basses sing "Home on the Range," key of E-flat, and the tenors "My Home's in Montana," also in E-flat (see ex. 39, Appendix C). See next example 19, "Kum Ba Yah" for two-part tenor-baritone with optional bass. Be prepared to adjust key!

Example 18   O COME ALL YE PEOPLE — Two-Part Song

Oh come, all ye   pee-ple, oh come one and all
To Beth- le-hem's sta-ble, to Beth-   le-hem's stall.O see with re-

joic-ing this glo-ri-ous sight our Fath-er in heav-en has sent us this night.

Example 19   KUM BA YAH — tenor and baritone, optional
            bass

Kum-bah yah
Kum-bah-yah my Lord,   Kum-bah-yah   kum-bah-yah   kum-bah-yah.Oh Lord.. kum-bah- yah
Kum-bah-yah

Part G.
Listening Lessons

Formal listening lessons are feasible but not recommended at this time. Boys at this age are not always amenable to sitting quietly for an extended listening period. It is better to keep such sessions short and for a very definite purpose. One valuable experience is for the boys to hear very competent male singers in a recording of songs which the boys themselves can sing and enjoy. For example, some twenty years ago the men of the Roger Wagner Chorale recorded a collection of "Songs of the Sea" and "Songs of the Western Plains" which are excellent for getting teenage boys used to the sound of adult male voices while providing some very usable songs for their own unison singing.

One enterprising junior high school teacher made use of a visiting artist-in-residence, who happened to be an excellent bass singer. This teacher persuaded the singer to make tape recordings of five or six English folk songs with guitar accompaniment to provide a model for his adolescent basses. This was so successful in capturing the attention of his students that he found a co-operative tenor to do the same for his boys in that section.

The formation of a bass-clef chorus has already been discussed. With membership by tryout, with distinctive name and uniform dress, quite often it can be an effective motivator and morale builder for the boys involved. It can also serve as a fine public relations group between school and community, "selling" parents on the worth of a fine male chorus. It can also be an organization to impress boys in the ten to twelve year old age group (who will be entering junior high school), arousing an eagerness for future membership when they are advanced to junior high school.

This was brought home to me when my boy students in the county farm school (a special school for problem boys) worked up a thirty-minute cowboy skit (complete with ten-gallon hats, chaps and boots, plus a genuine lasso-twirling exhibition by one of the more notorious fellows) that made the rounds of the community until it ended up on the local television station. We followed this the next season with a sailor routine, borrowing naval uniforms from all sorts of places, and adding some comic dialogue to a series of songs. People in the community were not accustomed to admiring the boys in this school, so the prestige of this "problem school" rose tremendously, and music became a bright spot in the school's curriculum.

Once a junior high teacher has advanced his bass clef chorus to a point where it has a good sound, there need be no hesitation to let his young men be heard. If faces are freshly scrubbed and hair is neatly combed, even if costuming is quite simple (a plain white shirt, a bright red bow tie and plain dark trousers, for example) most audiences will be impressed. If some practice is given to train the young choristers to enter smartly, stand erect and keep eyes on the director, they will surely win the attention of the listeners. Music can be simple, as simple as unison-octave, if it is the type that is appropriate to boys of this age. If there should be one lad with a distinctive solo quality to his voice for a short solo passage, and a bongo player for a calypso number, or a passably capable guitarist for a folk song accompaniment, this is all the variety needed. Once the word gets about among the service clubs, the parent-teacher groups and the women's organizations, the boys will be in sufficient demand to make them feel they belong to an "honors group."

Part H.
The Teacher and Singing Materials

There is one other factor that needs discussion. The teacher who guides boys through their voice change plays a vital part in determining the degree of success attained. That such a teacher must be well informed in matters of correct vocal production is of prime importance. That he be a competent choral singer himself is equally important. He must have the ability to adapt to the situation before him; no matter what unusual patterns of vocal development occur, he must be ready to adjust to them, which means he must have a repertoire of song materials and vocalises to fit any group or individual, and he must sense when and how to use this repertoire. Most important, he must have a liking for and understanding of boys in early adolescence and for their vocal potentialities. This teacher, as well as the boys in his class, must look on the phenomenon of voice change as a fascinating stage of vocal development, as an exciting adventure and as an opportunity for great increase in resources for musical participation and enjoyment.

Summary

We have thus far suggested four procedures to use in order to achieve better results in guiding adolescent boy singers through the earlier stages of voice change.
1. Segregate these boys from their classmates for a time until they have gained control of their deeper tones and have had some training in reading the bass clef and the tenor and bass part from that clef.
2. Convince them that voice change is an adventure, a discovery of a new voice, an increase in power and ability.
3. Use song materials, vocalizes and listening activities that will help the newly emerging lower tones to develop gradually, without physical strain or emotional embarrassment.
4. Motivate the boys to develop and improve their singing voices through special clubs and honors groups, as well as through choice of songs of interest, dressed up with costumes and attractive staging.

SECTION 4
THE NEWLY CHANGED VOICE - AGES 14 TO 18

Chapter XX

FIRST EXPERIENCES IN SINGING BASS, TENOR, ALTO, SOPRANO MUSIC

The purpose of this chapter is to discuss the choice of music for young singers ready to sing four-part mixed chorus music. Our discussion will be of immediate interest to:
1. Vocal music teachers in junior high school.
2. Directors of high school freshmen courses, especially in areas where students have had limited or deficient training in elementary schools.
3. Directors of church choir programs that include a unit for teen-agers.

This discussion will also be helpful to high school choral conductors who maintain training choirs for less capable singers and for college choral conductors who find students with deficient choral experience who need a preparatory course in choral singing techniques.

Let us suppose that it is early September, and you, ninth grade choral director, are meeting your SATB chorus for the first time. As you survey the students that arrive your heart sinks, for it is not the ideal enrollment you had anticipated. Instead of the 60 singers divided neatly into four sections of approximate size, you see only fifty-four pupils; thirty-six are girls and sixteen are boys. You suspect that your perennial foe, the athletic coach, has been dropping hints that no boys hoping to be on the team may sing in the choir. You also wonder if that prejudiced councilor has again steered some of those better boy singers you had worked with in grade seven into "more masculine" subjects like science or special mathematics. You even dare to wonder if YOU have been at fault and that you may have "turned off" some of the better boy singers.

This is the poor material out of which you must develop a performing group to appear in public to bring pleasure to an audience. If these are the singers who will wear the beautiful robes you have managed to purchase, you want them to add to the prestige of the school, the music department and to your reputation as a competent choral conductor. If you are a sincere dedicated teacher you want these students to get satisfaction, pleasure and a sense of accomplishment as they sing for you.

Those sixteen boys are a motley crew, ranging in size from the six-foot "bean-pole" to the four-foot-eleven cherub. A few display the very significant muddy complexion, the pimply skin, the faint traces of moustache that go with a changing voice. Others still have the smooth rosy skin of pre-pubescent little boys. The in-betweeners are nondescript.

You know that the voices of those gangly adolescents will be well into the changing stages. There will be some with restricted ranges somewhere down in the lower bass clef; some will be uncertain of pitch; some will be coarse and rough in tone quality.

There may be some definitely deep basses; with luck there will be a few true, settled tenors. There will be some that are not ready to be classified as anything definite. As for those little fellows, they probably should be sopranos or altos, but you know that they will resist sitting in the "girls' sections" for psychological-social reasons.

For the moment the girls do not pose so many problems. They have been singing soprano and alto for several years and are probably quite prepared to continue doing so. True, these thirteen-and fourteen-year-old girls' voices will tend to be colorless, breathy, rather restricted in range. There will be only a few who can be definitely classified as true altos, and there will not be many who can soar above the treble clef with ease as genuine sopranos. But right now they are ready to assume their roles as sopranos and altos; they are not your most urgent problem.

The most pressing problem, you know well, is that group of boys. They will demand most of your attention during these opening days of the semester. What to do? They have come expecting to sing, and they have a right to have some success and pleasure in that singing. (Presumably this is an elective course, and nobody has come reluctantly.)

Several decades ago I heard a noted choral director say, "If you have only one tenor, put him in the front row and give him the melody". Paraphrased to apply to our situation, this says, "If you have a weak, uncertain section, put those singers into a special prominent place and give them the melody, preferably one they know well."

The rationale is quite clear. The immediate need of these uncertain singers is to concentrate on "making their voices go where they are supposed to go". This may be quite a problem for some of those newly-emerged bass voices, especially after a summer of non-singing. It will be wise to avoid adding any complications like reading notes in an unfamiliar part or posing any puzzling problems of rhythm. Right now you want to down-play any factors that will distract their attention from the one challenge they have, "Finding those new tones down in the bass clef".

What do we see in so many commercially published "easy SATB arrangements?" An attractive melody in the soprano, an undemanding alto-line, a tenor part filling in a harmony and the bass following the I-IV-V-I progression, which means leaps of a fourth or a fifth. That is just the opposite of what the situation demands.

Obviously the voice part most in need of development is the bass. These boys have been singing in the treble clef ranges for some six to eight years, many of them on the highest soprano part. Suddenly they are confronted with some rather puzzling new requirements. They must sing in a radically different range. They have to use a vocal apparatus that has grown rapidly in size, with a frustrating loss of control. They are now buried below all the other singers, where they cannot hear themselves easily to be sure they know what they are doing. They must sing in a different idiom, i.e. not the melody "up on top" but a vocal line including widely spaced leaps and uninteresting contours.

To reduce the number of problems our new basses must solve, we will contrive some arrangements where as many problems as possible will be eliminated, or at least minimized. We cannot do much about their range or tessitura, but we can, remembering our statement above, give them a familiar melody to sing so they can concentrate entirely on adjusting their newly-enlarged vocal apparatus to the new sounds and on "making the voice go where it should".

For purposes of illustration, let us consider DECK THE HALLS WITH BOUGHS OF HOLLY:

1. It is a familiar carol which all the basses are sure to know.
2. The melody lies within the compass of an octave, presumably a manageable range if the octave is chosen properly.
3. It is a downward melody, built on the descending scale, so the basses will be working into the newly emerging lower tones.

Let us suppose that, after some quick voice checking, the key of A-major is the best one for our basses at this particular time. Some can sing higher, some can sing lower, but these are the tones that all can manage. We have the start of a bass section, a group of boys who can produce tones within that octave range without having to force or strain. We have given our basses a familiar melody on which to practice maneuvering their coarse and uncertain voices until they can achieve a passable homogeneity of tone.

The next section of the choir that needs special attention is the tenor section. There will not be many true tenors with a full, resonant quality at this age level. Some of these boy-tenors will be really treble voices, the immature boys who will strongly prefer not to sing with the girls. Keep in mind that these boys may be vocally immature in this first week in September, but within the coming school year many of them will become pubescent and will be ready to move into the bass clef ranges. There are those who believe that it is wise to anticipate the voice change by easing these boys into a low alto part occasionally, providing there is no forcing or straining.

The tenor part we will work out must be carefully contrived. We cannot give the tenors the melody, since the basses already have that, but we can give them a very obvious harmonic part, similar to the tune in melodic line. The range must be rather limited, not going below a G for those light treble voices, yet not very high, in case there are boys finding their changing voices moving into a tenor range. One hazard here will be the new, unfamiliar experience of harmonizing a melody "below them". This is compensated for by the removal of any temptation for these "tenors" to sing a soprano melody an octave lower.

Giving the tenors a part that moves in thirds or sixths with the basses and putting the two parts on a bass-clef staff, we get this arrangement. (see ex.20)

Example 20   DECK THE HALLS — for baritone and tenor

Deck the halls with boughs of hol- ly   fa-la- la-la- la -   la- la- la
"Tis the sea- son to be jol- ly
Troll the an- cient Yule- tide car- ol

Don we now our gay ap- par- el, fa-la-la fa- la-la fa- la- la . . .

D. C.
al Fine

This two-part arrangement will be quite satisfactory in itself if sung on the exact pitches written, so it could be used with an all-boy chorus. Some of our sophisticated choral directors may think it is trite and obvious. That is just the point—it is purposely so. We want our new, inexperienced basses and tenors to work into the "feel and sound" of their new voice-ranges in a song that is obvious and easy. This won't sound trite and obvious to them. It probably will intrigue and satisfy them, for it is new to them and their "new voices". If the boys' voices are uncertain, muddy, hesitant at first, and if the girls must be kept busy while this new material is being presented to the boys, parts can be doubled. Altos may sing lightly with the basses in their own comfortable range, while the sopranos double the tenor part an octave higher and very softly. As soon as possible the boys should carry on by themselves.

It is notorious that the most shoddily taught section of the mixed choir is the soprano section. These girls have been singing melodies since earliest childhood. Since most of the so-called "easy four-part songs for junior high" put the melody in the soprano, these girls are given nothing new. They meet no challenges, have few puzzling problems to solve. All too often these girls become adept at "singing the tune by ear" so they never have to acquire skill at harmonizing or even hearing harmonies, and they seldom experience a vocal line moving in counterpoint against a set melody.

To equalize matters we are going to challenge our sopranos by giving them a descant, a challenging one with a moving line involving sixteenth note figures and a few leaps involving intervals greater than a third. They will have to read the notes and figure things out. As part of our strategy, we also know that such a part will not tempt our immature boy-singers to try singing the soprano an octave or two octaves below the girls. We are going to insist that the sopranos sing lightly and crisply, so they do not cover the tune and so that they are aware of the sound of their voices moving against a melody.

The same applies to the altos, with a few modifications. If there are not many girls with *real* alto quality, we'll stay in the treble clef, making few forays into the ledger lines below. We may want to give these girls just as challenging a part as the sopranos if they are adept at singing an alto line, or we may choose to keep their part simpler, if they are not very capable.

While the girls are learning their parts, the boys can be singing their bass melody and tenor harmony, not only to give them ample practice in developing their new voices, but also to give the girls the needed experience of singing counter to the melody.

Our four parts may emerge as illustrated in example 21. Note that I have elected to put the tenor in the treble clef with the admonition to sing an octave lower than written. That is what these tenors will be seeing when standard, published SATB music is used. If preferred and if there is to be some singing from hymnals and liturgical scores, it may be advisable to put the tenor with the bass on the bass-clef staff.

Example 21   DECK THE HALLS — Carol for bass, tenor, alto, soprano

One of the purposes of this chapter is to motivate YOU, the reader, to arrange music that will fit your particular situation, not to give you something to copy. That is why I chose as an example a song that is not suitable for early September.

Suppose you take the familiar theme from Beethoven's Ninth Symphony, found in many collections as JOYFUL, JOYFUL WE ADORE THEE*. If you change the final note in measure twelve, the entire melody lies within the range of a fifth, so a wide choice of keys is possible to fit almost any restricted tessitura YOUR new basses find comfortable. On staff paper, sketch out the bass part in that comfortable range. Above it, pencil in a tenor part, one which will in general move in parallel motion, either a third or a sixth above the bass.

You will quickly discover that if you copy the tenor in the treble-clef, by putting the tenor notes on the same lines and spaces as the bass, you will get a pitch a sixth above. This will work whenever you want obvious harmonic writing, but some care must be taken to watch the cadences lest you come out in the minor rather than the major. In example #22, the notes are starred where the tenor line needs to move in contrary motion.

Example 22   JOYFUL, JOYFUL WE ADORE THEE

Once the boys' parts are in place, estimate how much challenge the girls should have and contrive some interesting soprano and alto counter-melodies.

Next, let us deal with another problem, that of the frequently weak tenor section. What if your boys in that part of the choir are immature of voice, feeble of tone, non-aggressive, and unable yet to hold their own against the sopranos and altos? Let's give THEM some arrangements where they have the melody. Choose an easy, familiar tune, with limited range and with step-wise progressions rather than leaps or skips. The hymn NOW THE DAY IS OVER, is

---

* Also, we are told, there is a popular arrangement extant, one with rather deplorable words.

one which fills these requirements very adequately. What key to use? Whatever key will best accommodate these timid voices. (See ex. 23)

Example 23   NOW THE DAY IS OVER

Choosing the key of E-flat for our example, we'll give the basses the traditional bass-line with some alterations to avoid the extended range of a tenth. We are assuming that by now the basses have attained some homogeneity of tone, some control of their voices, and are ready to handle something more challenging than an obvious tune.

We next give the altos the familiar counter-melody with the admonition that they must keep it softer than the tenor melody; no heavy, pushed, chesty tones will be acceptable. As for the sopranos, we won't give these girls a chance to sit back and sing a hymn by ear. Rather, we'll give them a fairly high descant, just difficult enough to keep them alert and interested, with the requirement that they keep their voices light enough so that they hear the tenors easily.

It must be remembered that the purpose of making these special arrangements is educational. These are learning exercises intended to attain certain goals, to introduce young teen-age singers (or inexperienced, deficient older singers) to SATB singing, efficiently and effectively. These arrangements make no claim to great artistic worth, and only occasionally will one of them prove to be so musically satisfying that you will want to keep it in the permanent repertoire of your choir.

We are presuming that within a few weeks your four sections will have attained enough assurance and control so that you can proceed to use the standard, published SATB arrangements available commercially, and that you will resort to specially contrived arrangements ONLY if one of your sections is persistently weak and is in constant need of attention.

A word of caution is in order. Only songs in the public domain should be used in these learning-arrangements. It is illegal to reproduce any score that is copyrighted; so if you take a currently popular tune or some song from a recent Broadway show, arrange it and reproduce copies mechanically you are breaking the law. Be advised to use familiar hymns (as we have, with a thought for our church choir directors), folk songs, old spirituals, both white and negro, the "old line" patriotic songs, and melodies dating back to the nineteenth century or earlier. For suggestions, consider these:

1. Give the tenors the melody for America, for All Through the Night, Oh Susannah, Home on the Range, Blow the Man Down.
2. Give the basses the melody for Skip to My Lou, The Water Is Wide, Joshua Fit De Battle of Jericho.

Your first attempts at making and reproducing your own arrangements may be slow and time-consuming. Will it be too time consuming for a very busy teacher? That depends on your philosophy and your attitude toward your job. How serious is your problem and how hard are you willing to work to solve it? How much difficulty do you have in fitting your voices to standard choral arrangements? How well prepared and vocally settled are your singers when they first come to you?

The results achieved by the above procedure will more than repay a director for the time spent. It takes only two or three attempts at this process to become rather adept; it is possible to reproduce a sixteen bar arrangement in as little as half an hour, once you have penciled in your proposed arrangement. Paradoxically, the more acute your problem, the more restricted your voices, the easier it is to contrive the arrangement. Those very limitations dictate the arrangement you must use. For example, if the tenors are very limited in range, their part will go into that range. The other parts will, perforce, have to be adapted to that tenor part.

If you, the reader, have never had experience with this process a few instructions are in order.

There are several very good ways to produce original manuscripts in quantity for class use. I personally prefer using ditto-duplicator masters, for with these I can run off as many as a hundred copies that are clearly readable.

Once I have blocked out the four-part arrangement in pencil on staff paper, and checked carefully for possible errors, I get a 12-staff music master,* remove the cushion sheet, and after I have decided how I plan to assign the staffs to the voice-lines (either a separate staff for each voice-part, or soprano-alto on one staff, or bass-tenor on same bass clef staff) I type in the words. Words are typed in first because it is easier to fit notes to words than to squeeze long words in under notes, especially if I am careful to separate word-syllables rather widely. The notes are then penciled in, using a firm pressure and being careful to keep notes on the several staffs in exact alinement. (A ruler or straight-edge to extend the bar lines through all the staffs and to line up the note-stems is a great help). Once the notes have been traced in, the master is placed on the duplicator machine (the carbon being removed, of course) and the desired number of copies run off. If an error is made in copying, the master can be turned over and the mistake scraped off with a sharp razor blade, the master put back on the carbon and the correction penciled in.

---

* Sure-rite Units #3500, Music Master 12-staff, American Stencil Manufacturing Co., Denver, Colo. 80216, is one source of supply.

Chapter XXI
FITTING THE MUSIC TO THE CHOIR

In this chapter I intend to adopt the philosophy that the choral program is to be child-centered, and the music to be sung is to be chosen to fit the present capabilities of the students present.

A corollary will be that music will not be chosen before the class/choir appears. If fifty girls and ten boys come to the first class session, the director will search for music to fit that particular balance of voice, and if none is found, he will make his own choral arrangements. If there is a reasonably good balance of voices in numbers, but one or more sections is deficient, (lacking in vocal maturity or musical awareness) adaptations to accommodate will be made in the music selected.

Part A.

Transposition of Published Material

One very mild adjustment to accommodate vocal limitations is to alter keys, transposing down or up; this device will be useful for a director who is still reluctant to abandon the traditional SATB pattern.

For example, suppose for some reason (e.g. long-standing tradition, community desire) your choir is to sing the Hallelujah Chorus from Handel's "Messiah". You have a choir of 64 voices, and on paper they appear to be properly balanced in numbers, but your tenors as a section cannot sing above g, and some of your young basses are uncomfortable above middle-c. You see that there is a steady succession of d's for the basses, and many high g's plus one VERY exposed high a for the tenors.

Suppose you transpose down a whole step, to sing the Chorus in the key of c-major. The bass range now goes no higher than middle-c, the tenors have one high-g. In one measure there is a single low F for the basses, but that is only ONE hazard, offset by the fact that the exposed entrance in measure 42 is now not a hurdle to be approached with fear and trembling.

Not only do the tenors have an easier time with the notorious entrance in measure 45, but the steady succession of g's is now a more comfortable succession of f's.

The altos will have one minor adjustment to make in measure 19. The sopranos must descend to an occasional c—but they will be much less under strain in the long, sustained rising passages from measure 48 to 68.

Some may cry "heresy and sacrilege" at the thought of changing such a venerable classic. Such cries are not substantiated by history. Since "a-440 dv" was not established as concert pitch until long after

104

Handel's day, we have reason to believe that what is written in the key of D in 1725 may have been sung in the present-day equivalent of D-flat or even C. It certainly is true that the orchestral accompaniment of Handel's first performance was not the one we hear today in the orchestration made by Mozart several decades later; it is just as probable that the use of male altos, counter-tenors and even possibly boy trebles, may have resulted in a different vocal "sound" than the one our purists label "traditional."

Most important to our adopted philosophical train of thought, our students are able to sing and enjoy and come to appreciate this established classic with less vocal strain and discomfort. I will add the personal belief that nine-tenths of the hearers will not be disturbed in the least by the change in key, but will be much happier at the better vocal sounds.

Part B.
Re-voicing of Published Materials

Very much in the same method of procedure is the practice of re-voicing certain sections of a composition.

Suppose that for ten bars the tenor line is quite high, ranging from d to a high a'-flat, and the bass line hovers almost entirely above the bass-staff. For those ten bars it would be quite feasible to ask a group of altos to take over the tenor part (asking a few sopranos to move over to the printed alto part to balance) and giving the tenors the bass part. I hasten to add that I am in total agreement with those who deplore the practice of re-enforcing a weak tenor section with girl "tenors"; for an adolescent girl to spend a year or even a semester singing entirely in her chest tones is to do harm, to impede proper vocal development. But we speak here of only a brief passage, well in the comfortable alto range.

Part C.
Making Special Arrangements for Special Cases

Consider the plight of a director arriving in a new situation to discover that the choir he sees on the first day of school is composed of 50 boys and 10 girls. For the director to attempt to develop a traditionally voiced choir is an almost impossible task. He will certainly get better results, both educational and musical, if he divides his singers according to some other scheme, e.g. bass-baritone-tenor-treble.

For dramatic effect, we have said "50 boys and 10 girls". Even the most tradition-bound high school choral director will cry "Impossible! There is not a school in this country with THAT imbalance". He would be right but there are many schools where 10 boys and 50 girls would be quite usual! The solution then should be to find music for SMAB.

For music of unusual voicing we can look at the madrigals of Elizabethan days or English composers under the Stuarts, where voicing is in FIVE parts; where the voices called for are bass-baritone-countertenor-treble. We suggest as an example "O Lamb of God" by Purcell, originally scored for treble, two

105

Example 24   O LAMB OF GOD — Purcell

Mixolydian Mode   originally scored for treble
two countertenors, baritone and bass

countertenors, baritone and bass. Transposing it upward we have an arrangement for soprano-mezzo-alto-baritone-and bass, with the baritone part not too low for a tenor voice. Since madrigals were sung *en famille* with women included (women did not sing in public usually) we can assume that women would sing the upper three voice lines, while in public male altos (countertenors) sang lines two and three. A work like the Purcell would not be difficult for a twentieth century composer to emulate in voicing and balancing of parts. If a tenorless chorus is satisfactory for Purcell, a modern arranger might be equally satisfied. If tenors are scarce or not yet ready to sing up above the bass staff very high why not find or arrange music where they sing with the high baritones?

Certainly sixteen sopranos, sixteen mezzos, sixteen altos is approaching a more equable distribution of voices in opposition to ten tenor-basses.

Extending this form of the 5-part madrigal further, and recognizing the scarcity of tenors, we might arrange music SMABrBs with the possibility of OCCASIONALLY dividing the boy-voices to allow the few tenors (perhaps re-enforced by one or two high baritones) to use and develop their higher tones. We suggest a very simple, obvious arrangement of a much-used, well-know hymn. (See ex. 25)

Extending this idea to the extreme, we can suppose that if there are 60 girls and only five boys who enroll, we could give those five boys a place in the front row, assign them a very obvious melody, with the 60 girls furnishing an overlay of harmonic enrichment or some contrapuntal passages developing out of that melody.

If this seems rather "far out" for a high school director to contemplate, please note that in the field of "pop-music" there are many examples, e.g. a male soloist with a female chorus backing him up, or female star surrounded by a male chorus of some ten to twelve singers.

106

Example 25   OH WORSHIP THE KING — for baritone-bass
with alto-mezzo and soprano

Chapter XXII
THE COUNTER-TENOR OR MALE ALTO *

The scarcity of tenors is ubiquitous and constant in American high school choirs. A survey of the enrollments listed in Appendix A reveals the fact that not *one* school in our State of Iowa sampling shows a 25% enrollment of tenor voices, the one-fourth we would expect in a four-part mixed chorus. The mean percentage is below 10% while sopranos make up 40% of all singers.

In the schools that claim a well-balanced choir of equal tenors and basses to sopranos and altos we discover that there are also one or more all-girls' glee clubs to take care of the greater preponderance of girls. This means that the director has taken EVERY possible tenor into his mixed choir, whether he was ready (mature and vocally settled), to match a carefully screened, select group of girl singers.

Obviously there is something in need of a change here, and it speaks ill of our senior high choral directors that they have made no great efforts to make desirable changes.

The most rational procedure is to cease grouping senior high choruses in the traditional SATB manner. Some practical, workable groupings were discussed in the preceding chapter. Unfortunately reason cannot always prevail. The enterprising director may be willing to make other types of vocal arrangements, but he may find himself coerced into singing music in the traditional soprano-alto-tenor bass arrangements.

Our high school directors have inherited a deeply entrenched SATB tradition. Literally millions of choral arrangements ranging from venerable masterpieces to trashy pot-boilers have been composed and published in the past for four part soprano-alto-tenor-bass. In contrast, there are comparatively few choral works written for other vocal combinations. The choir director who thinks of breaking away from the rigorous tyranny of the SATB tradition must either embark on a search for non-SATB composed works or must make his own arrangements.

Even if an enterprising person is moved to adventure into new territory, he can expect to find pressures exerted on him to get back into line. For example, if his choir is to participate with other choirs in a large scale festival, or to compete in one of the music contests so prevalent each spring, he will find that the assigned songs to be performed are all SATB in voicing. He may even find pressures put on him by administrators and parents, especially in a large city where several high schools are co-ordinated by a supervisor or curriculum

---

*Much of the material included in this chapter appeared originally in THE CHORAL JOURNAL, the publication of The American Choral Directors' Association, the May 1976 issue, and is used here by special permission of the editorial board of that magazine.

director. What then is the director to do if he does not have tenors who can handle such music?

The purpose of this chapter will be to discuss a type of voice not well known in America but quite widely used in Europe that may alleviate the scarcity of tenors. I refer to the countertenor, sometimes called the male alto.

I personally became aware of this voice rather late in my teaching career when I heard Russel Oberlin as soloist in a concert given by the old New York Pro Musica under the direction of Noah Greenberg. I later heard Oberlin as the alto soloist in a performance of Handel's "Messiah" at Augustana College in Rock Island, Illinois. About the same time I heard the recordings of Alfred Deller, the noted English countertenor. I must confess that my first reactions were negative, although I was not as much repelled as most of the Messiah audience who expressed their disappointment in not hearing the more opulent voice of the usual female contralto, and found the reedier, thinner voice of the countertenor not to their liking at all.

My negative reactions were considerably modified when, in 1967, I attended a two-week session for boys' and men's choirs in Addington Palace near Croydon, England, sponsored by the Royal School of Church Music. Here I met and rehearsed with several male altos—all of them bass-baritones, who, to serve the needs of their church, developed the head tone (the first-overtone, the faucette tone, sometimes called falsetto) until they could encompass the range of tones usually sung by the alto voice. These were sincere, dedicated men who were most generous in giving me explanations and demonstrations of this (to me) unfamiliar voice. I discovered in this almost male setting (there were only a few female choir directors in attendance) that the countertenor voice has a peculiar beauty and charm in its proper milieu, and in ensembles can be VERY useful.

The following two weeks were spent at Wroxton Abbey, near Banbury, listening to lectures and demonstrations of English music. Each day John Whitworth, professional countertenor, sang Elizabethan and Restoration songs while accompanying himself on the harpsichord. In this setting I began to enjoy and appreciate the peculiar, exotic (to my American ears) sound of the countertenor voice.

My latest exposure to the effective use of the countertenor voice was as late as June, 1976. On a sponsored tour I heard professional countertenors in Stockholm, in Warsaw, in Belgrade and Prague and finally in England—all of them members of superb musical ensembles. In England especially I discovered that quite commonly male altos will sing with female altos when the director wants to achieve a certain delightful and very appropriate tone quality. Of course, in Canterbury Cathedral as well as at St. Paul's where we observed a rehearsal and Evensong, there are no female voices so countertenors are used. There the divided choirs have two basses, two tenors, two countertenors and eight boy trebles on each side.

Each year as I work with boys with changing voices I have discovered that many boys can keep control of their boy treble tones and can sing quite effectively either as a boy treble or an adolescent baritone. I have no doubt that these boys could sing an alto part in the faucette voice if I asked them to, with no harmful effects to their vocal apparatus.*

Part A.
The Origins of the Countertenor

Historically the term countertenor (contratenor) was originally not a classification of a voice but a term used to denote a contrapuntal line of music. When part singing was first introduced and developed, the cantus firmus (melody) was "held" by the tenor. To this was added a lower vocal line, not surprisingly called the contrabass. A third vocal line appeared to move in opposition to the tenor, sometimes above, sometimes below (crisscrossing, so to speak), called the contra-tenor.

In certain monasteries and cathedral schools where young boys were present, a yet higher counter-melody began to appear, called sometimes a discant, and sometimes, because of its tendency to move in thirds above the tenor, the treble.

For liturgical reasons, it must be remembered, only males took part in church services. In secular performances it was not considered proper for women to appear on the public stage. Only in the privacy of the home and family, where the custom of singing part music after a meal became common, was it permissible for women to join in the singing. Therefore, music composed in these earlier centuries was usually written for male voices, tenor, contra-bass, contra-tenor and treble (discant). Presumably women took over the boys' part of discant when they joined in the singing, en famille.

After the reformation period, the exclusion of women from participating in church services was relaxed in the "reform churches". After the "invention" of opera, women began to assume singing roles in the court presentations and then on the public stage. Gradually the female soprano replaced the boy-treble, and a new voice appeared on the scene, the female contralto, to replace the countertenor. As a result in the nineteenth century the female contralto had taken over the countertenor part in all but the tradition-bound cathedral choirs, in which to this day only males may sing.** Even the solo parts in the operas of Purcell, Gluck and Handel, written originally for countertenor, were assumed by female contraltos. Thus in the nineteenth century we find female contraltos singing "trouser-roles" of males, replacing the countertenors.

Two terms or labels are in current use for this special type of male voice, countertenor and male alto. At least one noted authority*** makes a difference between the two terms. In the male alto voice, the

---

* Provided they did not sing in the "passagio" the area where the head tones and chest tones overlap, until they had learned how to move from one to the other smoothly.

** For an interesting "complaint" from one of the disappearing countertenors in 1836, see page 91 of *A Singularity of Voice* by Michael and Millie Hardwick, London, Cassel, 1968.

*** Alfred Deller as quoted in *A Singularity of Voice* by M. and M. Hardwick, London, Cassell 1968, p. 79.

fundamental voice is baritone or bass and the faucette is developed to the maximum range; the faucette voice is produced naturally (without strain) and it can be developed just as any other voice, but the singer can still sing "off the chest" as a baritone or bass. Deller classifies himself as of this type, as was (he says) Purcell. Most people would call this a male alto when used in chorus or ensembles.

The "true countertenor" is a high tenor who can dispense with the faucette entirely, or use it for the top fifth of the compass without perceptible break, (a' to e'.)

The difference in labels seems to be more academic than of practical importance. It is quite obvious that the use of the faucette mechanism is involved either part of the time or throughout the entire compass; the resultant tone, lacking certain overtones, is of a peculiar timbre, being thin, light, often reedy and penetrating. Usually the tone is quite straight, with no trace of vibrato, and rather limited in dynamic differentiation.

Part B. The Strengths and Weaknesses of
The Countertenor Voice

This unique timbre is at once its greatest recommendation and drawback. Heard in ensemble literature composed to include this male alto, and sung in the proper milieu it can be hauntingly beautiful. Employed along with boy trebles it blends admirably. In a large cathedral with walls of stone and high vaulted roof, singing in a mass or motet of the early renaissance period the male alto is highly effective. In an English drawing room with lute or harpsichord accompaniment, an Elizabethan air or French-Italian chanson-canzonetta sung by an accomplished countertenor is quite charming.

Conversely, when used in inappropriate compositions or uncongenial surroundings it can be ineffective, ridiculous, even repulsive. This voice would not be effective in a Puccini or Verdi aria in a large opera house. Attempting a dramatic concert aria with full orchestra would probably not work out well. Songs of the nineteenth century romantics are possible, but should be chosen with some care. Works of the Italian Verisimo school or from the Wagner-Strauss repertoire are not for the countertenor. Music of the Baroque, composed by Handel, Purcell or Bach and their contemporaries are very congenial to this voice. It is worth noting that twentieth century British composers are also writing music for this special type of singers, e.g. Britten and Tippett.

Not that a countertenor is too frail a voice to sing loudly. The fault is that in producing loud sounds there must be such intensity of placement that the quality can become quite cutting, even raucous.

I have said that the countertenor is not often found in the United States. That is not quite true. Quite often the high tenor in a "barbershop quartet" is a faucette singer, and some of the "singers" in the current rock-and-roll or country-western bands definitely and obviously develop the high faucette tones until their voices are so intense they can cut through the loudest battery of percussion, high

111

brass and squealing woodwind accompaniments. Whatever your opinion of rock and roll singing, you must admit it IS very loud, very high, very cutting, almost as ear-splitting and unendurable as the tones of the professional hog-callers who compete in our corn growing states (The champion hog-caller is the one who can produce the loudest, highest, most penetrating sounds to bring the pigs from the farthest remote field up to the barn lot for feeding.)

I hasten to add that the disagreeable examples just mentioned of misuse or abuse of the faucette are just as much caricatures of the legitimate countertenor as are the raucous emissions of the blues singer who "belts out" her song distortions of the legitimate contralto tone.

Part C.

Developing Countertenor Singers

How do you, as choral conductor, locate a potential countertenor or male alto, and how do you, as a teacher, train him?

The first step is to find three or four men/boys who have a very clear falsetto. Your procedure will be something like this:

1. Assemble a group of amenable men about the piano. Strike the c' (third space treble clef) and ask the group to match the tone on a well-rounded oo sound. If even after five or six tries some cannot succeed, tactfully eliminate them.

2. Ask these who remain to sing a five-tone descending scale passage (see example 26a) showing no dismay if the lowest tone tends to disappear or become fuzzy. Continue with five-tone descending passages, lowering the pitch by whole steps, noting which men stay with it the longest.

3. Tune the group on a'-flat. Ask the successful faucette singers to sing the first stanza of America, using the sound too-too-too instead of words (example 26b). Encourage them to sing lightly but to use plenty of breath, almost more than usual. Listen carefully at measures 11 and 12 "Land where by fathers died" for the high e'-flat. Any who can negotiate measures 11 and 12 are potential male altos.

4. Now consider these faucette singers. If any have a rich resonant baritone or bass that indicates possibility for soloist or section leader you will not want to put them on the male alto but keep them where they will be of greatest use.

If any of these baritones have rather indifferent voices and won't be greatly missed if removed from the baritone/bass section, this may be a chance for them to be an important cog rather than a section-filler, especially if they are rather adept at part-singing, and pitch discrimination. Quite often men/boys who play instruments and sing as a second, supplementary activity, are intrigued and challenged by this highly specialized and unique type of singing. Intending to be players rather than singers, they won't mind giving up the development of their full voices for a while, as they adventure into this quite unique, rather exotic voice.

Example 26a **Five-Tone Descending**

too—too—too—too—too..   loo—loolooloo— loo.   whoo—who— who—who—whoo.

Example 26b **AMERICA**

My coun-try 'tis of thee   Land where my fath-ers died   Let free-dom ring.

Example 26c **Two-Octave Descending Scale**

Whoo—who—who—who   who—who—who—who   who who who who who who who

Example 26d **WEE WILLIE WINKIE**

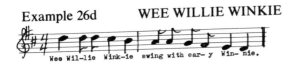

Wee Wil-lie Wink-ie swing with ear- y Win- nie.

Example 26e **Octave Leap**

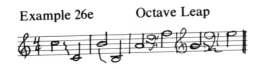

Example 26f **WHITE CORAL BELLS — also key of C, B♭, G, F**

White cor-al bells up-on a slender stalk, lilies of the valley by my garden walk

Example 26g **ALLELUIA, AMEN — Passacaglia**

Ctr.   Al- le- lu- ia, al-le- lu- ia, al-le-lu- ia   al- le- lu-ia.   A- — — men

Bar.
Bass   Al- le lu- ia Al -le-lu- ia, al-le- lu-ia al- le-lu- ia.   A-   men

Once three or four possible countertenors have been located, it will be quite desirable to schedule a series of "private sessions". The first vocalises of choice will be the descending scale; the purpose here is to carry the faucette tone as far down as possible, eventually all the way down (ex. 26e) to E (third space bass clef) with no audible "passagio" into the full voice. Failing that, every attempt will be made to smooth over the "passagio" so it is gentle and almost undetectable. Quite usually at first, the light falsetto voice will thin out and become breathy around middle-C and the voice will either cipher out, crack/break, or suddenly produce a full round tone a full octave lower than intended. Cautioning the students to use proper breath support and, paradoxically, *more* lift in the passagio than on the highest, lightest faucette tones, patiently work away until the lower tones are found.

Since pure vocalises are apt to be boring, and to mix in other vowels, song passages with descending scale progressions can be added, e.g. "Joy to the World" verses 3 & 4; "White Coral Bells" (Ex. 26f), "We Merry Minstrels" (Ex. 1, page 48).

Since the faucette tones at first lack volume and resonance, especially in the lower tones, the vowel EE is recommended (trying to keep the tongue from arching so high it closes the oral passage; a slight mixing of long a as in hay may be needed). One of my interviewees suggests that the singer imagine a board one foot higher than his head and one foot in front of his face, and to pretend he is drilling a hole in the board with his voice. This, like all devices, may work with some, not with others. Another suggests the nonsense song "Wee Willie Winkie swings with weary Winnie", on a descending scale. (Ex. 26d)

To counteract an over-bright sound as resonance increases, return to the vowel oo, where the singer imagines that the tone is following the back of his neck up to the top of his head and then is arching high above it.

The descending scale can be followed by the descending octave leap with a slight glissando, keeping the lower tone in the falsetto rather than allowing the tone to "pass" into the full voice. (Ex. 26e)

Only when the descending scale is well under control should much work on the ascending scale be attempted. To start a tone in this low faucette will be difficult at first. The recommended procedure is to start on a low tone (F, for example) in a mezzo-piano and proceed upward. The individual singer will have to experiment until he discovers just how much pressure he can exert, where he must make adjustments (the passagio) so there is no audible shift.

I am assured that once the ascending scale is reasonably smooth, there will be a slight blending of the full (modal, chest) voice that can be carried up almost to the top, to give more body and color to the thin colorless pure faucette.

Once some facility is gained, it is time to get out the English madrigal books to try the countertenors in music that was written for their particular voice.

As these willing young men develop their countertenor voices will they be restricting or impairing the use of their full "normal" voice?

114

Potentially, quite the opposite will occur. As the faucette is developed and extended the total range of the singing voice is enlarged. The fear of high notes is removed. Because of the strengthening of the "overtones" of the voice, chances are the chest tones will be richer and more resonant.

Is it possible for a man to sing countertenor in one ensemble and baritone in a chorus during the same period of time? Theoretically yes, if the singer has a sure, well-grounded technique. While he is seeking to find and develop his countertenor it is recommended that he avoid singing in the chest voice for awhile, just as it is recommended that when a trumpeter is switching to tuba he should get control of the "new" embouchure before he tries changing from trumpet to tuba and back again.

Part D.
Best Use of the Countertenor

What type of music should a countertenor attempt to sing? At first music written specifically to be sung by that voice is recommended. Seventeenth century was the heyday of the countertenor, so madrigals, glees, catches from that period are for him. Ensemble music previous to that time is certain to include some compositions intended for the male alto. In the early eighteenth century many of the Bach cantatas were intended for male altos rather than female contraltos, as were the arias. The same is true of Handel's choral works. Of twentieth century composers Britten and Tippett are composing for the countertenor. As mentioned previously, music of the late eighteenth and the entire nineteenth centuries is apt to be less congenial for male altos in solo, but in full chorus it should work.

In the area of solo song, the countertenor will need some protection by his director in many localities in the United States. Since this type of voice is not commonly heard in America and because it has such a light, impersonal quality, the first reaction of many audiences is apt to be one of revulsion, of dislike, and this negative reaction is likely to be demonstrated. When heard by less sophisticated people the male alto is apt to be made the object of derogatory remarks; even so established an artist as Alfred Deller confesses that he is occasionally the butt of belittling comments, not only from the general public but even from fellow professional musicians.

When a madrigal group sings and three or four boys take the countertenor part, it is probable that nothing will be said, since it is the total ensemble effect that will be heard. But if a director plans to feature one of the countertenors in an exposed passage or extended solo, it had better be before a sophisticated audience with some prefatory remarks from the master of ceremonies.

Since the tradition of all male choirs* has never been well established in the United States, why might a high school choral director or a director working with college students want to develop

---

* We except the "barbershop chorus" and certain localities where certain European racial stocks are concentrated.

115

and use a group of countertenors?

The first and best reason, already mentioned, is to sing certain music according to the original composer's intentions. A vocal ensemble performing a pre-Palestrina motet or an early madrigal would want to use male altos. Likewise a barbershop chorus, if you go in for that sort of thing. Is it possible that a high school chorus would attempt a rock and roll number? I am assured by several of my interviewees that, if properly produced and reinforced by sound amplification, there need be no harm done to the vocal apparatus. I personally do not recommend it: I await further comments from those who have tried it. Meanwhile there is a wealth of other, less dubious choral literature available.

The second reason is to add a resource to alleviate the shortage of tenors in high school choirs. How often we hear "The tenor part is just too high for my immature singers" or "As usual my tenor section is the weakest." What if the available tenors are augmented by a few baritones? I mean, using the methods for developing countertenors suggested here, the whole group finds the high g's and a's can be negotiated—and there are enough in the section so even the more fragile faucette tone comes through in proper balance.* It may take extra time and outside preparations—but that is better than just complaining!

A third situation where a countertenor group can help solve an awkward problem is where there are one or two late maturing boys, the fellows who are sixteen and in the junior class but still not well-advanced into puberty. Quite often these boys are very self-conscious about their immaturity; it may be difficult to persuade these uncomfortable youths that this is nothing to worry about, that in due time their voices too will drop down into the mature ranges. In a *mixed* group of from thirty or sixty singers there may be no good opportunity to ease their qualms. Such persuasion becomes much more feasible in a small group of boys their own age. If there is a countertenor group being recruited, how much easier to include these not-yet-changed voices in the group.

Should their voices finally, sometime in the middle of the school year, begin to change and some deep bass tones emerge, they need not shift groups in mid-season and learn a new voice part. Because of their practice in singing in the countertenor range they may continue to sing in what is now becoming their "faucette-voice". When they return after the summer break they can then be labeled bass or baritone or tenor. Should the voice change occur early in the school year, the shift can be made immediately after the Christmas holiday break. Note that this may not work out satisfactorily if they and the teacher are not in rapport or are not aware that the voice change is due or why it has been slow in coming. But if they and the teacher KNOW this may happen, proper vocalizing and advance practicing

---

* Simon Halsey of the Halsey Singers of London, England, reminds us that, while the countertenors will produce the high tones from f to d very effectively, they will not have much body of tone below middle-c, especially from G on down. The director will have to alert his augmented tenor section, so tenors in full voice sing out on the lower tones, to compensate for the more fragile tones of the countertenors.

can ease them through their late voice change with never an awkward moment.

The fourth recommended use of the countertenor idea is to ease the transition of younger teen-agers as they change from trebles into bass-clef singers. At the risk of over-simplification this is the recommended procedure.

As the first signs of puberty appear, the boys can continue to vocalise on their soprano-alto tones, so they do not lose them, while gently vocalizing downward into the bass clef ranges. If done consistently and properly, it is quite likely that their voices will never "break" nor develop those troublesome areas of silence around middle-C. Eventually there will come a time when the boy voice becomes the faucette, and the lower tones strengthen to become a bass-baritone-tenor in quality and range. Since the faucette has been kept functioning, and not allowed to atrophy, his range will not be restricted but will be greatly extended.

I say that the above is over-simplified because:

1. It is not always possible to "catch the voice" just before it begins to change. Voices that drop into the deep bass over the long summer holiday, when there is no supervised singing and much outdoor yelling, may present some very difficult quirks in September. Even during the Christmas holiday, a voice can deepen amazingly. Of course if the vocal music teacher does not recognize the infallible signs of early puberty, no anticipatory activities are possible.

2. It may not be feasible to segregate the boys on the verge of voice mutation from the other boys and girls for special vocal sessions, especially in smaller schools where there is only one vocal music teacher. Quite usually the time for voice mutation is in the junior high or middle school, so it is the junior high teacher who should be expert in guiding boy-singers through this challenging time. Alas, our junior high/general music teachers sometimes are burdened with large classes and tight schedules so any kind of special grouping or individual guidance is out of the question. Unsympathetic administrators work out unrealistic schemes like having a class in music five days per week for nine weeks and then no music at all for the other twenty-seven weeks of the school year. How then can a teacher hope to find these about-to-change-voice boys if they do not arrange to enter puberty during the exact nine weeks they are in music?

I have mentioned team teaching, which can work out fine in large schools where there are two teachers available to form a team. In a smaller school this would not be possible—unless somebody else could be on hand for just the right class. Sometimes I wonder if there is a senior high school teacher who would even consider going to the junior high or middle school for an hour or two each week so he/she could work with the boys in the eighth grade class in music who need special attention during voice change, or who might agree to take such boys before or after school for their special coaching. Is there a high school choral director so concerned about building up his boy singers' sections that he would seek to "win them over" before they enroll in senior high? And would the junior high director welcome him?

Suppose you have organized a bass-clef chorus for your junior high boys, and you have found a few boys where signs of puberty are appearing but the voice is still definitely treble; they are not yet in stage 3. They want to sing with the boys in the bass clef chorus and, for social-psychological reasons, you want them to be with their classmates.

You write out a countertenor part for them, really a low alto part, starting middle-high and working DOWNWARD into what will be the medium tenor range. Since these boys will not have the melody, you will caution them to "keep it light so you do not cover the melody". (See ex. 26g)

If they DO sing it lightly there is a very good chance most of them will keep these tones in their control even when the deeper baritone voice begins to emerge. Probably none of them will develop those "areas of silence" between the faucette voice and modal (chest) voice that can be troublesome and frustrating.

In this Alleluia-Passacaglia for baritone melody with ground-bass and counter-tenor, the counter-tenor is written in the actual pitches to be sung. If optional bass is used, key of G-flat or G may be better.

Chapter XXIII
THE CONTRABASS, A NEGLECTED VOCAL RESOURCE *

At the other end of the adult male vocal spectrum is the contrabass voice. This is the voice that can descend to the area BELOW the bass clef, a fourth, a fifth, or even an octave.

The men (and boys) who possess these subterranean voices are a neglected group in America.

1. They exist is a sizable number, yet there are those who deny their very existence, and others who seem to doubt their usefulness as choral singers. There are few solos that exploit these lowest tones properly, and few American composers who write music that makes use of them.

2. In America there are few teachers who recognize the teenage boys who sing in this lowest register. Music written for junior high school singers never (I use the word advisedly) puts the bass line in the lower part of the bass clef or below. In music labeled specifically "for senior high school choirs" there are few arrangements which extend a low bass to E'. High school choir directors who ask their singers to sing tones below the bass clef are rare. I except from this last statement those few schools that still feature eight-part *a capella* choruses.

3. There is a sizable number of boys in their early teens who can sing ONLY in the lower bass register (with perhaps some high treble tones also producible, with an "area of silence" between). These boys, if allowed to sing in this very low tessitura, can produce some very musical sounds, quite pleasant to hear and highly effective both in vocal ensembles and in solo passages. Yet there are many teachers who refuse to allow these boys to sing in their comfortable range and label them "deficient singers" if the boys cannot or will not sing music assigned to them by these ill-advised teachers.

As a result, the contrabass has all but disappeared from the vocal scene. This was called to my attention quite vividly when a group of noted choral conductors, men who work with singers at the adult, professional level, were decrying the absence of an adequate supply of such basses. These directors have ceased programming any of the liturgical music of the Russian-Slavic school because they cannot find the contrabasses required to produce the low tones written in such literature.

---

*Much of the material included in this chapter appeared originally in THE CHORAL JOURNAL, the publication of The American Choral Directors' Association, in the January 1977 issue, and is used here by special permission of the editorial board of that magazine.

It was not always so. Many of these directors, myself included, remember the two decades just after World War I, when the Russian Cathedral Choir, the Don Cassock Chorus and the Kedroff Quartet were touring extensively in America, amazing their audiences with the powerful bass sections that rolled out rich organ-like sounds in the octave BELOW G'. We recall the eagerness with which American choral directors attempted to imitate the Russian style of *a capella* singing in their repertoire and somehow found the bassi profundi to sing the contrabass part.

To this day most of the men's sections of Scandinavian and Eastern European countries include and feature these contrabass voices with highly satisfactory results. But alas, not in America!

Part A.

Some Reasons for Scarcity of Low Basses

Are the larynxes of modern American males smaller than those of their grandfathers? Are the Slavic vocal folds somehow different from those of our male singers? The answer to these questions seems to be "No".

American men, we are told, are physically larger in weight and height today than their grandfathers, so we can presume that their larynxes are, if anything, larger too. At least it seems unlikely that they are smaller. So if we follow this train of thought, we should have men with at least as large if not larger larynxes with vocal bands as large if not larger than those of the men of forty years ago.

It seems equally improbable that the vocal endowments of men of Slavic descent are much different than those of the men of America. In our melting pot, there are descendants of Bulgarians, Yugoslavians, Russians along with those of other countries. In localities where children of these Slavic immigrants have concentrated we should find these same native endowments. There are no reports that these voices are being found and used.

More reasonable was one director's suggestion that singers tend to reflect the trends of the times. Today, in the last third of the twentieth century, the emphasis is on producing HIGH tones. To be in step with the times, a tenor must boast of his ability to sing a succession of ringing high-C's. We hear of "lyric baritones" who can produce high a-flats and a's up in the range usually assigned to tenors. Contraltos have all but disappeared; they prefer to be mezzo-sopranos. The mezzo-sopranos have begun to assume roles formerly assigned to sopranos. Our basses (who are the subject of this chapter) are now expected to sing a high f with ease and sonority, and we hear of bass-baritones who go even higher.

We almost never hear of a tenor who boasts of his powerful LOW-C; few of them even attempt to sing down there. Baritones do not feature their LOW-A's. The contralto who could win an ovation

120

as she produced a powerful, rich low F# seems to have gone out of fashion*. The last concert bass to feature the low D′ in Flegier's "LeCor" was Pinza, and that recording has been out of print for some time. (At least my many attempts to find or order it have met with failure.)

Composers nowadays do not write solos exploiting the deepest tones of the vocal register, and probably singers would not prefer to sing them if such solos were written—at least not until the trend changes and audiences demand such sounds.

Small wonder then that teachers and vocal coaches work consistently and persistently on developing brilliant top tones, but slight reinforcing and developing the deeper tones to extend the range downwards. In other words, we lack the low basses and contraltos because our vocal coaches are not developing them.

Teachers of junior high particularly, and senior high as well, are abettors here. As recently as in the January 1976 issue of THE CHORAL JOURNAL we find this passage:

. . . a great deal of Renaissance music lies in a high range which is an advantage for the young voices, especially the young male voice. There are many examples where the range of the baritone part falls between the C below middle-C, and the E above middle-C. . . . and the tenor part lies between the G below middle-C and the G above middle-C. These vocal lines are ideal for the "changing voice" of the tenor and the "newly changed voice" of the baritone.**

I am sure that the author of that passage, writing in good faith, reflects the beliefs of quite a few music educators. Yet I have to state that if I were to accept that paragraph I would be eliminating from one-fourth to one-third of the boys with "changing voices and newly changed voices" I have worked with for some twenty years. Since I first began graphing vocal ranges of boys in early adolescence from about 1955 up to the present there has always been a significant number of boys who have dropped far into the LOWER reaches of the bass clef.

This was true in 1957 when I followed some 82 eighth grade boys through a complete school year;*** it continued to be so not only in the junior high schools in which I worked but for eight summers in the junior high vocal music camp at the University of Illinois. It is true today, when, out of the 18 adolescent males taking private lessons from me, six boys sing comfortably in the lower reaches of the bass clef, but experience an uneasiness as they sing above the A, fifth line of the bass clef.

Here are fifteen year old Paul, fourteen year old Nick, three Jim's and a Brad age thirteen or fourteen, who vocalize very comfortably down to the F below the staff, three of them a third lower than that, with open throat, no sign of tension or strain, and with plenty of

---

* For the story of a control to who DID win accolades for her LOW tones, see Homer, Sidney: MY WIFE AND I, New York, Mac Millan, 1939, pg. 79 line 9 ff.

** Drotleff, John: RENAISSANCE MUSIC AND JUNIOR HIGH SINGERS, The CHORAL Journal, Jan. 1976 parag. 1

*** Swanson, Frederick: MUSIC TEACHING IN THE JUNIOR HIGH AND MIDDLE SCHOOLS, New York Appleton-Century-Crofts (now Englewood Cliffs, N.J. Prentice-Hall) 1973 pp 288ff and 184ff.

resonance. Shall I refuse to develop these deep tones where the youths sing so comfortably and where they sound most promising because I am told I must endeavor, somehow, to get those voices to produce a tone on middle-C and even higher with control, and a satisfactory vocal quality? Why should I not take these voices where they are, and wait for gradual maturation plus unhurried practice and vocalizing to find and control those difficult upper tones?

I should mention that these are not deficient singers. These are boys who have graduated from a performing boys' choir, with four to six years of training and concert singing behind them, both as choristers and as soloists. Most of them can still produce the high treble tones of boy-sopranos quite easily; it is only in the area of middle-C that voices are "out of control". They are matched by two who have come from other communities with very little previous training in singing, who display the same pattern of vocal development.

I must mention also, that much of the music they sing is in manuscript. There simply is not vocal material published in any amount which lies within the octave Bass G' (first line) to baritone A (fifth line), so we write out the transposition.*

I have to wonder, then, if there is not a sizable segment of our male singers who are "turned off," who are discouraged from singing from the time of voice change into maturity. If the music I assign to these 8th or 9th grade boys should lie in the upper reaches of the bass clef, extending past middle-C into the treble clef, I would see heads shaking, see throats beginning to clinch, hear objections—or, worse, find a third of my boys simply refusing to sing. If I have been indoctrinated with the belief that only such high tones are appropriate for boys in my junior high classes (or early senior high) I might very easily declare these boys resistant to training, or deficient in singing voice and ability, and write them off as lost causes. The result could easily be that out of 100 boys, I might eliminate some 25 or 35 who might develop into very useful low basses, some of them, as we are saying in this article, very possible contrabasses.

Now why shouldn't the director of a ninth grade (freshman) choir or an eighth grade mixed chorus develop these lower bass tones and find music for them to sing to the enjoyment, vocal growth and improved choral sound of his students? Consider our instrumental colleagues. Is the organist reluctant to use his 16-foot stop? Does the arranger of orchestra music refuse to write his bass viol parts to include the low E-string, and does the string quartet composer avoid the cello C-string? Why do we have players of the contrabassoon and bass clarinet (provided with instruments at great expense) if it is not to have available the deep bass they provide? Granted that for special effect we may put the bass viols close to the bridge on the G-string. A cello melody soaring up into the thumb position can be highly effective. But it was the low E-string that brought the bass viols into

---

* Swanson, Frederick: a) THE CHANGING VOICE, The Choral Journal, March 1976 pg. 8 col. 2
b) ARRANGING MUSIC FOR FIRST EXPERIENCES IN BASS-TENOR-ALTO-SOPRANO, The Choral Journal, Sept. 1975, pg. 15 ff.

the standard orchestra and the low C that justified using a cello in a string quartet. The reason we have violas in our orchestras is that they have a C-string to encompass tones a fifth lower than the lowest note on the violins, not because the violists can, on occasion, play nearly as high as those same violins.

In like manner, the full, *mature* bass voice or the rich-toned contralto CAN be highly dramatic as they soar above the staff, especially when there is a full-textured orchestra accompaniment to support them, but it is a waste and neglect of potential musical resources not to make use of the deepest low tones of the vocal spectrum, especially when voices sing without the aid of an instrumental accompaniment.

As the director of a noted Yugoslavian chorus took the trouble to point out.* "In the orthodox church, we do not use the instruments. Our singers must sing unaccompanied. If we want a rich, full bass we cannot depend on the organ or bass viol to supply it. So we must develop the deep bass voices. That is why we have them."

To go back to the fourth paragraph of this chapter, what HAS become of the *a capella* choir that can produce the rich texture of sound built on a contra-bass that can support without benefit of any instrumental re-enforcement? What has caused the deficiency of American bassi profundi? I am suggesting as an answer that it is not that low bass voices have disappeared from the American population, but that those men with the very low bass potential are not discovered and encouraged to develop their singing voices. I am of the opinion that they are still in our midst, unrecognized, neglected and unexploited.

I am also suggesting that starting with our junior high and middle school teachers we should listen for, and accept as legitimate singers, those boys whose voices produce sounds in only the LOWER part of the bass staff. As a corollary, I suggest that there is a need for music written for these boys who can sing, for a time, only in that restricted range—music that is interesting, appealing, but not difficult.

It is equally important that junior and senior high vocal music directors recognize these boys with contra-bass voices as potential assets and use them where they are most effective rather than to urge them constantly to sing tones too high for their immature, limited-range voices, even if these ambitious directors have to forego the performance of some cherished work written originally for mature, professional singers in favor of something less prestigious.

Part B.
Fry Tones and Contrabass Voices

As a sequel to the above comments, a discussion of "fry tones"**is in order. I refer to those subterranean vocal sounds which are little

---

* An interview in Belgrade, Yugoslavia, in June 1976 with the director of the Belgrade Choir.

** A better label is "the pulse register" suggested by Dr. Thomas Shipp of the Speech Research Laboratory of the VA Hospital in San Francisco, California; another is "diocrotic dysphonia" suggested by Moore and Van Leden.

explored and discussed, at least in America. I find that this term is unfamiliar to many practitioners of the vocal/choral art, for when I speak of "fry tones" I very often see puzzled looks or faint smiles of disbelief.

Hollien, Moore and Wendahl* define "fry tones" as "a range of fundamental frequencies below those of the modal (chest) register." They report that out of twenty-three subjects, all untrained singers, they found sounds ranging from frequencies of 18 v. per sec. to 65 v. per sec., with a mean of 34.4; these are pitches matching those of the lowest notes on the standard piano. It is quite important to note that they found a very noticeable "area of silence" between the lowest modal (chest) tone and the topmost fry tone. Most of the subjects had no suspicion that they could produce sounds down there in the depths. Hollien** goes on to report that there is a significant reduction in airflow in contrast to the normal emission of breath in producing tones in the modal register. To explain the production of these deep tones, there is, he thinks, complete relaxation of the cryco-thyroid musculature, so there is no opposition of a high level of thyro-arythenoid muscles; the vocal folds (bands) are in a fixed and thickened position; the respiratory driving force (airflow) is adjusted to the subglottal pressure necessary to cause vibration of the vocal fields.

Fry tones are so called because, when first produced, they have a sound resembling that of bacon frying or steak sizzling on a very hot greased griddle. Moore and Van Leden*** prefer the term Dicrotic Dysphonia and define these tones as "an atypical vibration pattern in which the vocal cords separate twice in quick succession and then approximate firmly in a relatively long closed phase." Vennard**** used the word "popping" for this sound, and also the term "glottal scrape." Vennard also makes reference to Gillis Bratt, the great Swedish authority, who made use of the "scraspning" as part of his method. He suggests that with practice and strengthening, this "voiceless rattle may rumble into a tone by adding phonation." Shipp uses the term "pulse register" which identifies the characteristic variations in loudness. It should be pointed out that Hollien *et al.* state that this was a new experience for their 23 subjects, and it is possible that with additional practice and training they would have extended the range of the fry tones. (Presumably they could hope to eliminate the gap between fry tones and modal register.)

---

* Hollien, Moore and Wendahl: ON THE NATURE OF VOCAL FRY Journal of Speech and Hearing Research #11, 1966 p. 24, and 1967 p. 393.

** Hollien and Michel: VOCAL FRY AS A PHONATONAL REGISTER, Jrnl. Speech and Hearing Research #11, 1968, pp. 600-604.

*** Moore and Von Leden: DYNAMIC VARIATIONS OF THE VIBRATORY PATTERNS IN THE NORMAL LARYNS, Folia Phoniatrica #10 158, pg. 205 ff.

**** Vennard, William: SINGING, THE MECHANISM AND THE TECHNIQUE, New York, G. Fischer 1967 items #45, 115, 929.

Manuel Garcia, * writing more than a century ago, refers to these very low-pitched tones as "the contrabass register". Using the translation by Donald V. Paschke, used here with his permission, we read:

THE CONTRABASS REGISTER-Manuel Garcia

By this name we designate a series of low and rough (rauque) tones, rather similar to the tremolo of the organ or to a strong and sustained swelling. This kind of voice includes the lowest sounds of the basso profundo and can extend from the E-flat to the fifth below.

In order to form this range, it is necessary to raise the larynx and enlarge the pharyngeal cavity. The first attempts dry the throat which brings about coughing movements.

Comparing this register to the chest register, one sees not only that the tones which compose it differ by their nature from the first, but also that they remain in a much lower region.

To my (Garcia's) knowledge, this register has been used up to now only by some Russian bassi profundi. This register, although it has for the bassi profundi an admirable usage for accompanying other voices, does not seem to me generally applicable to the art of singing, and for two reasons. First, there exists, at least for ordinary voices, a gap between the lowest notes of the chest voice and the tones of the contrabass. This gap could, it is true, disappear in the basso profundo voices. For them it would be possible not only to join these two parts of the voice but even to form some tones common to the two registers.

The second inconvenience, and the most troublesome, consists in the deterioration of the other registers which the frequent and prolonged use of this one unfailingly causes. The Russian basses themselves justify this observation; after a certain lapse of time there remains for them only the contra-bass voice and a weak section of the chest voice.

In 1847, Garcia, one of the most eminent students of the voice, obviously took a dim view of the legitimacy of these very low tones as a part of the singers' usable vocal resources. Yet, noticing the shortness of this discussion in comparison to the entire length of the treatise, it seems fair to question the extent and thoroughness of Garcia's exploration of the "voice raque". Does the development of these very low tones have to result in a weakening of the middle and upper registers? Could these low tones be effectively used in SOLO passages if a composer wrote songs to exploit them?

Could it be that Shipp and the others, working in the present century, are opening up a long neglected area of inquiry of more than academic interest? Might there be male singers who could profitably develop these extremely low tones while keeping a very usable upper register to become a highly useful, yes even a spectacular singer in that seldom heard part of the vocal spectrum?

I have one answer to these questions. Vratislav Vinicky,**a member of the Prague (Czechoslovakia) Madrigal Group, stated in a personal interview in Prague in June, 1976, and later mentioned in a letter received October 1, 1976, that he can sing both in the basso profundo and the head voice equally well. He gives as his best range from

---

* Garcia, Manuel: A COMPLETE TREATISE OF THE ART OF SINGING, translated by Donald V. Paschke, Eastern New Mexico Univ. at Portales, obtainable from him on request. pg. xxxii.

** Vinicky, V.: bass with the Prague Madrigal Group. Interviewed in person in Prague, June 1976 and in a letter, available for reading as translated from Czechoslovakian by Bohumil Stulir of East Moline, Ill.; letter addressed to Frederick Swanson.

B'-flat, third added space below the bass staff, to middle-C, with possible D and E above middle-C. Since he has sung professionally since 1957, he obviously has suffered no vocal impairment by developing these contrabass tones, and presumably can sing in what we could consider the standard bass range as well.

Morris Hayes* has suggested a procedure for finding and developing these fry tones at a demonstration-lecture in St. Louis in March 1975, the occasion being the national convention of AMERICAN CHORAL DIRECTORS ASSOCIATION. Hayes had had the opportunity to watch the training of very low basses while on tour in Russia, and he tried to duplicate the procedures for us. It was encouraging to notice that even within that short period of time, some members of the University of Illinois Men's Glee Club were producing the tones we have been describing.

Here I would like to utter an appeal to any reader of this chapter. If you, as a vocal coach or choral director, have had some success in finding and developing these extremely low tones among your male singers, will you be willing to sketch out and demonstrate the procedures you have found successful?

If you have had no experience with these "fry tones" and have access to male singers of the bass persuasion, will you be willing to experiment to discover if you can get students to produce them? If you do, will you make notes on what works well, what are your best procedures, and how many contrabasses you are able to develop? Most important, when you have developed some contrabasses, what music are you then able to perform successfully that had formerly been beyond your capabilities?

Hollien et al. had only 23 subjects. Hayes worked for only about forty-five minutes; I have had only a few subjects thus far and for only a short span of time. Here is certainly a subject area ripe for research and experimentation.

The following procedure is suggested as one from which to start to develop these contra-bass tones:

1. Either individually or in small groups (two to four), schedule men who can sing effectively the F' below the bass clef, for a series of lessons.

2. Ask each singer to stretch his arms high and wide, and to shrug his shoulders until he feels quite relaxed. He then is to sigh several times to attain complete relaxation of the throat.

3. Before tension can return, ask each singer to produce the lowest tone possible, working down from low F by half steps. The resulting sounds will not be true musical tones but will sound more like a gargle or a gurgle with a faint overlay of popping and crackling (close listening is necessary here) much like the sound made by bacon or steak frying.

4. When each singer has found that he can produce these sounds, encourage him to fill his lungs with an ample supply of air, and, "using the diaphragm as a generative force" while maintaining

---

* Prof. Hayes, Morris: Head of Choral Music Dept. University of Wisconsin at Eau Claire, Eau Claire, Wis.

that complete relaxation of the throat muscles, to start and stop a series of eighth notes.

5. As these repeated exercises extend over frequent practice sessions (not necessarily supervised) the muscle tone of the vocal bands vibrating in *toto* will increase and the seldom used and weak muscles involved will gain strength; the uncertain gargle-like tone will become steady and smooth, until there is a definite pitch with sufficient volume to be heard.

6. The only vowel possible at first is probably the broad "aw" as in "hall" or "*Aw* shucks" but eventually the "AW" can be lifted and directed "into the mask" for a brighter "ah-sound" (as in "*Aha,* I've got it"). The most that can be hoped for in vowel modification and shaping will be the "Ay" as in "hay" and "oh" as in "no no" with the close "ee" or "ooh" difficult to achieve. It will be noted that in literature of this genre much of the low bass line is sung on a neutral vowel, rather than with text, and it is no coincidence that translators contrive passages featuring the low-formed vowel sounds as in "Like a choir of angels" when words are to be sung. (See ex. 27a).

7. Once you have a least six basses who can descend to the B-flat below the staff you can attempt one of the CHERUBIM SONGS, e.g. by Bortnyansky or Gretchaninoff. With those six or more singing the lower octave and the other basses singing the upper octave, presumably you will achieve the deep, solid sound of the Russian-Slavic school of choral singing.

Example 27a CHERUBIM SONG — bass and contrabass

Diercks* reminds us that, if a tone a perfect fifth above the bass is added, not only will the bass tone be reinforced, but a sub-bass tone an octave BELOW the sung bass will be heard. That being true, if the fifth above the bass F′ is added, there will be heard the F″, fourth-ledger line below the clef, with a fuller, richer sound resulting.

By an amazing coincidence, while I was writing the first draft of this article in May, 1976 , I got the report from a junior high school music teacher that he had found a student who could sing "down to the fifth note from the bottom of the piano," that is, the fifth added space BELOW the bass clef G′. With great eagerness mixed with some skepticism I went to the school with tape recorder in hand, and arranged to hear the young adolescent. Jim, it developed, was just completing the eighth grade, was 14 1/2 years of age, was physically well-developed (70 inches tall and 185 pounds in weight, with noticeable moustache and faint suggestions of a beard). He was well-mannered and quite willing to co-operate, although he admitted

* Diercks, Louis: THE INDIVIDUAL IN THE CHORAL SITUATION, The Choral Journal, March-April 1967.

that he has never cared much for music, that he has had no intention of continuing any singing activities and has never even momentarily considered developing his singing voice.

Using AMERICA as an audition song, I pitched it successively lower and found that Jim could sing down to a low B'-flat (third space below the staff) with no strain, with agreeable quality and considerable resonance. He expressed some doubt that he could go any lower, so I changed procedure. I asked him to sing a descending scale passage (so-fa-mi-re-do) on the word "No", and then on "Yah", suggesting that he stand erect but relaxed, and that he use plenty of breath. He began this passage on F', descending to B'-flat; then E' down to A'; then D' to G". On this low G" (octave below first line of bass staff) the "fry tone" appeared with its characteristic popping/scraping/pulsating sound. When I assured him that he was doing very well, we continued to lower the pitches until the lowest E" was produced, quite soft and tenuous but definitely audible.

To check the range going upward, it was noticeable that when we reached the A on the fifth line of the bass staff he was uncomfortable, the voice broke slightly and he asked that we go no higher.

Carefully packaging the tape of this audition, I made arrangements for a copy to be made to be available for anybody who might want to hear.

What will happen in Jim's vocal development is still not clear. He is mildly pleased to learn that he has an unusual voice, but he shows no great enthusiasm for developing it. As his family has heard of Jim's unique voice there have been stirrings of interest. The offer is made that if Jim will take a voice lesson once a week for awhile, we'll introduce him to the joys of singing that he has thus far never experienced. As we bring in other boy singers who play football (one of Jim's great interests) to sing along with him we hope there will be some personal motivation.

Jim's story is in miniature a summary of what this article is attempting to explain. Because he matured rather early and had a voice that "growled" down in the depths in grades 6 and 7, he did not fit the expected pattern. There probably were expressions of dismay or disgust or disapproval as he failed to sing along with his classmates. He certainly was discouraged when he could not make his voice "go where it should go". Convinced that he was a non-singer, he gave up trying, and found his satisfactions and pleasures in other activities. I can even suspect that his teacher may have been quite content to let him sit off to one side, not participating, as long as he did not bother anybody else.

Now, if we can find music that fits his voice, and develop his vocal control so the sound is full rich and round and put him shoulder-to-shoulder with some other deep basses of his own age, there may be one more basso profundo added to the short supply of such rare but valuable voices—and a potentially fine singer may be slavaged from the junk heap of discarded vocal drop-outs.

By a second coincidence, in the summer of 1976, a second boy, also named Jim, has come from a distant city to live in Moline. He has not sung for several years, having concentrated on playing the trombone in the junior band of his former city. At the request of his

128

parents, I consented to give him vocal training. To my great surprise, he too produced most acceptable tones in the lower reaches of the bass staff, down to the D′, and like the first Jim, he could sing only up to G comfortably; in fact his voice simply stopped there. As we have vocalized and sung, this Jim's range has extended downward very quickly to a usable low C′, and below that the ''fry tones'' described have appeared with almost no effort. His upper range is developing much more slowly. It is worth mentioning that he had absolutely no ''faucette tones'', and took several weeks of trying until he found those treble tones. Gradually we are working them down to meet the slowly ascending full (modal) voice but they have not yet joined.

See Appendix E for the history of a professional bass that parallels the story of Jim.

Chapter XXIV
SUMMARY

As a summary of the foregoing chapters, let us sketch an "ideal curriculum" for developing boy singers. Such an organized course will include:

1. A boy choir for singers age eight through twelve.
2. A changing voice class or "bass clef choir" in which boys with changing voices, usually age thirteen to fifteen, will participate.
3. A preparatory mixed choir where boys' voices have progressed into their approximate adult ranges, so first lessons in singing tenor-baritone-bass along with girl sopranos and altos can begin (ages fourteen to eighteen).
4. One or more advanced mixed choirs supplemented by male chorus, small mixed ensemble, chamber-music groups, male quartet as desired and as time permits.
5. A teacher available to give private, individual lessons for boys wanting to do solo singing.

Since communities vary widely in size, in financial resources, in ethnic and racial types of citizens, and in interest in furthering worthy community projects of an artistic nature, there will have to be adaptations to this seemingly simple five-item plan. Let us discuss some of these.

There are two types of "schools" that can adopt the five-point plan rather easily: the private, all-boy school enrolling students from grades three through twelve, and the church-sponsored choir progression where choirs are organized at various grade levels from nursery school to adulthood. Unfortunately there are not many such schools in America; perhaps less than 1% of the male population can avail itself of training in private all-male schools or in a large church choir training program.

The most obvious educational agency to provide this training would seem to be the public school music program. These schools are everywhere, attendance is mandatory (except for those enrolling in privately supported equivalent educational institutions).

At the senior high level there is a bright prospect. Most high schools of any size try to maintain a school choir of some degree of excellence. It presumably would be possible for the choir director in that school to offer points 3 and 4; the freshman boys are enrolled, so a scheme could be worked out to get them into a class or club once or twice a week.

In the junior high schools (where there are such schools), it should be quite possible to implement step 2. Quite often music is a required subject in grades seven and eight, and if there is a ninth grade present, step 3 would certainly be possible at least on an elective basis. Unfortunately, in far too many junior high schools the principal (the chief administrator) is not favorably inclined to give the music teacher the co-operation and support he gives to "more important,

130

major subject teachers." The back-of-the-hand-whispered complaint that too many junior high principals are ex-athletic coaches who have, in their older years, retreated into administration, while quite unfair, does hint at what I mean. Music is not often the first department-subject to be scheduled, or to be supplied with requested equipment; not always are the students, the teacher wants very much to have, scheduled for a music class. So a request for an adjustment in the scheduling of music classes is far too often met with indifference if not with actual resistance.* The junior high music teacher has to be certain that he wants to embark on segregated classes and clubs so he/she puts forth enough effort to convince his administrator that this is worth attempting. It may help in the convincing for the teacher to know that usually where segregated classes are scheduled, certain other scheduling problems are solved too, e.g. the best way to schedule boys-only physical education classes or double-period boys-only shop classes, as they alternate with boys-only music.

Yet despite the difficulties of inertia, passive resistance to change, it is worth the time and effort of a determined, dedicated music educator to fight for these segregated classes. The explanations, motivations and special teaching techniques possible in such boys-only classes should be available to ALL the young males in the community, since nobody can foretell WHO will develop a promising voice or who will get the strong desire to become a good singer, as the voice changes in range and timbre. Certainly if we are appalled by the imbalance between the numbers of boy singers and girl singers it is worth inaugurating a change that will help rectify this imbalance.

Should an administrator be adamant in his refusal to attempt something innovative in the vocal music department, it may be possible to organize a community teen-age male chorus. If a sponsor can be found, an alert junior high teacher can note who the boys with changing voices are and do some recruiting. With a sponsor furnishing the facilities for rehearsal and lending financial support, expediency may produce desirable results. Such a community chorus can become a source of pride and prestige as well as a worth-while educational project for young teen-age boys as its members prove that boys with changing voices can sing very well indeed.

While it is desirable to have membership in a boy treble choir available to all boys, there are some very strong reasons why it may not be feasible to have such a choir sponsored by a public school system.

There may be community resistance to a special group for selected students only. This resistance will not be very great in the senior high

---

* In one of my earlier years of classroom teaching I discovered that this indifference to my requests or recommendations changed to co-operative consideration when the principal (*not* an athletic coach) discovered that if he wanted a crowd out for a Parent-Teacher meeting, he had only to schedule a large choral group; parents turned out to hear and see their children perform. So a 60-voice glee club, an 80-voice freshman choir, even a 40-voice bass clef chorus swelled the attendance admirably. The co-operation improved to actual active support when he discovered that the fall operetta, Christmas Vespers and spring "pops concert" produced more revenue than all three athletic teams put together.

school or junior high where music clubs are contained within one student body and where there are many other clubs to choose to join. In a city-wide situation, where members will come from several student bodies and be restricted by tryouts, such resistance is apt to be much stronger and more vocal.

The boys will have to travel to a central location from many parts of the community. If boys must provide transportation for themselves, there may be boys left out because they have no way to get to the rehearsal hall. A school bus might be provided, but the expense could give resisters more cause for complaint. Moving children across town may produce problems of chaperonage and insurance coverage. If the choir develops into a performing unit so there is travel to more distant places there will be overnight lodgings and several meals to provide. This gets into the area of financial responsibility; the school funds cannot be used to provide for such items, yet a school-sponsored organization cannot get into the concert business with fees charged and ticket sales sponsored.

In many communities in the eighth decade of the twentieth century, there are strong objections to organizations in which membership is restricted to one sex. These objectors certainly will say nothing about item 2, since only boys' voices change and require special instruction, but at the elementary school level girls at least sing the same music, even if their vocal quality is different.* Even if an all-girl treble choir is also organized some of the most ardent feminists may still choose to express objections to an all-male organization, and the elected board of education may feel obligated to honor such objections.

In light of these difficulties, it may be expedient, even preferable, to have the boy choir recommended in step 1 function independently of the public schools. There is no reason why a privately sponsored boy choir cannot be organized and supported by any church, fraternal order, lodge, ethnic group or a group of interested citizens interested in promoting an artistic endeavor. The above discussion may explain why we find, in hundreds of communities, a flourishing boy choir administered by a body of private citizens or a community organization, often with the silent approval and active cooperation of the public school administrators.

As for item 5, almost nobody will try to justify a public school's hiring a coach or teacher for individual, private voice lessons. But if there is such a teacher in the community and he/she is obviously competent and able to communicate with young people there may be no objection to encouraging students to study privately with such a coach. I have heard of schools that make their music rooms available for such paid lessons after hours, justifying this privilege (as they do with the instrumental students), by wanting the assurance that students' coming and going can be supervised in a well-lighted,

---

* One argument supporting the propriety of an all-boy treble choir that is legally valid states that where a significant body of literature exists which is written specifically for certain voices, such a group of voices must be available to perform such compositions. Since there are many musical works written to be performed by boy treble choirs, such a choir can be organized and used for the performance of these works, just as works composed for a women's choir or an all-male chorus demand such organizations.

well-equipped building.

There is one other difficulty about inaugurating step 2 in certain communities. The junior high school is by no means a part of the school organization in every school district in the United States. Many communities still follow the 8-4 plan of organizing their instruction. This means that instead of assembling all the seventh and eighth graders in the district into one building, there are classes of only 25 to 35 children in many widely separated buildings. Obviously it would be impractical to attempt a bass clef chorus with perhaps 10 boys, and it would be difficult to find a way to segregate those boys with changing voices from the rest of the class, in a self-contained classroom. To organize a school-sponsored all-district bass-clef chorus would meet with the same difficulties we have mentioned in our boy treble discussion. In this situation it might be desirable to have a young teen-age boy choir sponsored by some civic organization, with membership open to any boy whose voice is changing, but with as much co-operation and assistance as the school administrators think is possible.

So now I return to the five-point plan for training boy singers, adding some modifications.

1. A boy choir for singers age eight through twelve. Ideally it should be school sponsored so all boys can be reached who want to develop into capable singers. In many communities it may be advisable to have some civic organization or special group sponsor this choir with the schools co-operating as much as possible in finding and recommending boys for membership, by granting permission to use school facilities if possible and encouraging members of the music staff to serve as directors or assistants for the choir.
   It is to be hoped that this choir will be large enough to accomodate a large part of the eligible boy-population. Ideally there should be enough boys enrolled to permit groupings by ability so orderly progressive instruction can be given and the boys advance from the beginners' group to the most capable choir according to his ability and ambition. The purpose of maintaining this choir is three-fold; the boys are to be given training in best singing techniques so their voices can grow and develop properly; there are to be other boy-oriented activities scheduled so the boys grow socially and psychologically; the community will come to look on the choir as a worthy, prestigious, enjoyable organization of which boys, parents and citizens in general can be proud.
2. When a boy becomes pubescent and voice change is imminent, there should be a changing voice class in which he can, along with his classmates whose voices are also changing, be given the special training needed so the voice develops properly. The emphasis here will be on keeping the boys singing so their vocal powers increase and expand. Each boy's voice will be charted in its development and music will be specially chosen to fit what the members of the class can, as a group, sing comfortably and happily. Every effort will be made to get the boys to look on voice change as a natural growth, as a fascinating unfolding of new vocal resources, and a source of pleasure and emotional satisfaction. Where feasible, a special chorus of "bass clef singers" will be organized, rehearsed and presented in public with tasteful showmanship so the community comes to take pride and pleasure in this group and it becomes a prestigious matter to be included in the choir. If school administrators are reluctant to schedule such classes, a community chorus may be a substitute.
3. When the boys have advanced in their control of their newly changed voices to an approximate adult range and they can sing with some control, there should be a preparatory mixed-voice choir in which the boys learn to read, hold and enjoy a bass or tenor part as the girls sing the treble parts. Since the boys have unique problems the girls do not have, i.e. reading notation in one or several unfamiliar clefs and in idioms quite different from the soprano or alto they sang as boy trebles, their first lessons in this choir group will be carefully planned to minimize their difficulties. Special arrangements will be sought out or even

133

manufactured that fit the ranges they can sing comfortably, and their voice parts should be relatively easy so they can concentrate on finding and holding their own part as the girls sing more difficult and challenging vocal lines.

4. After the boys have developed ability to sing their new voice parts, there should be one or more mixed choirs where they can experience, along with their girl classmates, music of the standard literature. If all has gone well and there is an ample supply of both boy and girl singers (ideally, about equal in number) there may be a need for small vocal ensembles, i.e. mixed quartets, chamber choirs, madrigal groups, as well as all-male chorus and a choir of girls only to sing music written for women's voices.

5. Since some students will be wanting to develop into solo singers it will be desirable to have in the community a teacher qualified to give private individual lessons, a teacher who understands the adolescent voice and who is congenial to teen-agers. While it may not be proper for members of the school administration to subsidize this teacher, it may be possible for members of the faculty to recommend that certain students enroll for a series of lessons. In some cases it is even allowable for school facilities to be made available for out-of-school lessons free of charge to this teacher.

It becomes obvious that such a five-fold plan will work best only if everybody concerned works as a team. If the director of the boy choir develops singers of great ability and high eagerness, and these boys go into the voice change unpracticed, untrained and deprived of opportunity to continue their vocal development, much valuable training has gone for nought. If the junior high teacher guides his boys through the changing voice period so the boys make the transition happily, easily and comfortably and with pride, his/her work is for nought if the senior high director "turns those boys off." In turn, the senior high director has a very difficult time of it if most boys are "turned off" in grade 7 or 8 so they do not even appear in the high school music room. It is much easier for a junior high teacher AND a high school director if the boys at an early age are taught to sing properly and have developed a high spirit of enthusiasm for that singing in a boy choir.

The administrators too have a large part to play as they make it possible or difficult for music teachers at any level to function at the best level. The general public also must be won over to lend its support, to give its blessing and to express its appreciation to this five-step plan.

So I address some remarks to each of these groups of people to give them a special summary of what they can do to support and maintain a proper course of advancement for boy singers from age eight to eighteen.

Part A.

From the Administrator's Point of View

Let us assume that you are the administrator of a public school system or a headmaster in a private school or the coordinator of music for a whole school district. You are inspecting your choral music program.

As one who is eager to have the support and approval of the citizen-taxpayer-patron you know that a good choral music program is one of the best public relations resources possible. A fine award-winning high school choir plus numerous quartets, sextets, madrigal and chamber ensembles available throughout the season for school and community programs create a fine image of what the schools are doing. Add to this flourishing junior high groups of boys' and girls' glee clubs that involve hundreds of children of that age level, and a fine boy-choir and girl-choir at the elementary level and you have a huge cross-section of the community proud of its schools and interested in participating—parents, grandparents, out-of-town relatives, chambers of commerce and city promoters, and especially the citizenry in general.

As one concerned with getting as much in return for tax dollars spent as possible, you realize that the choral music department is one of the best and cheapest "bargains" available. A high school choral director may work with five groups of over 60 each day and BE GLAD that he has that many, while most academic teachers would be complaining of over-work. One boy choir director can train three groups of boys, fifty to each group, working his influence on 150 children. A choir needs very little financial outlay-60 chairs, a piano, some choir risers and a library of choral selections that can be used over and over, year after year; choir robes are nice but not necessary. Compare this with the band with its costly tubas, bassoons, its uniforms and "extras;" or with the athletic team with its high-priced equipment and a ratio of one coach for every five players, plus the huge gymnasiums and swimming pools and playing fields required.

Most important, as a dedicated educator, you want to get satisfaction in the knowledge that MANY students are being initiated into one of the oldest, most durable art forms; one most readily available for aesthetic enjoyment, and an activity in which almost everybody can participate throughout his whole life.

For these three reasons and probably some more you will be happy if the choral music department is flourishing, with lots of students participating.

You can rightly assume that there is no native, inborn difference in musical talent or interest between males and females. You will realize that there is a greater demand for male singers than female singers in the adult world, and that Americans actually prefer to listen to men and boys as soloists or in chorus. You will therefore be greatly concerned if you do not find at least an equal number of boys and girls in choral music activities.

If you discover that in your senior high school there are five girls for every boy singer, or even two girls for every boy, you will be unhappy.

1. Every vocal music student should have the experience of singing in a mixed chorus in senior high school. Music for soprano-alto-tenor-bass is standard; most of the choral compositions over the centuries are written for that voicing. In the adult world, in church choirs (masses, oratorios, anthems, cantatas), in stage works (operas, operettas, musical comedies, revues), in secular works, this is the voicing most prevalent, most enduring.
2. No girls should be cheated by having to sing in a girls-only chorus all through high school.
3. Where boys are not enrolled in equal numbers, there must be a sizable number of potentially good boy singers who are being deprived of training they should be getting. They are undiscovered, untrained and not enjoyed.

135

4. The people in the community are cheated if they do not have an opportunity to hear choral music well performed by adequate, well-balanced choirs. They are cheated if a good supply of tenors and basses is not trained for community use after high school graduation.
5. The administrators and teachers are vulnerable to the charge that the music department practices discrimination by sex, with the males being discriminated against.

You will, of course, observe your high school choral director to see if he is to blame for that imbalance. Is he harsh, unsympathetic, impatient with his boy singers who are trying to learn to sing the new voice-lines assigned to tenors and basses while trying to get control of voices newly changed and immature? Does he select music that is too demanding, that is intended for ADULT singers? Is he more interested in putting on a "show" and earning a reputation than he is concerned with the best interests of his young singers?

But you will not stop there. You will realize that boys face certain hazards in their vocal development that they must overcome much earlier than the high school years.

In your junior high school or middle school (ages 13 and 14 especially) there should be provision for special classes or choruses for boys with changing voices. This voice-mutation is one of the most difficult hazards a boy singer must overcome, and there should be a teacher with great understanding of what happens when a boy's voice changes and with knowledge of what special techniques and materials he should be ready to use in his teaching. Every effort should be made to have the boys look on their voice mutation as a challenge and as an acquiring of new powers. Music should be found that fits their voices. There should be a time and place for teen-age boys to sing with pleasure not only in the classroom but also in public, staged with style and showmanship.

This is where you as administrator and coordinator can be a great help. The junior high music teacher should be considered a specialist, and a person hired who is congenial to teen-age boys. This is NOT a place for an inexperienced, non-career-minded teacher, nor a place to put a faltering, time-serving mediocrity.

Giving this specialist a time and place to work is equally important, and that is not always easy in the crowded junior high curriculum. Team teaching (if the school is large enough to warrant more than one music teacher), a special club period, classes alternating with other all-male classes like physical education and shop are for you, as administrator, to inaugurate, and you can aid in publicizing and scheduling a bass-clef chorus about the community. If you promote this program you will be amply repaid for your efforts.

Below the junior high, there should be a boy-choir (and a girl-choir as well). This boy-choir should be city-wide so any boy between the ages of eight and twelve will be eligible to try out for membership. Ideally the choir should be a part of the school music program, sponsored and supervised by the school administrators. Since there are many reasons why some public schools cannot sponsor such a community-wide project, the school administrators should at least co-operate as much as possible in furthering the development of such a choir. The use of school auditoriums for performances; allowing, even encouraging, members of the music staff to serve as directors, accompanists, prefectors-these are positive methods for supporting a boy choir. You are the one who can remove conflicts in scheduling and allow released time so that the members of the choir can perform for special occasions.

If the boy choir is under your jurisdiction you will hope that enrollment will be large enough to include a large number of boys from all parts of town. There should be a training class for the youngest and newest boys where they can learn the fundamentals of good singing and can develop desirable habits of working with other boys. There should be an advanced choir which sings in public. Where possible, intermediate classes should be organized so each boy can advance according to his own ability and industry.

If the school itself does not directly sponsor this boy choir an administrator is justified (since the choir if well run will affect the school music program favorably) in working closely with whatever governing board the choir elects. Laymen are not always aware of legal matters or the standard safeguards used in school for chaperoning and transporting children, nor of sound fiscal planning. Suggesting and making available one or more people to serve as members of the board of directors or to serve as liaison persons would do much to help the boy-choir function properly over a long term of years.

If you are the headmaster of a private school, much of what has been said up to here will be equally meaningful, but in some ways much easier to carry out, or put into practice.

If your school includes only students for the first eight years, you will be interested primarily in organizing a boy treble choir, and using it not only as an educational enterprise but as a very valuable means of adding to the prestige of your school. If your school is intended primarily for boys from age twelve through eighteen, the passages dealing with a special class for boys with changing voices and for singing in mixed chorus will apply. If your school is for boys only, then perforce you will have to organize a male chorus for tenor-baritone-bass voices at the fifteen to eighteen year age levels (unless there is a private school for girls nearby where you can find girl sopranos and altos to give your students the needed singers for mixed choral singing).

With the boys in your control all day you will have a problem in scheduling practices, finding the proper choir to put each boy in (training, intermediate, performing). If your faculty is too small in number to justify a full-time music teach, you are in a good position to hire a part-time person, for example an outstanding church choir director, a graduate student in a nearby university or an experienced voice teacher.

Part B. From the Standpoint of a
Senior High School Choral Music Director

Let us suppose that you are a senior high school choral director who is perennially hampered because you cannot get enough boys to form a balanced mixed chorus (You may take some comfort in the

137

knowledge that you are not the only one in that predicament. The majority of high school choral conductors suffer from the same frustration).

Let us further suppose that you are in a community where there is no very good vocal music preparation in the elementary or junior high schools that send their students to you. This situation is by no means confined to thinly populated rural areas or small village schools. There are, we hear, very large cities where elementary or junior high school music is badly taught, or in some places not taught at all.

In this situation you will be advised to offer as a first class in high school choral music a section for boys only and another for girls only. The boys' classes should be organized and taught much along the changing voice class decribed in Section III. This class need not be a dreary affair, for often boys who have had little or no vocal music training and who are already well into the voice change find few inhibitions and frustrations and are quite amenable to rather elementary vocal exercises. Your first emphasis will be on letting these boys experience the joys of singing in unison without introducing many problems for them to solve before they are ready for them.

For the purpose of arousing enthusiasm and spirit, you may choose to build this male chorus up into a performing group. The emphasis will be on winning applause and enthusiasm in the community until being a member of this boys' glee club is a prestigious, eagerly sought privilege. If unison or two-part music is all that can be achieved, this will not matter for the moment. Let the pleasure of singing in concert and the satisfaction of winning some applause be sufficient reward until the glee club is firmly established, and the boys are participating in gratifying numbers.

You may have difficulty scheduling this glee club at a time when all the boys who want to join can be there. For this reason you will seek the help of your administrator. You may have to settle for two meetings a week, before school or during noon break or after school (athletic events permitting). Nobody enjoys meeting at 7:30 in the morning or sacrificing a lunch period, but if it is "important enough" most boys will make such special efforts—IF you can make the singing so satisfying that they feel it is worthwhile.

Working on a long range plan you will not hurry this campaign to find and train boy singers, but eventually you hope the point is reached where you can "tap" ten or fifteen tenors and a like number of basses to join the girls to form a mixed choir. This will be a critical point. You will do well to be very aware of the two hazards these boys will face.

1. They will be reading music and singing from different clefs than the girls, so you must give them time and special practice for learning to match their voices to the position of the notes on those staffs.
2. The usual arrangement of music for SATB choirs is melody in soprano with basses and altos singing harmonic parts. At first this will be difficult for these untrained boys to follow, to hold and to enjoy.
   That is why you will want to simplify the problems for these boys. Reviewing the material in Chapters XX and XXI, you will try to give the boys the obvious, simple, familiar melodies and harmonies, while challenging the girls with more difficult voice parts.

3.   Once the boys are able to sing the bass and tenor against the girls' parts you
can begin to adventure into commercially printed, standard four-part music,
always keeping a careful check on the range and the tessitura of the boys' parts
to be sure they can handle them with no vocal strain. During the learning period
you may want to transpose a piece down or up, or you may want to reassign a
few measures to another voice.

Be assured that this simplification of music for boys will not
have to continue for long. Once they are comfortable in four-part
music, i.e. they can hold their own parts without constant effort, they
will be able to sing music printed commercially for the standard
repertoire.

So far we have dealt with immediate procedures. Over the longer
period of time, you are justified in trying to get more preparation in
the pre-high school grades.

In this sort of situation, a high school director might well explore
the possibility of getting a boy choir started in the community, may
even organize one himself. The emphasis, at first at least, is to get
citizens converted to the idea that boys can and should sing, and to
get the community used to the sound of boys' voices raised in song.
With a good supply of experienced boy singers coming to your school
with a favorable attitude and some experience in choral singing you
will get much help in attracting other potential basses and tenors into
your choral program.

In a rural situation, where schools are rather widely separated,
transportation to and from boy choir practices may be a problem.
That is why rehearsal times may have to be carefully planned so
parents can bring their boys into a central place. In a large urban
district there may be problems of heavy traffic and dangerous travel
through certain parts of town. Yet such problems can be solved, and
are worth the effort needed to solve them.

Now let us propose a situation in which you, the senior high
director, may need to revise your own procedures.

Let us suppose that you are the choral music director in a rather
large senior high school in an urban community. There are two or
more junior high schools that send their "graduates" to your school.
All of these junior high schools have very flourishing vocal music
classes, including ninth grade (freshman) elective choirs with between
60 and 100 singers.

If most of these ninth grade choral singers were to enroll in your
sophomore class/choir you would have to form two or even three
sections. Suppose for some reason such numbers do not enroll. There
are usually enough girl singers to make a sizeable sophomore choir,
but the boys simply do not appear. Never do you get enough tenors;
genuine tenors seem to be non-existent except for one or two
lonesome fellows. Some seasons you do not even have enough boys
of *any* voice part. This means that you have trouble developing
enough good singers to move into your "top choir." Sometimes you
even put sophomore boys, immature and vocally undependable, into
your senior choir, leaving your sophomore girls and many junior girls
in all-girl choruses. You ask the junior high teachers why they do not
send you more singers, get only shrugs or evasive answers. What is
the cause for this lack of singers?

139

First, look to the surface symptoms. It is not likely that there is a conspiracy on the part of these junior high directors to turn their students away from you. More likely you need to examine your own methods and procedures. Could it be that you have a record of discouraging boy singers? Do you find yourself "picking on the boys" because they are not as capable as the girls? Are you sarcastic and abusive when they cannot hold their part or are not so adept at reading their notes? Or could it be that you are selecting music that is not congenial to boys' voices in their immaturity? Is the music too hard, or does it lie too high so they must strain and feel uncomfortable? Or is it music they do not understand or which has no appeal to them in their lack of musical appreciation? Is this why the junior high school boys find excuses for not singing in your choirs?

If the answer to any of the above is "yes," do some deeper thinking. Why are you a choral director? Is it because you want to teach young people to sing properly, to read music, to experience some enjoyment and to develop their aesthetic appreciation? Or are you really hoping to develop a fine choir that YOU will enjoy, that will win the respect and admiration of others, especially other choral directors, and add to your reputation?

The two aims are not mutually exclusive, of course. But the order of priority makes a great difference! If you are thinking of your students first and how to develop them into fine singers, you will realize that you cannot teach the boys as you do the girls. The boys have two big hurdles that need special attention: they are fourteen or fifteen years old, singing with voices that are still undependable, not completely changed, limited in range and at times difficult to control; they are singing in idioms quite different from those of their boyhood soprano-alto. So instead of being sarcastic, impatient or abusive, you must take pains to accommodate them, to give them music they can handle with some success and comfort and to encourage them, not deride them.*

You may be advised to arrange for a special class for tenors only, in which you concentrate on such matters as finding head voice, extending range, developing a smooth "passagio" as they move from one register to another, and practicing the reading of notes in BOTH the tenor clefs (treble clef sung an octave lower than written; bass clef extending above the staff). Likewise you may want to meet your sophomore basses for special work in finding their lower tones, discovering the boys with very deep voices who cannot get up to an a

---

* An example of this problem needing consideration is a "simple four-part arrangement" of a hymn tune or familiar folk song written on two staves. It IS simple for a mediocre pianist to play, and an adult, experienced singer will probably have little difficulty following his/her proper voice line. But consider the sophomore choir. The familiar melody is in the soprano: what soprano has any difficulty in singing a familiar tune by ear in a voice line she's been singing since first grade? But our new tenor is looking at notes written in the bass clef, which means with added ledger lines above the staff. He must follow a harmonic part that is unfamiliar, that moves in awkward intervals and is not particularly interesting in its own right. So the sopranos sing easily and successfully but the insecure tenors must try to hold their own with their not-dependable voices and in an unfamiliar part. If the tenors are less than adept do you, teacher, express your disappointment or dismay while the sopranos win only praise?

or b without strain and adjusting the bass parts for these boys.

If special class sessions are not possible, you will certainly want to make a voice graph of each boy's voice (girls' voices too) indicating which tones are comfortable, where the two registers overlap. When you know what each boy can do , in September, the time when you will win or lose your boys, you find or arrange music that they can handle. You may not get to the published material in your library for several months, but you will be hearing pleasant sounds, you will be developing techniques and vocal resources, you will be giving ALL your students a chance to enjoy their singing experiences and have personal satisfaction as they gain power and skill. You may be sure that within the semester your sophomores will be able to handle standard choral music of YOUR choosing and preference. THEN you can select music YOUR taste and ambition desires, and you will have singers eager to attempt it.

You will also begin to experiment. If you are determined to sing SATB music and you have a chronic shortage of tenors, you will try developing some of your more plentiful baritone-basses into countertenors, so the tenors will have the reassurance of more numbers and the support of singers who can produce the higher tones of the tenor line that *they* cannot produce with absolute assurance. With the new countertenors swelling the ranks and adding reassurance, tension is eased, doubts are lessened!

You will also be very alert for several challenging types of male voices.

1. The voice of the slow maturing boy who at fifteen or even sixteen is still really an unchanged treble who sings very comfortably on a high tenor part (really an alto part) and who suddenly plummets down to a bass-baritone in mid-season. MAYBE you can keep him on first tenor by using the now-faucette voice of this boy treble, but more often he should be shifted immediately to the bass line (How you react to this situation reveals what your order of priorities is: the well-being of the students' vocal growth or the importance of having somebody somehow sing the notes of a composition you want to perform, no matter what!).

2. The very deep basses who sing very comfortably on the lower half of the bass clef and even several tones below, but who cannot sing above G (fourth space) comfortably. These are the voices for which music is scarce, especially in America where many arrangers, composers and even teachers refuse to believe they even exist. These voices, properly used and developed, can become valuable assets, adding tones and qualities highly desirable and beneficial to the choral ensemble. But for a time they may be unable to sing a standard bass part because it lies too high. So you find music for them.*

---

* For example, take the familiar Russian hymn, HARK THE VESPER HYMN IS STEALING, and let the contrabasses double the bass under then tenor melody; add soprano and alto counterpoint to achieve a full, rich choral sound. (example 27b)

Example 27b HARK, THE VESPER HYMN IS STEALING
— for tenor, bass, contrabass

Hark the ves- per hymn is steal-ing o'er the dis- tant mead-ow far.

Remembering that your boys have certain hazards to overcome, be willing to praise them when they succeed and give them learning materials with which they can hope to succeed. The word will spread through your school, to the junior high schools and into the community that the sophomore choir provides a very happy learning experience for boy singers as well as girls. You become known as a producer of tenors and basses and the director of well-balanced choirs. And it is quite possible you will be known as the only director in your district that has a really superb male section.

To enhance this impression, you will cultivate a better image in those junior high schools. If there is to be a musical program in x junior high, you attend, remain afterward to give compliments (there is always *something* to praise), shake hands, become known; you will carefully avoid any adverse criticisms except in the strictest privacy and then only if the director asks for them.

You offer to bring your choir to sing for the junior high students. If you are particularly interested in encouraging boy singers, you may find it possible to have an all-male chorus sing music junior high boys will enjoy hearing. You also offer free tickets to a performance or dress rehearsal of your choir concert.

If you are in a position to do so without over-stepping lines of authority you can offer your support and advice to any junior high music teacher who asks to have his changing voice boys segregated from the girls in required music. You may even dare to go so far as to offer to direct this boys' class or glee club as a guest teacher once in awhile. You may suggest an "all-city bass clef chorus" to be made up of properly selected boys from all of the junior high schools, perhaps for some special occasion or music festival. If it is a successful venture you might even help find other places for this chorus to sing in and about your community. You are careful to leave the direction of the choir and selection of the music to the junior high teachers, making your own services and advice available only if very cordial invitations are offered.

Two questions you might ponder, questions to which I have no final answer. Many high schools give a large scale presentation of a popular Broadway musical each year. Is this desirable? These shows were written for adult professional singers so make demands on your immature singers that may be more than their voices can stand. Yet such presentations arouse great enthusiasm and both students and the general public look forward eagerly to each year's show. Does the risk of damaging voices justify entertaining an audience?

Are choral and vocal solo contests justified? Is music really a competitive enterprise? Do students need the challenge of competition and possible "winning a first place?" Does the chance for winning justify the equally great chance for losing and being discouraged by defeat?

A few schools have answered the first question by the compromise expedient of staging scenes from several shows instead of one complete musicale. Only such scenes were selected as lay within the capabilities of the students present, with solos raised or lowered in pitch and troublesome passages altered. Thus many more students have a chance at solo singing or playing leading dramatic parts. I

142

remember seeing the second act of the opera *Martha* by Flotow sung by a quartet of beautifully blended voices (the high tessitura was avoided by transposition down as much as a minor third.) The quaint old-fashioned lines were cleverly brought up to date and the comedy played up to the audience's great approval. Best of all, to the business manager's delight, there was no expensive royalty).

There is an answer to the objections to the competition of contests, rather widely used in certain parts of the country. Several high schools band together into a "festival chorus." The music is chosen by mutual agreement, rehearsed in the home schools ahead of time, and then, under the direction of a guest conductor, the cooperating choirs gather in the morning, rehearse during the day, and in the evening present the program. To introduce a slight bit of friendly competition, each participating choir is also expected to perform one or more numbers by itself.

Part C. From the Standpoint of a Boy Choir Director, Present or Future

Whatever your motives were originally in becoming the director of a boy choir (there are *many* honorable motives), you will have discovered before long that there are two great satisfactions in directing a boy choir.

1. When your boys sing properly there is a unique beauty and charm inherent in the boy treble voice that is aesthetically pleasing and emotionally satisfying.
2. You have in your control an organization that can win many admirers, that can give much pleasure to many people, and that can gain for *you* respect and prestige.

You can add to these two the satisfaction that you are rendering a valuable service to the boys in your choir as you start them along the road to becoming competent singers; through their singing these boys are developing a capacity for enjoying and appreciating music; you are convincing boys, families and community that singing is rewarding, satisfying and a prestigious activity.

All of this is true if you are a COMPETENT director. You must know the technique of voice production so you can develop the clear, unforced yet resonant tones admired and enjoyed by people the world over. You must know how to develop clean part singing, correct intonation, clear diction. You must be able to choose repertoire suitable to young boys' voices, including compositions that are of artistic worth yet within the capacity of boys and their listeners to enjoy. You will want to present the choir effectively, so you must know how to stage a concert with tasteful showmanship.

This is not enough. You must also understand the nature and needs of boys age eight to twelve; you must enjoy living with and working with boys within that age span. You must discover how to find the fine line that separates the stern disciplinarian whom the boys respect and obey, and the "good fellow" that the boys can laugh with, play with and confide in, and learn to straddle that line.

An added desirable attribute is the ability to find and keep good assistants. While it is possible to maintain a small choir by yourself, you will do well to find a competent accompanist and a

143

prefector—the pianist to provide suitable accompaniments and the prefector to handle the many non-musical details connected with assembling a large group of people and having the proper equipment on hand. As the size and scope of the choir increases you may want a librarian, a costumer, a choreographer. Ideally you, the director, should concentrate your attention entirely on matters musical. Part of your success will be due to your ability to find capable people who will be loyal, dependable yet not obtrusive.

If you are planning to start a choir, there are several tried and true ways for you to proceed. It is possible to begin by gathering about you a number of boys recruited from family, friends, acquaintances. When they have learned enough songs to sing a program you can begin to present them, in and about your community, hoping that you will please your audiences, attract more boy singers and gain some supporters in the community.

A somewhat better way is to find or make a special occasion and form a boy choir to provide music for that occasion. With a definite purpose and a chance to perform at a prestigious event, you can expect to attract a sizable group of boy singers to develop a good choir. If all goes well and you win admiration, you can then propose that the choir continue to function, and to give immediate purpose to this, you may have one or two other appearances scheduled.

Many times the opportunity to form a boy choir is thrust upon you. A church, a fraternal order, a civic organization may advertise for a director. Along the same line, you may approach several organizations with the proposition that a boy choir would be a good project for them to sponsor. This situation has some very strong points in its favor. You will have an organized group helping you to recruit singers, you will have a place to rehearse and a sense of permanence that permits long range planning. Best of all you will probably have a budget for necessary expenses and a suitable salary. But there are also limiting factors to beware of. You may be restricted to boys of certain religions, races, ethnic backgrounds, economic status. You may be confined to only certain types of music. You may even find that you must abide by certain behavioral standards in your personal life.

If you are a public school music teacher, you may want the Board of Education to sponsor the boy choir and make it a part of the school music curriculum. The advantages here are your access to an entire population of boys within the age span of eight to twelve, you can have rehearsal rooms and auditoriums for concerts and the co-operation of many administrators and fellow faculty members. There will be an organization equipped to provide chaperonage, transportation, legal advice. But here too there are drawbacks. An organization that belongs to the public is subject to the whims of the public or its elected representatives. Pressures may be applied to include boys for reasons other than their musical ability, disappointed parents may apply negative pressures, other departments may resent money allocated to the choir's maintenance so desired equipment cannot be purchased; there may be restrictions on travel.

If there is any best advice to give here, it is that you as director must be able to keep your own integrity. You must be free to admit

144

any boy you want into your class of singers. You must be the one to choose the music that is to be sung; you must develop your own methodology for getting the boys to sing that music as you feel it shoud be interpreted.

The best way to prepare yourself to become a boy choir director would be to find a college or music school which gives a formal course of study in that field, with a functioning boy choir on campus for you to observe and eventually to get practice in directing. Unfortunately there are few colleges that offer courses specifically in boy choir organization and management, nor do many music schools sponsor a boy choir.

This need not deter you. Much of the preparation for choral conducting in general will apply. For direct training for boy choir work, there are each year in many parts of our country workshops and short courses for credit. The American Choral Directors Association or the Music Educators' National Conference sometimes have lecture-demonstrations at the state, district or national conventions. There are functioning boy choirs in every one of the fifty states, and most directors are willing to allow visitors who come in good faith and with advance permission to observe and learn. It has even happened that such a director has later offered a post as assistant director to a would-be boy choir conductor after such a visit. There are recordings of many boy choirs available for listening, and nearly every large city has scheduled concerts by touring boy choirs from time to time. There are not many textbooks written, but the determined seeker can find the few extant if he has access to a large library.

As for acquiring the ability to communicate with boys and to enjoy them as talented fellow human beings, there is no substitute for actual experience. If there is no boy choir on campus, there are always other types of boy-groups: YMCA classes; boy scout troops; organized teams of baseball, basketball or swimming; churches or synagogues with children's groups to teach. All of these have use for a willing assistant leader. A term of service will usually determine if you experience pleasure in working with children of this age and whether you can find ways to lead or teach them effectively.

Your chances for getting employment as a boy choir director on a full time basis upon graduation will not be good, but you may with luck get a chance to serve as assistant for one of our large, well-established boy choirs, for there are not presently many applicants for such jobs. Much better are your chances for finding a part-time boy choir directorship, to be combined with a job as music teacher in a large elementary school or junior high school. It has happened that a community organization or members of a lodge or church have used their influence to get a director appointed to a public school position with the understanding that he also direct a sponsored boy choir as an extra job.

There is always the possibility for a would-be music teacher who has not found a position or been hired for a music teaching job to take a temporary, non-music type of employment temporarily, and then to organize a boy choir and build it up to a prestigious concert group. In fact, this is an excellent way for a novice to "break into" a

145

profession that is presently over-populated at so many levels, with competent people unable to secure full-time employment as senior high or college choral conductor, elementary supervisor or specialist or any related jobs.

There is also the possibility, along with starting and developing a boy choir, of making yourself available for giving individual lessons to students, boys especially, who want to develop their solo singing voices and who want to be guided through the changing voice period properly.

Part D. From the Standpoint of a
Junior High School Vocal Music Teacher

Competent junior high school vocal music teachers are scarce. It seems probable that for a long time to come there will be a constant demand for people to teach junior high vocal music when most of the other levels of music teaching are over-supplied so these would-be teachers have rather meager chances for employment.

The reasons for this scarcity are many, but they can be compressed conveniently into three. The music teachers of children ages 12 to 15 must be both excellent musicians and persons able to understand, attract, control and enjoy those youths in their early teens. Add to this the third item, that he/she is willing to dedicate his/her professional life to this special area, realizing that there are great rewards and satisfactions to be enjoyed in what is sometimes labeled a "difficult area." The sum total of these three characteristics is a rare, valuable teacher, one who will be sure to win respect, acclaim and prestige—and steady employment. There are some music educators, and I count myself one of them, who think the competent junior high teacher should have better preparation and be more expert in his/her teaching than any other staff member on the music faculty, and should be paid more.

The teaching of boys with changing voices is one aspect of the junior high teacher's challenges that points up the need for skilled teaching backed up by special knowledge. This is the area where most junior high school music teachers falter, and all too often fail miserably. This is why most schools have an ample supply of girl singers but such a deficiency of boy singers. The teacher who can produce as many tenors, baritones and basses as he/she can develop sopranos and altos is rare indeed. That is one reason that some think if such a capable teacher were in every junior high (or middle school) the senior high choral director's job would be much easier; some go so far as to suggest that a less experienced, less skilful choral director should be assigned to the senior high school post (where students come willingly, already prepared in fundamentals, from the upper ranges of natural musical ability) and the most knowledgeable, personable, skilled teacher should be promoted to the junior high assignment.

Voice mutation in the adolescent male is a natural development; all normal males go through this maturing phase. Therefore it should be regarded as a time of expanding vocal resources, a fascinating experience, an exploration of new types of vocal sounds and a chance

146

for more complicated, challenging types of choral and solo singing. It is not to be regarded as a frustrating phase, a difficult hazard, a disaster or an end to a happy singing career. By no means should a boy cease his singing activities when his voice begins to change, for then he would allow his singing skills and his vocal control to atrophy. Rather he should keep as much of his boy-treble still functioning as possible, while adding a whole "new voice" of several octaves to enable him to sing over a large range of tones.

How can you, junior high school music teacher, get YOUR boys to sing comfortably, happily, eagerly during the time of voice change? Here is a sketch of procedures that work well.

You, the teacher, start with the mental assurance that most boys like to sing, they have within themselves the capacity and equipment to sing, and they will be especially eager to sing if their boy classmates sing with them. Very important is it that you LET THE BOYS KNOW you have this assurance and want very much to give them the chances to enjoy singing as a group, and as a soloist.

You must have a clear understanding of what happens when a boy's voice changes; you must know the physical causes for voice change and what socio-psychological growth the boy is experiencing at the same time. You should know how the onset of voice change can be predicted quite precisely and thus anticipated. You should have a good idea of the possible patterns of voice change that can emerge and what you, as teacher, can expect a boy to sing at this time.

You will find some way to separate boys with changing voices from their classmates for singing activities, justifying this to all concerned on the sound educational practice of grouping students with special abilities and problems into homogeneous classes. When you have the boys alone, you can give them the explanations they should have, but which is for their ears alone, so they know what is happening and why they should be interested, yes, fascinated, by the growth they can expect. You can do voice checking and charting, in surroundings where boys will not be embarrassed but reassured as they discover their vocal development is much like that of their boy classmates; they will be intrigued, even amused but not frustrated when they experience temporary vocal difficulties if they know other boys alongside are having the same difficulties. Most important, they must sense that the teacher, you, look on this class as most interesting, most challenging, where you share their experiences and note their progress with special interest.

In this class of boys only, you discover what tones each boy can sing comfortably at a given time. You make voice graphs so both he and you know what these tones are. You and he can follow the individual path his voice is taking as he adds new bass-cleff tones and KEEPS his treble voice.

You find the common tones the boys AS A CLASS can all produce, either in unison or unison-octave and find or manufature songs that lie within that range, being prepared to raise or lower the pitch from week to week. You note which songs appeal, either through words or rhythm or style, and build a repertoire that all the boys sing comfortably and with spirit, so well they can "carry them home with them".

You find or manufacture vocal exercises (vocalises) that aid the newly emerging tones to gain in strength, and that help the boy to find and control these (for a time) uncertain tones. You will not let the treble voice atrophy but will have the boys practice in blending this "faucette voice" (falsetto) with the modal "newly emerging bass-clef voice "hoping that they will be able to shift smoothly from one to the other so they INCREASE THEIR RANGE GREATLY.

You will understand that this would be difficult, even impossible, in a mixed class with girls and less mature boys present. That is why you will consult with your administrator to work out some way for you to get these boys into this special class.

Once your young men have gained some control over their bass clef tones, you find ways to build up their confidence, give them a strong motivation and a chance to "show off these new voices" favorably. You organize them into a bass-clef chorus, maybe only a unison chorus, or if they seem capable and there is sufficient time, into a two-part or even three-part male glee club. You work up a program of songs, with enough variety and appeal for at least a thirty-minute program. You plan some sort of effective but inexpensive uniform dress. You work on stage appearance, adding a few touches of showmanship, e.g. adding a guitarist, a bongo player, a few spoken lines or a bit of choreography.

You find places for these boys to sing, beginning with small scale, informal and uncritical groups of listeners so the boys can experience the satisfaction of winning admiration and applause. Most important, you try to include EVERY BOY POSSIBLE, even those who have the reputation of being "difficult" in other school activities, those who are often resistant, withdrawn, over-excitable or accustomed to defeat.

Over the months you hope to build up the reputation of this bass-clef chorus until the boys in your school consider it a matter of prestige to be in it, people in the community begin to make favorable remarks, and the younger boys not yet in junior high school get the idea that there is something exciting and prestigious for them to join when they get into your school.

You will not be in a hurry to put these adolescent tenors and basses back with their girl classmates, but eventually there will come a time when they are ready. You will realize that for these young fellows to sing bass or tenor to the girls' alto and soprano will be a new and somewhat difficult experience. Since they were, as little boys, sopranos and altos themselves, they will have a tendency to sing the soprano line or alto harmony. If they are reading the music, they will have trouble in finding the pitches in the "new bass-clef" unless you have been giving them practice and experience in correlating their new voices with the position of the notes on that "new staff". Psychologically you may have to build up their enthusiasm for mixed chorus singing so you predict the amazement and admiration the girls will display when they hear these new deep tones coming from the boys whom they remember as treble singers, and explain how the girls will need and enjoy the support of those lower, fuller sounds below their thinner high voices.

148

This is why you may choose to find or make special arrangements of songs for the first mixed chorus experiences. You may give the basses a familiar melody and the tenors an easy, obvious harmony and have the boys well-practiced in singing their two parts in advance. Of course you will see that both voice parts lie within the comfortable ranges of those particular boys, no matter how unusual or unorthodox those voice lines may look on paper.

As for the girls, they deserve a bit of a challenge as they find they do NOT sing the melody "by ear" but have a rather complicated, less obvious contrapuntal counter-point that they must hold against the boys' parts. A few simultaneous songs can also be used, where each voice section sings its own song which must mesh with the others. Once mixed chorus singing has been introduced successfully, you can begin to use standard, commercially printed SATB arrangements, analyzing each arrangement to be sure not only that the range is suitable but that the tessitura (the "lie" of most of the notes within the range) is suitable for your particular boys. You may have to transpose the key or reassign certain passages to be sure that no boys (or girls, either) are being forced beyond the point where they can control the tones and produce them easily.

Part E. From the Standpoint of a Student Preparing to Become a Teacher of Vocal Music

You will want to plan realistically as you prepare to become a teacher of vocal music or a choral director. You will have to realize that your chances for getting just the position you want are much slimmer than they would have been ten years ago. With public school enrollments declining and budgets being trimmed, fewer music teachers are needed and hired. As older teachers retire, they are not always replaced. Teachers presently under contract are not moving on to other jobs, but are holding onto their present assignments.

There are two exceptions to the above and you will do well to realize this and plan accordingly. Junior high school music teachers, vocal and choral, who are well-trained and professionally dedicated, are in short supply, so chances of getting such a position are quite good. Directors of boy choirs (treble voice) are not plentiful. With some 600 boy choirs known to be flourishing presently in our United States where there were only perhaps one-sixth of that number thirty years ago, obviously there has been a demand for such directors; with a probable increase in the number of such choirs in the next decade, the chances for a prepared college graduate to get such a post promise to be fairly good. If a future music teacher were to present evidence that he is specializing in the training of boy voices both at the boy choir level and in the junior high age brackets, chances for getting a job are more than doubled.

Teachers who understand the boy's changing voice, its nature and needs for specialized training, are not plentiful. People who are congenial to adolescents age 13 to 15, and who understand their behavioral patterns and know how to direct their energies into proper channels are equally scarce. Those who know how to work with such young people, enjoy them, know how to win their respect and loyalty

149

and also have the musical training to direct them in vocal music are rare people indeed. If you can prepare yourself to be such an individual, you will find an area of specialization worth your lifetime dedication, and your rewards in musical satisfaction, respect and admiration from students and community, and even on the larger national scene will be very considerable.

A career as the director a boy choir can be equally rewarding, especially if you develop your choir to a fine concert group. There is a tremendous appeal in the voices of well-trained boys' voices raised in song that wins universal admiration. It is always a source of amazement to laymen when they hear to what high levels of performance a group of boys can be developed.

There is a difficulty in preparing yourself for either of these fields. Very few schools give courses specifically designed to train future boy choir directors. All too often the course in junior high school music methods is a rather superficial survey taught by people worthy and sincere, but inexperienced in actual junior high school teaching.

The subject of the boy's changing voice with which we deal in this book is an example. Very few textbooks are written on the subject so readings tend to be sketchy and very generalized in nature. Since the day when teacher training schools had a "practice school", where future teachers could observe, then put into practice on actual subjects what they have learned in theory, there is not much chance that a group of adolescent males will be available for the future teacher to hear, see, study and try to direct. And alas, if the future teacher is sent out "into the field" to work in a nearby public school, he may be assigned to a place where the classroom teacher is no more knowledgeable than he is.

I know of no college or university that maintains a boy choir under its direct control. There are a few where a member of their faculty also directs a boy choir as a separate entity, and others where there are established boy choirs in the vicinity. I do not find much provision for would-be boy choir directors to do any "practice teaching" with these boy choirs.

This lack of formal training need not deter you in your preparation. If the college or university you are attending does not give courses in either of these areas, you can often find organizations in the community where you can work with boys or youths in early adolescence: a YMCA, a settlement house, a boy scout troup, a church. You might be allowed to organize a small boys' choir on your own, or to gather a group of boys ages 13 - 15 into a singing group and quite on your own try out both your conducting skill and your ability to control and enjoy such boys. You might even convince the sponsoring group to pay you! As for learning to work with boys, there are also little league baseball and swimming and basketball teams, scout troops and Sunday School classes looking for people to volunteer their assistance.

This practical experience plus your formal training in choral conducting will give you an advantage when you apply for a teaching position. If your "sponsors" can add a few lines of recommendation this will be to your advantage too. But most important, you will have discovered if you WANT to work with boys and early-teenagers, if

150

you find them challenges and sources of enjoyment. And if you can develop your little boy choir or "changing voice singers" to the point that a possible employer can watch you teach them and hear your results you are even further ahead in your chaces for getting an appointment.

If you are unlucky in that there are just NO jobs available when you graduate there is also the very great possibility of persuading some organization, church, lodge, or civic group, to sponsor you as you start a boy choir on your own while supporting yourself in a temporary job in a non-music field, and using that choir to build for yourself a reputation that will win you a desired contract before long.

There is one more possibility, if you are interested in doing studio teaching. Along with your embryo boy choir you may advertise yourself as available for private voice lessons, specializing in boy singers. Not many teachers are *willing* to take on the high school boys who desire to begin voice training for possible future careers, and almost nobody is willing to coach boys in the changing voice period, helping them to get through this period of rapid change properly, safely and without loss of singing ability.

Part F.
From the View Point of a Parent

If you are the parent of a young boy, you will be fortunate if you live in a community where there is a boy choir. No matter if the choir functions rather modestly rather than at the professional, touring and recording level. It WILL be better if the number of boys participating is large enough so there can be at least one group. When your boy is ready, you hope he can advance into a choir which performs in public, singing music of artistic worth and some technical difficulty.

You will want the director of this boy choir to be more concerned with the vocal development of the boys than with putting on an impressive show of prestigious numbers. You will be glad if there is provision for social enjoyment to surround the music-making with the environment that young boys enjoy, e.g. games and competitions, play days, camping trips, overnight travel.

Knowing that your son will be learning skills, finding enjoyment and getting aesthetic experiences that will last him his entire life, you will be willing to pay a tuition fee and to do your part in any fund raising enterprises, or doing committee work, or helping with costuming or chaperoning or transporting. If called upon, you will be willing to serve on a board of directors to set the policy that will affect your son, and to manage the business and financial matters connected with the best interests of your own son and his fellow singers.

If there is no boy choir available in your community, you will do well to help get such a choir started. You may appeal first to the school music coordinator or to the choir director of your church. You may find some civic organization or club to sponsor the choir. Whatever you do, you will be performing constructive work for the welfare of your son, and also for the community in which you live.

When signs of puberty appear in your son, you will hope that the

151

junior high school vocal music teacher will have the proper training and knowledge to direct your boy's singing activities as his voice changes. You may join with other parents in supporting the school administrator as he tries to find, hire and keep a dedicated career teacher rather than taking on an inexperienced teacher wanting only a short-term job. You will be happy if there is a glee club for changing voices that your son can join, where he can learn to use his "new voice" and the new types of music-making in which he can use that voice. You will be ready to lend support in helping such a boys' glee club to get uniform dress, or provide transportation and chaperonage as these young adolescents sing in and about the community. You will not find this a chore, but a source of pleasure and satisfaction as you see your son finding his place in the group of youths that are developing into young men with the voices of adult-like tenors, baritones and basses, in a worthy enterprise and a well-disciplined group.

You will also be happy if your church or club or civic group sponsors a group of boys with changing voices. You will help to see that a minister of music or choir director is hired who is trained in developing adolescent boys' singing voices.

When the boys are ready and able to sing the standard mixed chorus literature, you will want to know that there is a high school director who is prepared to introduce the boys to the new idiom of singing with girl sopranos and altos. You hope this high school director will be patient and careful as the boys try to sing this new type of material for the first time. If you find that the high school director is interested in finding out what your son is capable of doing and then selecting or arranging music accordingly, you will give him due compliments and expressions of approval. If he seems to be choosing music that is too difficult or inappropriate for immature voices, you can assure him that you will not be judging him or criticizing him according to the prestigious difficulty of the works he performs, but rather on the vocal development your son is displaying.

If there is a voice teacher in your community who works well with adolescent boy students and produces good results, and if your boy displays interest in doing some individual work, you will try to arrange for a series of private lessons, not just because you want him to be a fine soloist, but to be sure that his newly emerging adult voice is properly developed.

Part G. From the Standpoint of a Director of Music Education or Voice Coach

Two areas of music education still offer good chances for graduates of our music schools to be gainfully employed after graduation—junior high or middle school vocal music teaching and the direction of a boy choir. What is more important, both forms of music education offer excellent opportunities for aesthetic satisfaction and professional advancement. Competent practitioners in both areas are in noticeably short supply.

Section I of this book defines the situation. Both areas of musical directing deal with the male singing voice, and too few educators face up to the fact that boy singers need special teaching—in fact some educators refuse to admit that this is the case. The hazards facing boy singers are summarized thus:

1. Boys as a group are slower to "find their singing voices" in the primary grades. Often, therefore, they are labeled deficient singers or even non-singers, and are discouraged at an early age from any desire to join in singing activities.
2. Voice mutation in the junior high and middle school can be a discouraging and frustrating time for boys who are not aware of what is occurring, even boys who have been excellent singers up to that time. When a normal maturation process should be a time of expanding vocal powers and of adventuring into new territories, too often this is a time of bewilderment and of discouragement. Much of this undesirable situation is due to the teacher who is not informed about what causes voice-change, how it can be precisely predicted, what are the patterns of development most voices follow during mutation and what special materials and techniques are most successful as voice change becomes an advancement and increase of vocal powers. This is the time when far too many of our potentially fine male singers are "turned off" and lost to the choral music director, and the future enjoyment of singing activities, never to be won back.
3. In the senior high (or ninth grade) too many directors are unaware of, and hence unsympathetic with the boys' bewilderment as they try to control their newly changed voices while learning a new idiom of singing and reading music from new clefs. Of those boys who have survived up to this point, another sizable group is turned away from further singing activities.

In contrast, when boys are properly taught, great satisfaction can result. The boy choir is a notably popular singing organization, as witness the fact that there are presently over 600 boy choirs functioning in our United States, as contrasted with few girls' choirs; the boy treble voice is capable of considerable technical advancement and has a unique beauty universally liked. Not so obvious is the fact that when a boys' glee club is organized in junior high and the peculiar charm and potentiality of the adolescent male voice are properly displayed, a very popular performing group is available to win much loyal admiration from the listeners while the boy singers develop a high level of enthusiasm and *esprit de corps* and the director gains professional prestige as a specialist in what many mistakenly call a difficult area of teaching.

Section II discusses the boy treble voice and its training from four points of view.

1. The value of a boy choir in training boys vocally between ages eight and twelve.
2. Successful methods for starting a boy choir; how to recruit and audition (with a detailed step-by-step audition procedure); how to develop the ideal tone quality; how to introduce part-singing; what repertoire to select; how to present the choir in performance with tasteful showmanship.
3. Administrative aspects of maintaining a boy choir; how to organize; how to finance—whether to be a part of a school or church program, to be privately supported by a patron, or to be entirely independent; how to find and use a supporting staff; methods for publicizing and promoting the choir.
4. The boy treble as a soloist; how to train him; what and when he should sing.

Section III deals with voice mutation in the adolescent male, one of the most troublesome because least understood aspects of vocal development. Much new material based on actual case studies and years of research is presented here. A straightforward explanation of why a boy's voice changes (including discussion of "the castrati") is followed by a description of the three general patterns of voice

153

change and the many ramifications that occur. There is a refutation of some widely held erroneous beliefs and theories. Two highly useful teaching aids, the graphing of voices and the finding or arranging of song materials to fit the voices present, are discussed in detail.

Most innovative is the plan to segregate boys with changing voices from their classmates to permit specialized instruction. Various administratiive devices to do this are described. How to motivate, train and enjoy the boys in this class as they develop their new "bass clef voices" are all well discussed in detail. The values of organizing a "bass clef chorus" for boys with changing voices and (contrary to most current practice) how to make this choir into a performing group to display the unique beauties and potentialities of the male voice are carefully explained. Much of this discussion is innovative and at times controversial, yet its demonstrable soundness merits careful study and trial.

Section IV is particularly pertinent since the senior high vocal music program is shamefully lacking in good boy singers (in some states, over 75% of the high schools). A discussion of the special hazards boy singers must overcome as they move into the tenor and bass idioms of singing is followed by a detailed exposition of how to overcome these hazards and to change frustration to pleasurable success.

Two chapters, dealing with subjects little understood by many American choral directors, open new vistas for high school music teachers.

The chapter on THE COUNTERTENOR, besides being of general interest, offers a step-by-step procedure for bolstering a deficient tenor section with the re-enforcement of a very reputable type of voice much used in Europe.

The chapter on THE CONTRABASS brings to America, (where this voice is not only not appreciated but actually thought to be non-existent or to be such a rarity it is not usable) the awareness that this very low bass voice does exist in considerable numbers, and that far too many adolescent contrabasses are rejected as non-singers to be unused, undeveloped and not enjoyed. Here there is a description of how to recognize these voices even in junior high classes, how to develop them and how to use them to good advantage.

There is in this section an innovative discussion about the restrictions of the SATB heritage of mixed choral singing in high schools and the desirability of experimenting with other voice groupings, especially where voices present do not fit that prevalent soprano-alto-tenor-bass voicing.

One of the most obvious aims of the teacher of music education is to prepare students for careers in teaching. The private voice coach also plays a part in giving the future teacher a valid method for developing singing voices properly. It follows then that if there is a demand for vocal music teachers at the junior high level, and also a market for boy choir directors, students in the music education course should be made aware of this situation and given opportunity to get some training and experience in these two fields.

The day when a university or teacher-training college maintained an auxiliary school, grades one through twelve, to give students the opportunity to observe master teachers and then to "practice teach" seems to be past. It is now the prevailing practice to find some public or parochial school to take on the burden of accomodating these "practice teachers", hoping that some classroom teacher will make a satisfactory "critic teacher". Unfortunately there are almost no schools that maintain a boy treble choir in which would-be boy choir directors can get experience. Candor compels me to state that not many junior high schools or senior high schools have teachers who are expert in guiding boy singers through the period of voice-mutation and into mixed choir singing.

How then can a future teacher, observe and then practice? Where shall these future teachers get proper experiences? I make bold to suggest that a teacher training college try to maintain a boy choir to be used not only as a worthy addition to the choral music program but as an organization which future choral directors can observe. Then as student directors they can put into practice their choral conducting techniques. Even more boldly I wonder if any teacher training institution might organize and train a bass-clef chorus made up of boys in their early teens whose voices are changing. Such a chorus would provide opportunity for future music teachers to study and record the vocal development of the various boys in the class and to get some guided experience in working with boys during this notoriously difficult but importantly challenging stage of vocal development.

If there are difficulties in having either boy-group under the direct sponsorship of the college-university, it might be possible and legitimate for those responsible for teacher training to give the impetus and furnish moral support to some public school, civic group, church/synagogue, or private individual to organize either or both choirs.

There is one more area of discussion which can interest those engaged in teacher training or voice coaching. There are obviously many aspects of voice mutation in the adolescent male still in need of careful research. Any of these could well furnish a graduate student a subject for his master's or doctor's dissertation. There are surprisingly few such investigative reports available to those wanting information. The boy treble voice, also, is a subject not very well examined, hence a very possible area for investigation.

Appendix A

From time to time I find occasion to compare the enrollment of boys to girls in senior high choirs. The first such survey, made in 1958 in the state of Wisconsin is shown in Examples 28, 29, 30. A full recording of the data and conclusions are recorded in VOICE MUTATION IN THE ADOLESCENT MALE: a doctoral dissertation completed at the University of Wisconsin in 1959 and obtainable on microfilm from Ann Arbor, Mich. For our purposes here this brief summary will suffice:

1. Ratio of boys' choruses to girls' choruses was approximately 1 to 5 in 1956
2. Ratio of boy singers to girl singers was approximately 1 to 8 in 1956
3. Ratio of boys' choruses to girls choruses was approximately 1 to 5 in 1957
4. Ratio of boy singers to girl singers was approximately 1 to 8 in 1957
5. In a sampling of 36 schools in 1956
    a. ratio of boys to girls in choral music was approximately 2 to 5
    b. ratio of boy choruses to girls choruses was approximately 1 to 5
    c. ratio of boys to girls in mixed choir only was approximately 1 to 2 (disregarding any count of girls-only or boys-only glee clubs)

The latest survey was made in 1976 in the state of Iowa. Data were secured by polling every eighth school in the Iowa directory. The results are displayed in Examples 31 and 32.

1. Total girls enrolled in choral music is 5,151 or 29.2% of total girls' population
2. Total boys enrolled in choral music is 2,123 or 12.0% of total boys' population
3. Total enrollment in choral music is 5,621 or 16% of total school population
    A. Basses = 1,126 or 20%   C. Altos = 1,719 or 30.5%
    B. Tenors = 795   or 14%   D. Sopranos = 1,988 or 35.3%
4. Girls-only glee clubs (not counting duplication) totaled 1,444 members
5. Boys-only glee clubs (not counting duplications) totaled 202 members
6. In no school were there more boys than girls enrolled
7. In no school were there as many boys as girls enrolled
8. Variation was from a 2:3 ratio in E-2 to D-8 which had no boys at all.

157

9. One school, G-2 had an almost equal balance of the four voice parts, but to do so had to put the 141 girls left over into several girls' glee clubs

The results of other surveys have been much the same. In twenty years I have yet to find any co-educational school where more boys

Example 28
Wisconsin District Music Contests—1956

District	Boys' Number	Choruses Students	Girls' Number	Choruses Students
Abbotsford	2	71	10	465
Adams	4	130	13	494
Algoma	1	31	9	369
Ashland	0	0	9	261
Berlin	1	20	14	673
Brillion	6	166	11	411
Brodhead	2	74	11	441
Eagle River	0	0	7	249
Eau Claire	1	35	19	747
Edgewood (Madison)	2	54	8	364
Green Bay	3	91	9	468
Kimberly	2	81	9	481
LaCrosse	2	56	24	988
Mauston	4	162	15	698
Milton	0	0	3	102
Mineral Point	1	19	10	460
Peshtigo	2	43	12	578
Phillips	1	22	10	334
Port Washington	2	48	13	572
Prairie du Chien	1	27	13	426
Rhinelander	2	57	7	394
Rice Lake	2	57	7	231
River Falls	0	0	9	425
West Allis	2	130	7	539
Whitewater	5	116	20	886
Wittenberg	3	63	4	66
Total	51	1,553	283	12,122

Ratio of boys' choruses to girls' choruses
51 to 283 = .18 or approximately 1 to 5

Ratio of boy singers to girl singers
1553 to 12,122 = .128 or approximately 1 to 8

158

than girls enrolled in choral music, nor where boys equaled girls in numbers of enrollment. Always I find a significant number of schools that have almost no boys in choral music. Always when there is a fairly well-balanced mixed choir there are one or more girls' glee clubs for the overflow of girl registrants.

There are, of course, fifty states, and most of my inquiries have been made in the north central part of the country. Perhaps some day in some state as yet unsurveyed I will find a place where boys equal girls in enrollment in at least one school's choral music classes. I dare not hope that an entire state will report that its choir directors are

Example 29
Wisconsin District Music Contests—1957

District	Boys' Choruses Number	Students	Girls' Choruses Number	Students
Ashland	3	86	8	231
Baraboo	5	167	12	571
Birnamwood	3	58	11	381
Clinton	0	0	2	75
Cadott	0	0	3	122
Eau Claire	1	39	18	746
Hartford	2	53	12	493
Reedsville	1	33	7	234
Juda	2	56	8	285
Kaukana	2	50	8	417
LaCrosse	1	26	23	859
Laona	0	0	5	117
Abbotsford	2	71	9	432
Marinette	3	69	10	488
Park Falls	0	0	7	277
Port Edwards	4	135	11	424
Plattesville	2	59	25	846
Rice Lake	4	91	12	389
River Falls	2	66	10	473
Shawano	3	95	8	531
Sheboygan Falls	2	40	8	259
Sturgeon Bay	0	0	7	256
Sun Prairie	3	84	5	284
Waupun	0	0	10	428
Milwaukee	2	67	5	283
Whitewater	2	45	14	633
Wisconsin Rapids	1	24	6	276
Total	50	1,414	264	10,810

Example 30
COMPARISON OF BOYS AND GIRLS PARTICIPATING IN VOCAL MUSIC IN WISCONSIN, 1956 (EVERY 10TH SCHOOL)

City	Total Enrollment	Boys enrolled No.	Boys enrolled %	Girls enrolled No.	Girls enrolled %	Boys' Chorus	Girls' Chorus	Mixed Chorus Boys	Mixed Chorus Girls
Drummond	100	5	5	35	35		35		
Ea. Troy	260	30	12	80	31	8	80	30	50
Fennimore	250	16	6	40	16			16	40
Fish Creek	215	20	4	50	23		28	18	26
Hortonville	285		0	36	12		36		
Independence	245	14	6	58	24	4	40	10	18
Mauston	350	15	4	70	20	9	35	10	40
Mt. Horeb	290	15	5	55	19	4	35	15	45
Nw. Richmond	380	25	7	95	25		53	19	25
Nw. Holstein	306	40	14	55	18		50	40	55
Osseo	180	19	11	45	25			19	45
Peshtigo	250	30	12	60	24	30	60	24	36
Pardeev'l	182	40	22	80	44	30	40	35	70
Poynette	165	12	7	44	24		40	12	20
Random Lk.	200	12	6	40	20		12	12	40
Regis of Eau Claire	580	55	10	90	16			48	79
Salem	450	12	3	48	11		16	12	32
Sheboygan	500	35	7	100	20		30	20	45
Sparta	540	35	7	90	17		45	35	55
Tigerton	160	25	15	63	39	25	63	20	41
Two Rivers (Washington)	700	45	7	100	14	22	45	25	55
Walworth	250	40	16	79	32	25	45	24	34
Wausau	1400	40	3	150	11		30	20	30
White Lake	120			20	17		20		
Pulaski	555	24	4.3	82	15	22	72	18	33
Waupaca	400	6	2	17	4				
Maple	280	10	4	59	22		16	10	59
Plainfield	251	65	30	90	36	65	90	21	21
West Allis	600	45	8	70	12	45	70		
Cudahy	600	30	5	113	19		90	30	23
Glenwood Cy.	260	25	10	50	19		50	25	40
Monona Grove	580	18	3	40	7			48	40
Campbellsport	240	30	13	70	29			30	70
Turtle Lake	193	85	44	85	44	25	10	60	75
Westboro	96	14	15	36	38			14	36
Williams Bay	92	8	9	28	38	8	28		
Totals		940	336.3	2323	820	322	1264	720	1278

Ratio of boys to girls Ratio of boy choruses to girl choruses
940:2323 = .40 or 2:5 322:1264 = .25 or 1:5

Ratio of boys to girls in mixed chorus = 720:1278 = .56 approx. 1:2

160

giving equal treatment to both males and females—not in my lifetime.

Meanwhile I wonder how many tenors and basses must be walking in the halls of our high schools undiscovered, untrained and unused. I also wonder how many girls go through high school without ever singing in a mixed chorus or hearing the sound of a bass or tenor. I even wonder if some day some citizen is going to level the charge that our choral music directors are practicing discrimination—against the boys!

TABLE 3
RATIO OF BOYS TO GIRLS
IN CHORAL GROUPS—WISCONSIN

Year	Choruses	Total Participants
1956	51:283 or about 1:5	1553:12,122 or about 1:8
1957	50:264 or about 1:5	1414:10,810 or about 1:8

Thus there was in 1956 a ratio of 51 boys' choruses to 283 girls' choruses, and in 1957 the ratio was 50 to 264; the enrollment in 1956 was 1553 boys to 12,122 girls, while in 1957 the ratio was 1949 boys to 10,810 girls.

161

Example 31
MIXED CHORUS ENROLLMENTS IN IOWA: BOYS vs. GIRLS

School	Total Enroll.	Boys	Girls	Total	Bass	Tenor	Alto	Soprano
	School Enrollment			Mixed Chorus Enrollment				
A-1	116	55	61	33	6	5	13	9
A-2	1,300	650	650	119	18	18	37	46
A-3	287	143	144	85	16	5	27	37
A-4	228	116	112	63	7	8	19	29
A-5	774	397	377	86	13	13	28	32
A-6	289	137	152	104	14	14	39	37
B-1	1,450	725	725	155	32	20	53	50
B-2	288	146	142	65	11	9	21	24
B-3	185	92	93	68	11	10	20	27
C-1	104	38	66	78	20	18	22	18
C-2	275	128	147	75	10	6	28	31
C-3	570	267	303	96	15	15	32	34
C-4	344	160	184	67	15	8	23	21
C-5	1,500	750	750	207	55	40	40	72
C-6	265	140	125	40	4	5	12	19
C-7	1,500	800	700	104	18	18	27	41
C-8	1,454	730	704	162	37	22	43	60
C-9	368	183	185	170	40	31	51	48
D-1	1,150	575	575	66	15	6	19	26
D-2	1,107	543	564	70	9	6	21	34
D-3	523	249	274	86	22	19	24	21
D-4	2,039	1,071	968	242	50	30	76	86
D-5	266	132	134	52	10	8	16	18
D-6	140	75	65	42	7	2	15	18
D-7	117	58	59	25	5	4	8	8
E-1	280	120	160	85	15	12	28	30
E-2	750	375	375	50	12	8	15	15
D-8	142	74	68					
D-9	1,037	539	498	70	14	8	24	24
F-1	199	91	108	50	3	8	16	23
G-1	600	300	300	75	27	6	20	22
G-2	377	189	188	73	20	17	17	19
H-1	150	80	70	74	22	10	19	23
H-2	285	151	134	68	15	9	22	22
H-3	227	124	103	80	14	17	23	26
J-1	181	98	83	35	6	4	11	14
K-1	600	223	377	93	19	15	24	35
L-1	625	315	310	103	18	6	27	52
L-2	68	29	39	24	4	4	8	8
M-1	200	100	100	24	3	4	9	8
M-2	110	50	60	16	1	1	8	6

(Continued on next page)

School	School Enrollment			Mixed Chorus Enrollment				
	Total Enroll.	Boys	Girls	Total	Bass	Tenor	Alto	Soprano
M-3	112	49	63	76	18	11	26	21
M-4	800	400	400	49	12	5	17	15
M-5	1,500	740	760	80	19	13	25	23
M-6	401	200	201	60	11	9	18	22
N-1	1,062	573	489	177	38	29	50	60
N-2	216	112	104	48	6	6	22	14
N-3	143	71	72	38	9	4	12	13
O-1	298	167	131	75	16	9	26	24
O-2	1,500	750	750	201	31	29	66	75
P-1	99	11	88	52	11	8	13	20
P-2	189	86	103	34	9	5	11	9
P-3	360	181	179	89	17	8	30	34
R-1	450	224	226	65	16	7	18	24
R-2	272	123	149	92	10	10	28	44
R-3	360	200	160	50	11	8	15	16
S-1	335	176	159	53	13	9	16	15
S-2	485	242	243	76	28	6	20	22
S-3	1,170	586	584	179	39	24	55	61
S-4	469	235	234	109	19	20	39	31
S-5	175	95	80	45	8	6	13	18
S-6	94	47	47	48	5	7	20	16
S-7	139	72	67	57	11	12	14	20
T-1	257	126	131	98	19	13	27	39
T-2	180	90	90	29	6	3	10	10
W-1	200	103	97	52	10	5	21	16
W-2	280	139	141	64	13	9	18	24
W-3	204	103	101	33	12	4	8	9
W-4	400	180	220	150	24	26	40	60
W-5	300	149	151	47	12	5	17	15
V-1	414	212	202	115	20	11	39	45
	35,314	17,660	17,654	5,621	1,126	795	1,719	1,988

Example 32
MIXED CHORUS ENROLLMENTS IN IOWA:
BOYS vs. GIRLS GLEES

| | Girls' Chorus Enrollment | | | | Boys' Glee | | |
| | | Voicing of | | | | Voicing of | |
	Girls' Glee	Girls' Soprano	Glees Mezzo	Alto	Boys' Glee	Boys' Tenor	Glees Bass
A-1							
A-2	25	7	9	9			
A-3							
A-4	39	19		20			
A-5	77	20	25	32			
A-6							
B-1	26	8	9	9			
B-2							
B-3							
C-5							
C-1	26	10	8	8			
C-2	55	20	20	15	14	7	7
C-5	55	15	20	20			
C-7	13	5	4	4			
C-8	55	15	12	28			
C-9	99	30	30	39	71	31	40
D-1	47	1	10	20			
D-3	57	30	14	13			
D-4	29	10	10	9			
D-5	57	17	21	19			
D-6	8	4		4			
D-7	25	8	8	9	21	10	11
D-8	21	11	5	5			
F-1	38	11	17	10			
G-2	141	42	67	32			
H-3	34	15		19	21	10	11
L-2	35	18	9	8			
M-4	35	15	10	10			
M-5	51	11	15	25			
M-6	21	7	7	7	21	10	11
O-2	41	10	17	14			
P-2	37	14	13	10	19	8	11
P-3	12	4	4	4			
R-3	35	13	10	12			
S-1	70	26	21	23			
S-4	49	17	16	16			
S-5	15	5	5	5			
W-3	51	17	19	15			
W-4	50	20	15	15	35	17	18
W-5	15	6		9			
Totals	1444	497	459	521	202	93	109

Comparisons

Female Singers to Male Singers = 129 : 447 = .288 or approx.
1 to 4   7.16: 24.8 = .288

Appendix B

I have said that vocationally there are more chances for a male singer to be gainfully employed than for a female singer. It is not my intention in this modest volume to go into extensive proof but I do offer two bits of evidence that suggest how such proof could be made more extensive. Along with this evidence I also make the claim that the American public DOES prefer male singers to female singers and the great cross section of our population does ask for and get more male singers than female.

Part I

One type of survey examined the number of solo roles in opera and similar stage performances.

Twenty-three of the most frequently performed operas were chosen (sometimes called "the standard repertoire") and the cast of singers required for each opera was listed according to voice-classification and according to major roles or minor roles. A major role was defined as a part in which the character appears throughout the opera and in which he/she has one or more solo arias or ensemble numbers. A minor role was one where the character appears briefly in no more than two scenes and in which he/she has no solo aria nor part in a small ensemble.

As we inspect Example 33, we find that to cast a season of so-called standard operas, 35.7% of the parts must be filled by women, and 64.2% must be filled by men. We disregard the small parts to be sung by boys. Put in vocational terms, chances are twice as great for a male singer to appear in a solo role as for a female singer.

If we consider major roles only, we find 51 female parts and 74 male parts, or approximately 40% women, 60% men.

In minor roles there are only 18 parts for women, but 75 for men, or 19% for females and 80% male.

As opera companies increase in number throughout the United States and the length of the seasons becomes longer, it is obvious that more than twice as many male singers can find employment in either major or minor roles as can female singers. If we add the four parts for boys (not girls) the scales are tipped even further in favor of the males.

Part II

Comparison of male and female singers on coin-operated record-players

I include this information for two reasons:
1) The data support the hypothesis that Americans prefer to listen

to male singers rather than female singers
2) The reaction of certain individuals to this project reveal some unexpected, puzzling but provocative deep-seated prejudices.

Over thirty years ago, before air-conditioning was common in automobiles, we were crossing Kansas on a torrid summer day. The thermometer registered over 100° Fahrenheit as we arrived at noon in a town with the picturesque name of Annie Oakley. A sign on a restaurant proclaimed "Air conditioned" so we were glad to stop and enter. The little place was well filled with deeply tanned men, workers in the wheat fields who were seeking to escape the blistering sun over the noon lunch break. A harried looking waitress said "It'll

EXAMPLE 33
Distribution of Voices in Twenty-three
Frequently Performed Operas

| | Major Roles | | | | | Minor Roles | | | |
	Sopr.	Mezzo-Alto	Tenor	Bar.	Bass	Sopr.	Alto	Ten.	Bar.-Bass
Aids	1	1	1	1	2		1	1	
Trovatore	1	1	1	1	1		1	1	
Rigoletto	1	1	1	1	1	1	2	2	2-2
Traviata	1		1	1		1	1	2	2-2
Forza delDest.	1	1	1	1	2		1	2	1-1
Lucia	1	1	1	1	1			2	
Boheme	2		1	2	1			1	2-1
Tosca	1		1	1		1 (boy)		2	2-2
Butterfly	1	1	1	1			1	1	2-2
Pagliacci	1		2	2					
Cav. Rust.	1	2	1	1					
Rosenkav	2	2	2	2	3	2	6	3-2	
Fidelio	2		2	1			1	1-2	
Lohengrin	1	1	1	1	1				1
Tristan-Isolde	1	1	1	1	1				2-1
Tannhauser	1	1			1			3	3
Don Giovanni	3		1	2	1				1
Marriage Fig.	2	2	1	1	2	1			1 1
Magic Flute	2		1	1	2	2	1		1 2
Faust	1	2	1	1	1 + 3 boys				1
Samson-Delilah		1	1	1	1				2-2
Carmen	2	2	2	2					1-2
Barber-Seville	1	1	1	1	2			1	1
Totals	30	21	27	27	20	8	10	24	27 24
						(+ 4 boys)			
Combined totals	51			74		18			75

166

be at least an hour. We're awfully busy. There's a couple chairs back there if you care to wait."

The chairs, it developed, were next to a coin-operated record player. We saw a steady succession of men coming to make a selection and deposit a coin. We had no trouble hearing the music chosen, nor was there any time that elapsed between the finish of one selection and the start of the next. Since music of the type heard on the juke-box is rather unfamiliar to me and not much to my liking, I ventured a few questions to these Kansas farm hands. One of them was more amiable and voluble than the others for he stayed to provide me with much information about the current popular songs, and the various singers in vogue at the time.

Facetiously I asked one question that elicited a response that was to affect my thinking for a long time. "I notice," I said, trying to be a bit humorous, "that you fellows all seem to pick the men singers. I should think a young fellow like you would prefer a pretty girl singer."

Example 34
Survey of male and female singers on juke-boxes   1957

City	Males	Females	%-males	%-females
Montello, Wisc.	25	6	80.7	19.2
Waupun, Wisc.	16	8	67.7	33.3
Tomah, Wisc.	15	2	88.1	11.9
Augusta, Wisc.	11	6	64.7	35.3
Fall Creek, Wisc.	28	10	73.7	26.3
Elk Mound, Wisc.	15	5	75.0	25.0
New Richmond, Wisc.	35	4	89.6	10.3
Freeport, Ill.	35	10	77.7	22.2
Minneapolis, Minn.	14	5	73.7	26.3
East Moline, Ill.	18	7	72.0	28.0
Columbus, Wisc.	40	5	88.8	11.1
Richland Center, Wisc.	23	10	69.7	30.3
Cross Plains, Wisc.	23	10	69.7	30.3
Spring Green, Wisc.	45	11	80.4	19.6
Viroqua, Wisc.	15	3	83.3	16.7
Berlin, Wisc.	29	10	74.3	25.6
Scholfield, Wisc.	35	7	83.3	16.7
Total	447	129		
Average	24.8	7.16		

Comparisons
Female Singers to Male Singers = 129 : 447 = .288 or approx.
1 to 4   7.16 : 24.8 = .288

He grinned and answered, "Oh sure, I like to look at a pretty girl (not his word) who sings, but when it comes to just listening like now on the recording, it takes a man to really sell a song."

Another month, this time a trip in Ohio, our car developed engine trouble. We limped into a small town and found a garage. "Sure I can fix it," said the machinist-repairman, "but it will take a couple hours." Again we looked for a restaurant where we could lunch at leisure, and again there was a juke box. The father of the little family group was the first to deposit his money and make his choice; then one of the middle aged ladies with shopping bags came over to select a favorite; next the single girl having a "Coke and smoke" made a choice. A group of high school boys and girls came in chattering, and one of the group selected several recordings. When they had gone, the fellow talking to his girl over their drinks looked up, noticed the silence and decided to provide us with his favorite. Remembering the Kansas conversation, I noticed that all but one of the chosen songs featured male singers. I walked over casually to look at the printed listing of records available. There was a much greater number of male soloists listed than female singers. I began to wonder if the Kansas farm boy might be speaking for others, and that when it comes to just listening "it takes a man to really sell a song."

Since that time I have continued to make a quick survey of juke box listings whenever I am near one of the record-playing machines, and not once in thirty years have I found this distribution to vary greatly; between three and four times as many male singers are featured as are female soloists, or ensembles.

Since my contact with juke-boxes is rather limited, I have on occasion asked for verification by others. I will describe two such verifications, one in 1957 and one in 1976.

I was teaching assistant in a class in advanced educational psychology. One Friday I asked if each member of the class, as he commuted to his home over the weekend, would find a juke box in some bar, restaurant or other public place, and write down a count of male singers vs. female singers. Their findings are listed in Example 34.

As I was preparing a newsletter to be mailed out to several hundred choir directors, I enclosed a prepared post card and asked each recipient to make a count of male and female singers on a juke box in his community. The responses to my request were unusually high (ordinarily a response of less than 10% can be expected in mail surveys, I understand). I list them here by states. See Example 35.

You will note a rather consistent ratio of male singers to female singers, with no great difference apparent in any state or district or section of our country, as noted in the Summary, Example 35.

The ratio of female soloists to male soloists is about 2 to 9 or 1 to 4½
The ratio of female ensembles to male ensembles is about 1 to 3
The ratio of all-male to all-female is about 4 to 1

Of great interest is the reaction some people have had to this "survey of the juke-boxes" and its results. Three instances will illustrate.

As I discussed my procedures and findings with one choral

168

Example 35
Survey of juke-boxes by correspondents

State	No. of Reports	Male Soloists	Female Soloists	Male Ensembles	Female Ensembles
Alabama	2	41	8	6	2
Arizona	3	60	15	9	2
Arkansas	1	19	6	8	2
California	5	175	20	15	6
Colorado	2	48	12	10	2
Delaware	1	25	6	3	1
Florida	6	182	28	20	6
Georgia	2	32	10	8	1
Illinois	10	302	79	60	19
Indiana	4	56	14	16	5
Iowa	8	245	58	44	12
Kansas	2	42	11	15	3
Kentucky	1	21	5	6	2
Louisiana	1	22	15	7	2
Maryland	1	20	5	6	2
Massachusetts	2	39	9	10	4
Michigan	3	66	15	9	6
Minnesota	2	42	6	16	5
Nebraska	1	26	6	6	2
Missouri	4	81	19	21	7
New Jersey	3	69	17	16	4
New Mexico	1	15	4	5	1
New York	7	141	30	38	14
North Carolina	1	25	5	5	1
Ohio	3	63	16	17	5
Oklahoma	1	19	5	7	1
Oregon	2	42	10	11	4
Pennsylvania	4	89	16	19	8
South Carolina	2	39	11	12	3
Tennessee	2	43	10	14	4
Texas	8	165	42	44	16
Utah	1	21	6	7	2
Virginia	1	27	5	5	2
Washington	1	17	4	7	1
West Virginia	1	23	4	7	1
Wisconsin	5	126	24	25	18
Totals	104	2468	556	534	176
Average		23.7	5.35	5.13	1.6

Comparisons
Female soloists to male soloists = 556:2468 = .225 or 2:9 (1:4½)
Female ensembles to male ensembles = 176:534 = .329
   or approx. 1:3
Females (solo + ense.); males (solo = ens.) = 732; 3002 = .243
   or approx. 1:4

director, she began to laugh. "Don't you know," she said a bit scornfully, "it's because of the teen-age girls there are so many more men singers than women. These silly little teen-agers get all sorts of romantic ideas at this age."

I protested that my observations included people of all ages and of both sexes. I pointed out that many of my "contributors" had secured their data from all sorts of places, many not frequented by teen-age girls. It was to no avail. She stubbornly insisted that the owners of the coin-machines catered largely to romantic teen-age girls.

The second illustration concerns my postcard survey. Most of the cards came back properly marked and signed and in a rather gratifyingly large quantity. Three came back unsigned, with adverse comments. One was actually obscene and abusive. Apparently he/she found the connotation of juke-box and male singers so emotionally upsetting he/she (presumably a college graduate with some command of the English language) was reduced to using the lowest common denominator of expression, the words associated with illiterate men of the street. "Not only was this survey worthless, it was actually disgraceful and the subject was not one to be mentioned in 'respectable society.' "

The third instance involved several men, all choral directors. In a discussion group, as I described my findings they assured me with leering looks that I was on the wrong track. All of the male singers, they insisted, were really homosexuals and it was the boys in the "gay bars" who created the great demand for men singers in this low type of music. I explained patiently that my data came from many sources, that the members of the graduate class could hardly all be homosexuals, that the father of the family, the laughing high school group, the middle-aged women shoppers could hardly be labeled homosexuals, nor could some 100 choral directors. It was all in vain.

These three instances open up an intriguing side issue, a question to be answered at some future time. Why would a straightforward compilation of data factually presented arouse such stubborn resistance or such obviously strong emotional outbursts? What deep-seated prejudice or suppressed experience connected with juke box and "pop singers" could cause educated people to refuse factual evidence so stubbornly and abusively?

Certainly they missed the point. When I go out into the highways and byways to find boys of talent, I take them where I find them, and I speak the language they understand. If they understand the names Crosby, Sinatra, Presley because those are names they have HEARD, I am quite prepared to start there. Of course once the boy is in the choir group we lead him to where we think he should go.

Meanwhile I will take the interpretation of these data that explains the most with the least ramifications. I suggest that the reason there is a great preponderance of male singers is that the great American public, untrained and unsophisticated in its musical tastes, prefers to hear male singers; those who own the coin-operated music machines display the recordings that will attract the most money from the purses of the patrons; if it is the recordings of male singers that "sell" they supply the machines with such recordings.

I suggest that the explanation for this preference is the one given by a Kansas farm hand. "When you are *looking* it's nice to watch a pretty girl sing, but when you are just listening it takes a man to sell a song."

Occasionally, not often, I find a family where there is some reluctance to have a son included in a cadet class of my boy choir, wondering if it might be that people would scorn him as "one of those singers." I have found the above statistics a great help in convincing a hesitant father that people will admire his son if he sings well. It has always worked, particularly when the father (or other members of the family) tend to be limited in good taste or musical training. I am also very careful to make it clear that I do NOT CARE FOR POPULAR SINGERS MYSELF NOR DO I hold out hope that the little boy will become a "hit" on some future juke-box.

Appendix C

A SUGGESTED AUDITION PROCEDURE

The following step by step routine for auditioning a choir candidate is transcribed from a taping of an actual session.

The Roman numerals will refer to the sections on the Audition Sheet, Example 36.

The passages to be played or sung are in notation in Example 37.

I. To check range, the song "America" is displayed and the boy is asked to sing it in the key of F; he repeats in the key of G, then A, etc., until he can sing no higher, and the upper limit of his range determined.

   The song is then lowered to E-flat, D, C, etc., until the lowest limit of his range is determined.

II. For determining a boy's ability to discriminate in variations in pitch, the auditioner says:

"You know what a bugle is? I'm going to play four notes on the piano and I ask you to blow them back to me using the word "toot". To show you what I mean we'll listen to Jim (the choirboy) do it first.

On the piano the four tones of IIA are played in arpeggio-order and Jim illustrates by singing. The pianist plays the tones again as an arpeggio, then as a chord and the tester says "Now you sing them as Jim did."

The pianist plays the four tones as a chord. If the auditioner fails the pianist plays the arpeggio again, but NOT the chord. If there is a second failure the pianist plays the arpeggio while the boy sings with him. According to the number of tries needed, the tester writes 1 or 2 or 3.

"Now my boy, we're going to do this again, but this time one of the tones is going to change. Listen." The pianist plays IIB, as a minor arpeggio, emphasizing the f-natural, then the d-minor chord. As before the boy gets three chances to repeat/sing the four tones, with the addition that on the third try the tester may say, "It's number 2 that changed. Listen to it more carefully."

Similarly IIC, D and E are presented, with the tester saying, if necessary, it's number three this time; (for d) . . . now listen for number 4; (for e) . . . it's the *first* tone that changes now. Obviously the boy who gets all five on the first try is superior in pitch discrimination, the one who needs three or more chances is not very aware of pitch changes.

Item II f′ and f″ are also intended to check pitch discrimination. The pianist plays the octave leap and the candidate is asked to sing both tones "right in the center." If he misses or smears the first attempt, "Jim" may illustrate.

EXAMPLE 36
Figure 1. Audition Sheet

Fill out the blanks down to the double line. When you enter the room to sing, hand this sheet to the director. He will fill in the blanks below the double line. Some time in a week or so you will get this sheet back, with some comments that will tell you if you are ready for boy choir training.

Your name_____ Telephone _____

Father's or
Mother's name _____ Street address _____

School you
attend _____ City (if out of town)_____

Grade_____ Teacher's name _____ Your birthday _____
Month, day, year born

Church/synagogue you prefer_____

I   Song of choice____   Comments   Range____   Quality____
    & America   Words____   Sureness____

II   Pitch detection:

   A. Tonic, major____   B. Tonic, minor____
   C. Augmented____

   D. Dominant 7th____   E. Diminished 7th____
   F. Octave up____ down____

   G. Remembering 7-tone melody, trials needed 1, 2, 3.

IIIA. Holding middle tone of
    (1) a major triad, trials needed 1____ 2____ 3____
    (2) a minor triad. Trial 4____ 5____ 6____
   B. Holding common tone as chords shift.

IV   Repeating rhythms   A. _____   B. _____
   C. _____   D. _____   E. _____
   F. _____   G. _____   H. _____
   I. _____

V   Sing "Home on the Range" against another song
   A. Trial 1____   B. Trial 2____   C. Trial 3____

COMMENTS AND RECOMMENDATIONS:

173

Example 37   **Manual for Auditions**

Arpeggios A. major   B. minor   C. augmented D. dominant 7th   E. diminished

F. octave up octave down   7-tone melody.

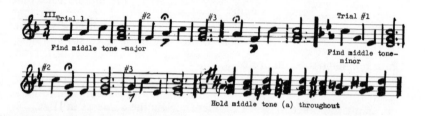

Find middle tone —major   Find middle tone—
                                                        minor

Hold middle tone (a) throughout

SIMULTANEOUS SONGS

Candidate sings:

Oh give me a home where the buf-fa-lo roam, and the deer and the an-te-lope
Where sel-dom is hear a dis-cour-ag-ing word, and the

Assistant sing

My home's in Mon- tan- a I wear a ban-dana my spurs are of sil-ver, my
While rid- ing the rang-es my luck nev-er changes, I

play skies are not cloud- y all day   Home... home on the

po-ny is gray gal-lop. and gal-op my pon-y all day Gal-lop-ing, gal-lop-ing

range where the deer and the an- te- lope play

gal-lop all day, gal-lop-ing gal-lop a- way...

Chordal accompaniment F–F; Bb–Bb; F–F; C7–C7; F– F; Bb–Bb;F–C7; F–F Fine
                       F–C7; F–F; F– G7 ; C 7 –C7 D.S.

174

Item II 5 is a good test for ability to remember tones in succession. "CAN YOU REMEMBER THE SEVEN NUMBERS IN YOUR TELEPHONE NUMBER (wait for boy to affirm)? I'm going to play seven tones in a row and Jim here is going to sing them to you as I play. Then will you toot them back to us?" If he fails to get all seven, the tester says "You only sang six" or "You got as far as the fifth perfectly, listen again," etc.; Jim sings the 7-tone melody again. If the lad fails again, "Once more, I'm going to help you with that number 6 (or whatever)" and this time you play softly along with him.

Item III is one of the most discriminating of all those suggested here. The ability to hear one tone in a cluster is not very common, even in adults; you can be sure that any boy who can perform well in this is well-gifted in pitch discrimination. The tester says "I am going to play three tones (play f-a-c in order, then as a chord). Will you blow me a toot on the MIDDLE TONE?" If the boy fails (he will most likely sing the highest tone, or quite possibly the lowest tone) say "Listen again. Here is the low tone (play f), the middle tone that you are to sing for me (play a) and the high tone. Now sing that middle tone." If he fails again, you say "This time I'll give you the middle tone first (play a) and ask you to sing it (he does so) and hang on while I play the lowest and highest tones and then the chord. Now take a breath and sing that middle tone."

For a second check on this you say "This time we'll start with the highest tone (play c'), the middle tone (g) and the lowest tone (e-flat). Now sing the middle tone." The procedure is the same as in IIIA.

"Now I'm going to try to pull you OFF that middle tone. As you sing it, I'm going to play other chords and as these chords change I want you to hang onto that middle tone. Here it is (sound a). Hang on (sound the f-major chord as in IIIB). Now hang on, no matter what you hear (play IIB 1, 2, 3, 4, 5, 6 in succession, allowing the boy to stop and breathe after #3)." On the first trial the pianist plays loudly; on the second if the boy fails, mezzo-piano; on the third, pianissimo.

For rhythm discrimination, see IV on the audition tryout sheet. The tester says "I'm going to play (sing) four tones. You sing them back to me" (play four firm steady quarter notes, moderato). "Now I'm going to swing a little. Will you toot these four tones back to me?" Play IVB. (If he fails, try again, saying "Watch out for that second note." Proceed similarly through patterns C, D, E, F, G, H, I.

Number V is intended to discover if the auditioner can hold a melody against another voice line. "I'm going to ask Jim here to sing a familiar cowboy song. If you have ever heard it, nod and smile." Jim sings Home on the Range. If the auditioner has never heard it, you ask Jim to sing it again with the boy singing softly along with him; a third and fourth time Jim should fade out, and the boy should be carrying on with an assist from the pianist.

"Now we're going to try to mix you up. As you sing 'Home on the Range,' Jim is going to sing a different song. We want you to go right on singing 'Home on the Range' and don't let Jim throw you off. Ready?"

Jim goes across the room and sings softly "My Home's in Montana," the pianist giving the auditioner a boost if necessary. If

175

the auditioner succeeds, say "Now Jim's going to be a bit meaner. He's going to come closer and sing louder. Don't let him bother you." The procedure is repeated, the pianist giving only a rhythmic chordal accompaniment this time, unless the boy falters and needs help.

If all is going well, challenge the boy to a third trial, with Jim standing very close and singing out quite loudly.

At the close of the audition, the tester/director smiles pleasantly at both boy and father and says "Now, that wasn't so bad, was it? Did you know, dad, that your young son here could do so many of these things? Of course you understand it will be a week or so before you get this sheet back with his scores. There are lots of other boys to hear yet, before we can tell how this lad stacks up against the competition. We'll mail this score sheet back to you with our recommendation."

The experienced auditioner makes some quick notations after they are gone and before the next boy comes in, including some distinguishing items that will help him remember the boy—e.g., short, tall, brown eyes, purple shirt, and on the back of the page in code impressions about appearance, personality, parent's attitude and status. This must be done immediately; since this whole process takes at least ten, maybe fifteen minutes; by the time two hours have passed impressions of each auditioner become blurred.

How fine the screening process is to be depends on the number of boys to be admitted into the training choir. Obviously any boy who gets all of section II and III and IV on first trial, and can go all the way up to trial 3 on item V is excellent material, musically speaking, but how far down to go below that level will vary at the discretion of each director.

Once the boys have been ranked in order of excellence in musical aptness and voice qualities (that is, free from faults), the notes on general behavior, appearance, responsiveness can be considered. Calls to school teacher, instrumental instructor, clergyman, leader of group activities and clubs, can be made. Supplementary information like parental attitude, social/economic background, cooperative attitude, can be considered if they seem important.

Appendix D

As a further discussion of the possibility that many low basses are lost to us because nobody looks for them or even admits that they exist, I quote from a letter sent to me quite voluntarily by a professional singer who opened a correspondence with me after reading one of my articles in THE CHORAL JOURNAL.

"My voice changed when I was in the 8th Grade at age 13. It took about a week for it to happen. Whereas before I was an alto in our church choir, a week later, I was a baritone. I had to learn to read a whole new part! You should understand that, though my family always enjoyed music, *I never intended to study it,* or even consider using it professionally. I attended a parochial school connected with the church which required every student to participate in the choir. That's why I was singing at all.

The next year, in my 9th Grade at the same school, one of my teachers thought I sounded like Larry Hooper on the Lawrence Welk show, and so coaxed me into singing *My Grandfather's Clock* two octaves lower than written for a Home and School meeting (something like a PTA). In the audience at the time was a lady who had taught voice at one time, but had gotten married and was raising a family. She volunteered to teach me free of charge if my parents would bring me to her home each week. It was her patient enthusiasm that sparked my fledgling interest in music. My range at the time, as I remember it, was C' (second added line below the bass staff) to G (fourth space bass staff).

I do not know what my faucette range was, as she did not even attempt to work with it.

The next year, she moved away to another city. My parents were interested in continuing my training and found a teacher in the local junior college to take me. He worked diligently on expanding my upper range, doing little to deepen or develop my lower notes. I remember that I had to *laboriously transpose* all my music by hand *in order to sing at all.* He had one song that I could sing, "Meersleuchtung" I believe it was called (Sea Lightning). It was a nice art song for bass, but I have not been able to find it anywhere for my file. If you run across it, let me know. He was able to raise my range one full step. I did not know at the time that I could sing lower than *low C,* because neither of these teachers ever took me lower than that.

The next two years, I attended a private boarding school in central Michigan. By this time I was thoroughly interested in music, and signed up for the choir and for voice and piano lessons. I also learned another Basso Art Song—*Asleep In The Deep.* I believe the highest note in that song is B or B flat. I could just barely reach it. The low D at the end was nothing—it made up for the struggle of the rest of the song. I continued to study voice to the present, the latest teacher being Mr. J. K. here in California. Of all the teachers I've had so far, Mr. K. has done the most for both ends of my range, even making use of my faucette.''

James A. Ayars
Bass in THE KING'S HERALDS QUARTET
The Voice of Prophecy Hour
P.O. Box 1511, Glendale, California 91209

178

APPENDIX E

The Case of Ernest Lough

A supplement to the discussion on the "waste" of the custom of "retiring" a boy treble when his voice "breaks" is the story of Ernest Lough. In the early 1920's there was an English boy soprano whose voice was so unusually beautiful that his fame spread far abroad.

I have in my possession a very ancient recording, badly worn, scratched and warped, of this boy singing the solo part of Mendelssohn's "Hear My Prayer".* Despite all the distortions of this faulty recording the beauty of Ernest Lough's voice comes through strikingly. In due time his voice "broke" and he was no longer featured as a treble soloist.

In the 1930's there was a story, widely disseminated and believed, that several former admirers of Lough's singing resolved to locate him to inquire about his musical progress. The story goes that to their dismay they found him earning his living in an occupation far removed from musical involvement. When he was asked why he had not continued his musical career, he explained that he had no financial backing, his parents could not afford to provide him with musical instruction so he was compelled to earn his living in another field. The story further goes that when he was asked if he would consider resuming his career at this late date if support could be found, he shook his head and said that his voice was a broken thing, good for nothing.

Within the past year I have had hints that this story has been exaggerated. The first hint was found in a novel, Amis' THE ALTERATION, Viking Press, New York, 1976, page 48. Amis makes the composer of "Hear My Prayer" somebody named Bartley and states that Lough did continue to sing as a baritone with an indifferent voice. Since this is a work of fiction certain liberties may be justified in the interest of story development.

Since then I have had the assurances from two different sources that Ernest Lough did indeed continue to sing as a baritone in the Temple Church choir and that he has recently retired. Oddly enough, attempts to find the present whereabouts of Ernest Lough have been unsuccessful; neither of my informants can find an address or location, and inquiries by mail from obvious sources have as yet been unanswered.

This does not negate the point of the story, although the apocryphal tale of the 1930's is much more dramatic. Here was a boy who had years of fame, the result of careful training and opportunity

---

* This recording was found by Mr. Richard Fling of Spring Valley, Illinois, who presented it to me as a gift.

for "exposure". If the people in charge of his training had not looked on the voice change as a "break", a hazard and a deterrent to further singing for awhile, I must wonder if Lough might have become a distinguished soloist as baritone or tenor or bass. Consider the fine vocal technique he had already developed, plus the exposure to fine music and the ability to sing such music most satisfactorily. Add to this a reputation already won that would open doors and command attention that most aspiring singers cannot hope to acquire for many years.

Much is made of the belief that a boy with a strikingly beautiful treble voice loses that beauty during voice mutation. I find the implications here rather disturbing. Is beauty of voice entirely native, in-born, God-given? Can a competent voice coach develop a fine singer only if that singer already possesses a voice of great beauty? Is such a voice coach helpless if a person of ambition, musical sensitivity, and willingness to work patiently and carefully appears if this person does not have a voice of striking beauty at the first audition?

What if a boy already has a beautiful voice as a treble singer? Cannot a competent teacher keep that boy singing correctly, if in a less exposed milieu, until the "new" voice has developed, keeping all of the skills, habits, techniques he has already acquired in continuing practice and use? Isn't it the function of voice teachers to maintain or DEVELOP a voice of beauty?

This is why I wonder what might have occurred had this fine boy treble been put under the tutelage of any of the competent voice coaches in London, to keep his already considerable singing techniques in control while moving the voice from the treble range to the bass-clef. Might we have had a leading baritone in the field of oratorio, opera, recital singing?

I find most repugnant the opposite implication—that a boy with an outstandingly beautiful treble voice is doomed to having a mediocre voice after his voice "breaks"—capable as a "filler" in the large choir, but no longer usable as a solo singer.

180

DATE DUE

NOV 8 79			
OCT 1 8 1993			
DEC 1 7 1997			
NOV 1 1 2002			
DEC 1 3 2002			
APR 2 2 2005			